JOHN EVELYN

A STUDY AND A BIBLIOGRAPHY

JOHN EVELYN

AET. 21

John Evelyn

A STUDY IN BIBLIOPHILY
with
A BIBLIOGRAPHY OF HIS WRITINGS

BY

GEOFFREY KEYNES, Kt.

CLARENDON PRESS . OXFORD
1968

Oxford University Press, Ely House, London W.1
GLASGOW NEW YORK TORONTO MELBOURNE WELLINGTON
CAPE TOWN SALISBURY IBADAN NAIROBI LUSAKA ADDIS ABABA
BOMBAY CALCUTTA MADRAS KARACHI LAHORE DACCA
KUALA LUMPUR HONG KONG TOKYO

FIRST EDITION 1937
SECOND EDITION 1968

Printed in Great Britain
at the University Printing House, Cambridge
(Brooke Crutchley, University Printer)

Preface to the Second Edition

THE FIRST EDITION of this *Bibliography of John Evelyn*, dedicated to the memory of A. T. Bartholomew, was published in 1937 in an edition of only 300 copies; of these 130 were distributed by the Grolier Club of New York under their own imprint, and the remaining 170 were quickly sold by the Cambridge University Press. The book has consequently been out of print for many years and its present high market value shows that it is still in some demand. The rights having been transferred from the Cambridge University Press to the Clarendon Press, I am glad of having been given the opportunity to revise the whole book. The Preface of 1937 has not been materially altered and no important changes have been made in the Bibliography other than the inclusion of the translation of Le Gendre's *Manner of Ordering Fruit Trees* (1660), this having been added to the Evelyn canon. Other less important additions and minor corrections have been made throughout. No attempt has been made to record every known copy of Evelyn's books, though the holdings of a few American libraries with important Evelyn collections have been registered. Other libraries have been occasionally mentioned on account of their having books of special interest, but it must not be assumed that they have no other books by Evelyn on their shelves. Wing's *Short Title Catalogue* will be sufficient guide to the rest.

The new edition of Evelyn's Diary forecast in 1937 was completed with consummate scholarship by Dr Esmond de Beer and published by the Clarendon Press in 1955. The *Bibliography* now issued from the same Press may be regarded as a pendant to this fine book, bringing up to date more detailed knowledge of Evelyn's literary activities. Again I have to acknowledge with gratitude Dr de Beer's interest and help, and on this occasion the courtesy of Dr John Mason and his assistant at Christ Church in their capacity as custodians of the Evelyn Collection deposited there by Mr John Evelyn. I have profited also by being allowed to see the notes made in the first edition of my book by the late College Librarian, W. G. Hiscock.

July 1967 GEOFFREY KEYNES

Preface to the First Edition

AT THE END of 1914 my *Bibliography of Donne* had reached a war-time birth, and another subject for research was wanted. Even a world war could not suppress so deep-rooted an instinct as the desire for books, though the kind booksellers who in spite of everything kept their catalogues in circulation can scarcely have realized how much pleasure they were giving to disconsolate bibliophils in dug-outs and windy tents in France and Flanders. I was particularly fortunate also in having as my most faithful correspondent in England the late A. T. Bartholomew, who, unable to serve in the army owing to physical disability, remained at his post at Cambridge University Library throughout the war. In 1915 I had begun buying books connected with John Evelyn, and early in 1916 Bartholomew and I agreed to collaborate in collecting and investigating Evelyn's writings, which seemed to be an interesting though neglected subject. His Diary was well known, but his numerous other writings were almost unrecognized in spite of their various attractions, and even the text of the Diary nearly a century after its first publication was still far from satisfactory.

One of our first steps was to compile a hand-list of Evelyn's works during one of my brief periods of leave in England, and this was printed in June 1916 by Fabb and Tyler.[1] Only twenty-five copies were printed for our private use and for distribution to our friends, and these may now all be destroyed and forgotten. Naturally the list proved to be both inaccurate and incomplete, though it served its purpose well as a basis for detailed investigation. A copy of the pamphlet, together with a manuscript list of the publications of William Pickering, accompanied me in the retreat of 1918, when all my less important possessions had disappeared behind the German lines, and this copy is beside me still. By the time the war ended we had gathered a useful collection of books by Evelyn and connected with him, and from that time to this the task of collecting and recording has slowly proceeded as opportunity offered, until twenty-one years after the compilation of the hand-list the full Bibliography is ready for publication.

Meanwhile, through the kind offices of Captain Evelyn Broadwood and his

[1] *A Hand-list of the Works of John Evelyn, Author of Sylva, and of books connected with him* (Cambridge, 1916), 25·5 cm, title and 17 leaves printed on the recto only; printed grey wrappers.

cousin, the late Miss Joan Broadwood, Bartholomew and I obtained permission in 1920 to visit Wotton House, which was still the home of the Evelyn family. The John Evelyn then living there was not the direct descendant of the Diarist, whose male line ended with the death of Sir Frederick Evelyn in 1812, but most of the Evelyn books, papers, and pictures were still preserved at Wotton. Miss Broadwood had also lived at Wotton for some years and knew more about the library and its contents than anyone else. Her knowledge and the goodwill of the late John Evelyn and his wife enabled me in the course of several visits to Wotton to gather a good deal of new information concerning Evelyn's books and manuscripts, and served greatly to increase my interest in his life and character. The present Mr John Evelyn has continued the courtesies extended to me by his parents, and I have much pleasure in acknowledging these, as well as the constant help given me by Miss Broadwood during the years in which she shared responsibilities at Wotton House with the late Mrs Evelyn. Another result of our first visit to Wotton House, as related in the proper places (pp. 29, 268), was the revision of the whole of the published text of the Diary.

After 1921 Bartholomew did not take any further active part in the work on Evelyn, though his interest was unabated until his death in March 1933.

My investigations at Wotton House were enhanced in value by the permission given by Mrs Evelyn to take photographs of book-bindings, manuscripts, and pictures on the spot, and these have added greatly to the value of the present volume. I first utilized some of the material I had gathered in a paper read to the Bibliographical Society of London on 16 March 1931, which was afterwards printed in *The Library*, vol. XII, no. 2. This was revised and extended when I was appointed Sandars Lecturer at Cambridge University for the year 1933–4. The two lectures delivered at Cambridge were not published, and have been incorporated in a much altered form in the present volume. The purely bibliographical part of the work was unsuitable for presentation in lectures, and now appears in print without having been used before in any form.

My obligations to members of the Evelyn family and to Miss Broadwood have already been recorded. In the course of twenty-one years I have been indebted to many other friends and correspondents whose names will be found in their appropriate places in the book. In particular I am grateful to the late Howard Levis, who, having formed an Evelyn collection, disposed of it in 1924 and immediately sent to Bartholomew his annotated copy of the hand-list which we had lent him some years before. Also to Dr A. S. W. Rosenbach, of Philadelphia and New York, for so readily supplying information about Evelyn's manuscript Life of Mrs Godolphin, with a photograph of the binding and photostats of several leaves. I was indebted for help to many librarians, and particularly to Mr R. H. Hill, Secretary of the Bodleian Library, Oxford, for verifying the class-marks of all the Evelyn books in Bodley, a tedious task which I ought never to have asked him to perform. The late C. G. des Graz, one of the Directors of Sotheby's, gave me the results of his investigations into the heraldry of the Evelyn and Browne families, without which I could never have begun to elucidate the problems presented by the book-bindings at Wotton. Further help in the same connexion was given by G. D. Hobson. Lastly, the largest debt of all, I acknowledge with gratitude the ungrudging help received from my co-labourer, Dr Esmond de Beer. He had worked for several years as editor of the revised text of the Diary, later to be published by the Oxford University Press, and his knowledge of Evelyn is immense and unrivalled. He read the proofs of this volume with critical care, and no statement that he believed to be in the least degree inaccurate (apart from the pure bibliography into which he did not enter) was allowed to pass unchallenged. The result was a considerable increase in the cost of corrections, which is more than compensated by the greater authority acquired by this book as a source of information about Evelyn. Dr de Beer shared with me all the results of his own researches which he thought might be relevant to my purpose, and I fear that my counter-contributions to his store of knowledge were relatively few. I can only record my grateful thanks to Dr de Beer for his unselfish and scholarly attitude.

The general form of the Bibliography conforms to that used in my earlier works on Donne, Browne, and Harvey. There are no new features to mention except the registering of all the class-marks of copies of books in English public libraries, so that these may be the more readily identified. The general atmosphere of the book will, I hope, be found even more humane than that of its predecessors owing to the inclusion of the preliminary essay on Evelyn's character and his attitude towards books, and of full prefaces before the descriptions of the various works.

It is perhaps unnecessary to state that an attempt has been made to attain completeness in this study of Evelyn's writings, though it would be rash to make any claim that this has been achieved. Evelyn was apt to publish both original works and translations anonymously or under a pseudonym, and the recent discovery of a very interesting, though undescribed, work by him relating to the Jesuits[1] may serve as a warning that other books may yet remain to be identified as his. It has been difficult, too, to know exactly where to draw the line in admitting or rejecting items connected with Evelyn's name. Thus I have rejected a printed form[2] dated 1665, concerning the conveyance of Sick and Wounded Seamen to His Majesty's Fleet, although this was almost certainly composed in accordance with Evelyn's directions. On the other hand I have admitted a broadside[3] concerning a family quarrel which was taken up to the House of Lords in March, 1698/9, because it contains '*some Remarks thereon, by* Iohn Evelyn *of* Deptford, *Esq.*'.

Evelyn himself compiled a list[4] of his works which he sent in a letter to the antiquary, Dr Robert Plot, dated March 16, 1682/3. This list, however, is incomplete and gives no information of any value. Bray and Upcott, editors of the Diary in 1818, gave a list of Evelyn's writings[5] taken from *Biographia Britannica*. This included a few bibliographical details, though too few to be of any use, and it has been reprinted in some later editions of the Diary in spite of its imperfections. The only real attempt to compile a brief account of Evelyn's writings was made by H. B. Wheatley, who in 1893 appended a list to a paper on 'The present condition of English bibliography and suggestions for the future'.[6] Again, however, this was no more than a hand-list, and still left the field clear for the compilation of a full Bibliography such as is presented in the pages following. Evelyn has already waited too long for proper recognition of his merits as writer and bibliophil, and it is to be hoped that this volume will add something to the honour in which his name is held.

March 1937 GEOFFREY KEYNES

Amended July 1967

[1] See no. 79, p. 177.
[2] BM: SP. 29/134, fol. 93*a*, with Evelyn's signature in the margin.
[3] See no. 130, p. 263. [4] Wheatley, III, 189.
[5] *Memoirs*, vol. II, p. 119.
[6] *Transactions of the Bibliographical Society*, vol. I (1893), pp. 77–90.

Contents

Illustrations

REPRODUCTIONS IN LINE

Abbreviations

DE BEER: The Diary of John Evelyn, edited by E. S. de Beer. In six volumes. Oxford: At the Clarendon Press. 1955.

HISCOCK: John Evelyn and his Family Circle. By W. G. Hiscock. London: Routledge and Kegan Paul. 1955.

WHEATLEY: The Diary of John Evelyn, to which are added a selection from his familiar letters, Edited by William Bray. A new edition in four volumes with a Life of the Author and a new preface by Henry B. Wheatley, F.S.A. London: Bickers and Son. 1906.

BL: Bibliotheca Lindesiana.

BLO: Bodleian Library, Oxford.

BM: British Museum.

CCE: Christ Church, Oxford, Evelyn Collection.

CH: H. E. Huntington Library, San Marino, California.

CLC: William L. Clark Library, Los Angeles, California.

GLL: Guildhall Library, London.

HCL: Harvard University, Cambridge, Mass.

K: Library of G. L. Keynes.

PL: Library Company of Philadelphia.

PML: Pierpont Morgan Library, New York.

PUL: Princeton University Library.

QCO: Queen's College, Oxford.

R: Rothamsted Agricultural Experiment Station.

TCC: Trinity College, Cambridge.

ULC: University Library, Cambridge.

VAF: Victoria and Albert Museum, Forster Collection.

Y: Yale University Library.

JOHN EVELYN

A STUDY IN BIBLIOPHILY

THE NAMES OF JOHN EVELYN AND SAMUEL PEPYS are so closely associated as the two great 'diarists' of the reign of Charles II that any mention of one inevitably recalls the other. Yet for every reader of Evelyn's Diary, probably there are a hundred or two hundred who have read the journal kept by Pepys. Evelyn's seems a dry record of facts and events compared with the rich human fare provided by Pepys's self-revelation, and parts of Evelyn's may even be called dull. Yet Evelyn was in some ways the bigger man of the two, more versatile, less self-seeking and self-indulgent—and it is exactly for all those qualities that it is so easy to like him less. Pepys himself summed up the matter in 1665 when he wrote of Evelyn: 'In fine, a most excellent person he is, and must be allowed a little for a little conceitedness; but he may well be so, being a man so much above others.'[1] Six months later, however, Pepys added, 'The more I know him, the more I love him,' and their correspondence shows that they formed a close and generous friendship. Both of them were lovers of books and culture, though Pepys was more the antiquarian collector than Evelyn. Pepys liked curiosities of typography, such as incunabula and Caxtons; Evelyn, on the other hand, had none of these and acquired books rather for the sake of the new information they contained, or because he was genuinely interested in them for their literary, philosophical, theological, or scientific content. He would not have despised Pepys's tastes, for he reverenced all means of cultivating the mind and regarded the formation of a library as one of the chief of these. It is unnecessary to drive the comparison between the two men any farther. Pepys has had almost more than his due of attention from modern scholars, whereas Evelyn has had noticeably less, and it is one of the objects of this book to present a study of Evelyn's character observed from the bibliophilic angle, and to try to communicate to others some of the writer's affection for the man. In this essay his general attitude to books and the methods he used in his library will be examined, and in the bibliography which follows he will be presented through the medium of the books he actually wrote and produced; most of them are both rare and obscure, and have remained quite unknown even to the readers of his Diary.

*   *   *

[1] Pepys, *Diary*, 5 Nov. 1665.

John Evelyn, born at Wotton in Surrey in October 1620, enjoyed the advantages of a good family and ample means. The family fortune had been derived chiefly from the manufacture of gunpowder, but Evelyn's nature in spite of this was gentle and pacific. He was always the scholar and virtuoso rather than the cavalier, and aggressiveness was entirely foreign to him. According to his own account his education was scrappy and imperfect. He was first instructed by a man named Fryer in the Church porch at Wotton, and was later sent to school at Lewes in Sussex. He refused, when he was thirteen, to go to Eton from his fear of the discipline he would encounter there, and insisted on returning to Lewes. He protests that when he left school at the age of seventeen it was rather because he was ashamed of staying there any longer than for any fitness to go to the University. One of his first acts on entering Balliol College, Oxford, was to discharge his duty as 'benefactor to the Library' by presenting eight volumes of theology by 'authors (it seems) desired by the students of Divinity there'.[1] These books are still in the College Library, and bear the inscription: *ex dono Johannis Evelyn filij Richardi Evelyn Armigerj et hujus Collegij Socio-Com.*

Of his three years at Oxford we know little, and it can only be inferred that his love of learning was given free scope to develop. He seems, at least, to have acquired a working knowledge of the Latin language and literature, though he speaks very modestly of his knowledge of Greek.[2] In 1640 he took up residence in the Temple, but he did not find the study of the Law at all congenial. It lacked the polish that he had already begun to value as one of the chief amenities of life and so it was soon abandoned. In 1641 he spent several months in Holland and Belgium, and already exhibited a marked taste for all forms of learning.

By nature and upbringing Evelyn was a Royalist, but he did not court adventure, and in 1643 he retired for the summer to his brother's house at Wotton, where he built himself a study and began to develop his latent taste for horticulture and ornamental water-works. In the autumn of that year he went to France, and for the next four years travelled in Europe. As we know from his Diary he had an insatiable zest for curiosities and sightseeing, and a receptive mind which could profit from all the things he saw. When he returned to England

[1] de Beer, II, 19.

[2] 'myne owne defects in the Greeke tongue and knowledge of its usefulnesse, obliges me to mention that particular with an extraordinary note.' Letter to Dr Christopher Wren, 4 April 1665. Wheatley, III, 305.

PLATE I

JOHN EVELYN AET. 28

by Robert Walker

in 1647 he was a gentleman of good general culture, and acquainted with several languages. This knowledge of men and affairs was further widened by a second long stay in Paris from midsummer of 1649 to the beginning of 1652.

Our impression of Evelyn at this period of his life, between the ages of twenty and thirty, will be made more vivid by considering two portraits, attributed to Vanderborcht[1] and Robert Walker,[2] which were at Wotton House. In the first, reproduced as the frontispiece to this book, we see a serious young man with a book in his hands, an excellent representation of him, we feel, as he really was in 1641. In the second (plate 1), done in 1648, the artist has expressed his sitter's fantasy of himself as he wished to be, carefully posed as a young philosopher, his elegant hand with its long tapering fingers resting uneasily on the emblem of mortality. Above is the Greek motto:

Ἡ δὲ μετάνοια αὐτὴ φιλοσοφίας ἀρχὴ γίνεται,

which may be rendered: 'Second thoughts are the beginning of philosophy.'

A less fanciful likeness was taken soon after this in Paris by the famous engraver Robert Nanteuil. His drawing was made in 1650,[3] and he also made an engraving on copper. Prints from the plate were no doubt circulated among Evelyn's friends, though it was not published until a long time afterwards, when it was employed as frontispiece to an edition of *Silva* in 1706.[4] In the meantime, however, Nanteuil's drawing or engraving had served as the basis for a very remarkable piece of portraiture, carved in high relief by a skilled hand from a block of oak (plate 2). Evelyn had made the acquaintance of Grinling Gibbons in 1670, and he laid the foundation of Gibbons's distinguished career by introducing him to the King on 18 January 1671.[5] According to Horace Walpole, in his *Catalogue of Painters*, Gibbons in gratitude 'made a present of his own bust in wood to Mr. Evelyn, who kept it at his house in Dover-street'.[6] Nothing further is known of this 'bust in wood' by Gibbons, though it seems probable that the oak carving in the National Maritime Museum at Greenwich is actually the work mentioned by Walpole, who may have used the term 'bust' rather loosely. The finer details of the carving have suffered somewhat by having been scraped down at some time, though the photograph reproduced here shows well enough the bold and life-like character of the head.[7] The work is

[1] de Beer, II, 29. [2] *Ibid.* II, 541. [3] *Ibid.* III, 9.
[4] See pp. 137–8. [5] de Beer, III, 568. [6] Wheatley, II, 255.
[7] Gibbons was a skilful craftsman in this kind of portraiture and made a fine relief of Sir Christopher Wren, now in the library of the RIBA. See David Green's *Grinling Gibbons* (London, 1964), p. 37.

undoubtedly contemporary with its subject, though representing him at an age many years younger than its actual date of execution. If it is not by Gibbons, it must be by some one not greatly inferior to him in skill and judgment. The carving is set in an oak panel on which Evelyn's name is inscribed, and has a contemporary frame as shown in the reproduction.

When Evelyn first went to Paris in 1643 he had immediately visited the English Ambassador, Sir Richard Browne. There are few references to Browne in the earlier parts of the Diary, but we may infer that from this visit in November 1643 sprang a friendship which was to influence profoundly the course of Evelyn's life. There is no further reference to Browne until in May 1647, in the course of describing how he had been robbed by a valet, he suddenly announces in a parenthesis his betrothal to Browne's daughter Mary. They were married in June, and later in the year Evelyn was visiting his father-in-law's house, Sayes Court, at Deptford. Browne forfeited the estate after the execution of Charles I, but six years later Evelyn bought Sayes Court from the authorities who held it, and it was to be his home for the next forty years. For many years Browne lived with his son-in-law, dying at the age of seventy-eight in 1683, and we may picture the two enjoying their books and manuscripts together at Sayes Court. Indeed, from this association has arisen a bibliopegic mystery which I hope presently to elucidate.

We may regard Evelyn's bibliophilic education as having properly begun in 1643 when he first went to Paris and met Sir Richard Browne. He could not in his wander-years have cultivated to the full his taste for books or have arranged a library, but there are various indications that he did not neglect the opportunities that offered themselves.

In later years he told Dr Wotton, 'I ever look upon a Library with the reverence of a temple'; the pages of his Diary bear witness that he neglected no chance of going to any famous library and that he carefully appraised their treasures. In his earlier travels he saw many of these. In the Luxembourg he noted in the library of the Duke of Orleans that it was 'well furnished with excellent books, all bound in maroquin and gilded, the valans of the shelves being of greene velvet, fring'd with gold',[1] so that even in 1644 he was interested in the details of library furnishing. He saw also the Vatican Library, and those in Florence, Bologna, Venice, Milan, and Geneva. Everywhere he notes the quality of their books and manuscripts. In later years he was familiar with the

[1] de Beer, II, 128.

PLATE 2

Evelyn's head in oak
attributed to Grinling Gibbons

University and College Libraries in Oxford and Cambridge. He found the Public Library in Cambridge 'but meane', though perhaps he was a prejudiced witness, for he says of Cambridge that 'the whole towne is situate in a low dirty unpleasant place, the streetes ill paved, the aire thick as infested by the fennes, nor are its churches anything considerable in compare to Oxford'.[1] He had, however, thought much on libraries and their arrangement, and in 1689 he wrote to Samuel Pepys a long letter[2] on the subject. This contains advice concerning the furnishing of Pepys's library with medals and portraits, and leads Evelyn to pass in review the state of English libraries at the date of writing.

There can be no doubt that he saw other libraries during his travels besides the large ones mentioned, particularly in France. Also he was in France in 1644, the year in which Gabriel Naudé, the celebrated *savant* and librarian, published a revised edition of his well-known book *Advis pour dresser une bibliothèque*, first published in 1627. Evelyn admired this so much that he made a translation, *Instructions for the Erecting of a Library*, published some years later in 1661. Naudé expressed the essence of bibliophily when he urged that there is no book whatsoever, be it never so bad or decried, but may in time be sought for by some person or other, and Evelyn was probably an apt pupil when Naudé recommended him 'to rummage and often to revisit the shops of frippery booksellers'. He already had an eye for manuscripts, and he would be attentive to Naudé's example of 'Pogius, who found Quintilian upon the counter of a cook's shop'. Late in life Evelyn himself wrote a short essay on manuscripts,[3] in which he said, 'Nor are (the Learned and Curious) to disdaine the rumaging sometimes of the most neglected corners of Shops, & other obscure places, however cover'd with dust & cobwebs, whereever one may heare or suspect some old Parchments may have ben cast; and to enquire what Trades & other Crafts (besides the Leafe Gold beaters, Book-binders, past-board, & the makers of Musical Instruments, who use it about the ribbs of Lutes, and other occasions) employ them in their works.' This breathes the true spirit of the game. On the whole he seems to have heeded Naudé's warning to 'neglect such books as are only valuable in respect of their antiquity, figures, paintings, binding and other weak considerations', though, as we shall see, he must have been wounded by Naudé's contemptuous observation that 'it becomes the ignorant only to esteem a book

[1] de Beer, III, 140. [2] Wheatley, III, 435–56.

[3] Printed in *Memoirs*, ed. Bray (1818), vol. II, pp. 334–48, 'Of Manuscripts'. The manuscript was at Wotton according to Wheatley, III, 190.

for its cover, so that it is a great deal better, and more necessary to have a good quantity of books well and ordinarily bound, than to have a little Chamber or Cabinet full of [books] washed, gilded, ruled, and enriched with all manner of nicety, lux and superfluity'.

During these fifteen years, 1640 to 1655, he had clearly learnt much about books, so much so that by 1652 his fame as a bookman was already beginning to spread. In December 1652 William Rand, a physician practising in London, was in a bookseller's shop in Cornhill when he overheard a description of a person of whom he had been for some time in search, namely someone worthy to be the dedicatee of his forthcoming translation of Gassendi's *Life of Nicolaus Claudius Fabricius, Lord of Peiresc, Senator of the Parliament at Aix.*[1] He even cried out *Heurica* in his joy, for at last he had found a man, the only one he had ever heard of in England, whose 'Peireskian virtues' did challenge his dedication, and upon enquiry learnt that this unique character was none other than John Evelyn, then of Sayes Court, Deptford, whose mother his kinsman Dr Ralph Rand of Godalming had attended professionally at Wotton in her last illness in 1635. The chief 'Peireskian virtue' was the assiduous cultivation of the mind, and Peiresc himself was the embodiment of wit, industry, and scholarship, a man 'whose sprightful curiosity left nothing unsearcht into, in the vast and all-comprehending Dominions of Nature and Art'. His interests ranged over astronomy, science, medals, genealogy, mathematics, geography, and heraldry. Evelyn may have been embarrassed by the weight of virtue with which Dr Rand endowed him, but that his choice was just none could deny, for Evelyn stands out among the figures of the second half of the seventeenth century as an example of industry, learning and width of interest. Even in wit, though it was often overlaid by his heavier virtues, he was not deficient, and Pepys himself has enthusiastically testified to this. In September 1665, after the news had been received of a minor victory over the Dutch fleet, Pepys supped at Greenwich at Captain Cocke's and met there Sir William Doyly, Sir John Minnes and Mr Evelyn.

This newes [he says] inspired into Sir J. Minnes and Mr. Evelyn such a spirit of mirth, that in all my life I never met with so merry a two hours as our company this night was. Among other humours Mr. Evelyn's repeating of some verses made up of nothing but the various acceptations of *may* and *can*, and doing it so aptly upon occasion of something of that nature, and so fast, did make us all die almost with laughing, and did so stop the mouth of Sir J. Minnes

[1] For details of this book see p. 283.

in the middle of all his mirth (and in a manner so agreeing with his own manner of genius) that I never saw any man so out-done in all my life; and Sr. J. Minnes's mirth too to see himself out-done, was the crown of all the mirth.[1]

In his writings, too, Evelyn frequently exhibits a dry wit which has been largely overlooked. Our chief concern, however, at the moment is with the 'Peireskian virtues' as they bear upon the knowledge and love of books, and Gassendi makes it clear that in this sphere Peiresc was indeed pre-eminent. He bought books in all the capitals of Europe, and instructed his friends to look out for them on his behalf at all times and places. 'Also where-ever any Libraries were to be sold by out-cry, he took order to have the rarer books bought up, especially such as were of some neat Edition which he had not.' Further, 'he would be sure to have them neatly bound and covered; to which end, he kept an industrious Book-binder in his House, who did exquisitely bind and adorn them. Yea, and sometimes he kept many book-binders at once; for one man was hardly ever able to bind up such store of books, as came trowling in from all parts!' All books bound for himself were stamped with his mark, a monogram of the Greek letters ΝΚΦ, neatly interwoven. He would even give and lend books almost as lavishly as he bought them, and of those that were lent an innumerable company was never returned. And now comes the crown of the 'Peireskian virtues', for he would return good for evil with an almost incredible generosity. It is related of him that 'it happened frequently that such Books as he borrowed, being neglected by their owners and ill-bound, he delivered to his binder to be rectified and beautified, viz. when their subject matter or rarity deserved that cost; so that having received them ill-bound and ill-favoured he returned them trim and handsome'. His care would extend even to 'fragments of Books and Leaves half eaten', and he would justify the charges he was at by saying that 'inasmuch as the best Books, when they fell into unlearned men's hands ill-accoutred, were pitifully used; he therefore endeavoured that they might be prized at least for the beauty of their binding, and so escape the danger of the Tobacconist and Grocer'.[2] But although Peiresc bought books so fast and tended them individually so well (and perhaps because of this), he failed in their collective arrangement. When the shelves were full the books remained stacked in the porch of his study, and piled in heaps and scattered over the furniture in every room of his house. He annotated his books profusely in the margins, and showed an almost modern passion for association copies and authors' manuscripts. He

[1] Pepys, *Diary*, 10 Sept. 1665. [2] *Life of Peiresc* (1657), p. 195.

even kept a faithful and laborious scribe, so that, should he wish, he might have anything transcribed in any language. He also kept a tortoise, and several

E Libris Evelyni
emptus: Lond: 1643.

Omnia explorate, Meliora retinete.

Evelyni Catalogo Inscriptus.

From the Westminster School *Institutio Græcæ Gram.*, 1640

Ex Libris Evelyni emptus apud Tours
16: Junij 1644: pret: 2: [illegible]
Omnia explorate, Meliora Retinete.

Dominus providebit.

H. 2. 4

From the *Symbolica Ægyptorum Sapientia* of Nicolas Caussin, 1634

Catalogo Evelyni Inscripti
Provove All-things,
Retaine the Best.

From an unknown book

INSCRIPTIONS IN EVELYN'S BOOKS

nightingales, and was ever to be found surrounded by cats. Yet there was a purpose in the cats, for they defended his books against the destroying teeth of rats and mice.

Evelyn could indeed challenge most of these virtues, and even transcend some of them. He was evidently a born and inveterate collector, and began acquiring books about 1640, when he was twenty. Naudé makes some observations on the getting of books by gift, the least expensive method of collecting. He says:

E Libris Evelynis: emptus
Lond: 21: Feb: 1647.

Omnia Explorate; Meliora Retinete

From an unknown book.

E Libris Evelynis emptus Lond: 1648.

Omnia Explorate; Meliora Retinete.

From an unknown book

Ex dono J: Crassi
Amici optimi. 1649

From the *Paradisus Precum* of Luis de Granada, 1589

INSCRIPTIONS IN EVELYN'S BOOKS

'We have only to publish and make known to everybody the affection which we have to books, and the extraordinary desire which we have to erect a Library; for this being once divulged and communicated it is certain that if he who designs it be in sufficient credit and authority to do his friends pleasure, there will not be a man of them but will take it for an honour to present him with the most curious Books that come into his hands.' We can see from the inscriptions in his books, that Evelyn pursued this method with some success, the names of his generous friends being punctiliously entered on the fly-leaves.

From the beginning of his collecting days he made a habit of setting his individual marks of ownership on his books, a duty which he performed with all the loving care of a bibliophil, and a number of these are reproduced on the preceding pages. His signature he wrote with elaboration, often combining the initials into a monogram. The place of purchase is sometimes recorded with the date and the price paid, or the name of the friend who had been privileged to enrich his library. When the book had been entered in his catalogue the fact is duly recorded, the case and shelf-marks being added below. Nearly always he wrote somewhere in the book his motto,

Omnia Explorate, *Meliora Retinete.*
or Proove All things, Retaine the Best.

It has been suggested[1] that the second part of this motto, *Meliora Retinete*, was inspired by the Greek words *εὐ ἐλεῖν*, which Evelyn would have pronounced *ev heleen*. Occasionally, however, he wrote the motto in Greek and then in the form, *πάντα δοκιμάζετε· τὸ καλὸν κατέχετε*, so that the other ingenious suggestion is unlikely to be correct. The original source of the whole motto was doubtless the words in I Thessalonians v. 21, 'Prove all things: hold fast that which is good.' Occasionally he used also the motto *Dominus providebit* accompanied by the mystic pentacle, with or without the words *Un Dieu*, *Un Amy.* The pentacle, a five-pointed star drawn with a single line, is not to be confounded with the six-pointed Solomon's seal, or hexagram, made by one equilateral triangle superimposed on another. The pentacle is a magic symbol of uncertain significance. It was generally used by Evelyn as a secret sign to express a sense of preciousness and particularity, as when he made a book of Devotions for his much adored friend, Mrs Godolphin. In the example illustrated (see p. 10) the longer motto seems to have been written in as an afterthought.

Many of Evelyn's contemporaries inserted an armorial book-plate in their books. He observed this custom as far as having a book-plate made when he succeeded to the estates at Wotton, and an example of it is to be seen in the Franks Collection in the British Museum.[2] This plate belongs, however, to the last years of his life, since he did not obtain possession of Wotton until 1699. It cannot have been inserted in many of the books he possessed before that date, as

[1] By the late Lt.-Col. W. E. Moss. [2] Franks Collection, Brighton plates, no. 241.

I have not noticed it in any of the numerous volumes examined at Wotton and now in the Evelyn Collection at Christ Church, Oxford. The Collection contains two drawings in pencil and pen for a book-plate made by Abraham Bosse (1602–76).

The mention of his catalogue in the inscriptions introduces one of Evelyn's most curious and characteristic foibles. There have been many methods of arranging libraries, the method having in many instances, even in some of our greatest libraries, grown up haphazard as the books accumulated. Gabriel Naudé had a good deal to say about this subject, and Evelyn took note of his dictum that books should be arranged in classes and faculties, this order being 'much better and easier than that of the Ambrosian Library, and some others, where all the Books are indifferently ranged *pell mesle*, according to the order of their volumes and Ciffers, and onely distinguished in a Catalogue, wherein every piece is found under the name of its Author'. The simplest might have seemed to be the best, but Evelyn's mind did not work in that way. He and his friends of the Royal Society were much exercised at this period about scientific method and classifications, and tried to apply their new ideas to all branches of intellectual activity from entomology to language. Evelyn must have been aware in later years of the method adopted in his library by Samuel Pepys, who arranged his books entirely according to their size, so that the eye should not be disturbed by irregular lines along the tops. Pepys even had small leather-covered pedestals of wood, or 'stilts' as he called them, made for books whose sizes could not otherwise be accommodated to that of their fellows. No such method satisfied Evelyn: it was much too primitive. He certainly started cataloguing his books from an early stage of his book career. Three different catalogues were sold with the Upcott papers at Sotheby's in 1846,[1] and there are at least two now in the Evelyn Collection. One of these is a list with a title-page elaborately penned by Evelyn's amanuensis, Richard Hoare, and dated 1653. The other corresponds with the description of lot 60 in the Upcott sale, and it may then have been secured for restoration to the library at Wotton. It is a much more elaborate

[1] 60. Evelyn (John) Alphabetical Catalogue of his Library in his own hand, russia. fol.
  *** Illustrated with proof impressions of the portraits and prints from Evelyn's Memoirs.

61. — a Classified Catalogue of his Library, written with his own hand, russia. fol.
  *** Proof impressions of the portraits of Evelyn and his wife, and of his father-in-law, Sir Richard Browne, inserted.

62. — Catalogue of the Library at Wotton, imperfect—Catalogue of the Library of Dr. Ralph Bohun, of Oxford (Evelyn's Tutor) in his own hand, with the price he paid for each book.

affair and carries inside the cover the faded vellum label from the original binding. This has an inscription beginning: *Catalogus Evelynian[us]*, 1687. The rest is illegible, but at least the date is clear. This volume Mr John Evelyn has allowed me to borrow and examine at leisure, so that it can be described in some detail. The catalogue appears to be complete, though Upcott's binding of russia leather is becoming shaky, and many of the leaves of the manuscript are loose.[1] It is partly in Evelyn's hand, and most of it is carefully and clearly written. By this date his method had become somewhat elaborate, and on the first leaf of the catalogue, both sides of which are reproduced here (plates 3 and 4, reduced), he has indicated the principles which commended themselves to him. First he tabulates a 'Method for a Librarie According to the Intellectural Powers'. The *Intellectual Powers* are subdivided into six heads, three of which employ *Memorie*, and three *Judgment*, the subheadings amounting to nearly 120. Certainly Naudé was being followed to his logical conclusion!

In the actual cataloguing and shelf-marking further complications followed. Twenty years before the date of this catalogue Evelyn mentioned under the date 12 March 1668 a visit to the famous Cottonian Library,[2] where, as is well known, Sir Robert Cotton's manuscripts were arranged in presses, each of which was surmounted by the bust of a Roman emperor, the presses being named accordingly. They ranged from Julius to Domitian, and were supplemented by Cleopatra and Faustina. The shelves in each press were then lettered and the individual books numbered. Evelyn saw and noted, and went home determined one day to go several better than this. He sat down to his catalogue in 1687 and first made some abortive attempts to provide a suitable system of naming for his shelves. He tried letters and numbers for the different subjects, but abandoned this after getting as far as O in the alphabet. He then began writing out the names of the Greek gods—Mercurius, Apollo—whereupon he broke off into the nine muses, Calliope, Clio, Euterpe, Thalia, Melpomene, Erato, Terpsichore, Polymnia (whom he first wrote Polyphymia), Urania. This did not seem satisfactory and he set off on the Roman emperors, running through the dozen from Julius to Domitian. But it was not enough to supplement them with Cleopatra and Faustina as Cotton had done, so he added instead the seven sages of Greece, Cleobulus, Periander, Pittacus, Solon, Bias, Thales, Chilon, and supplemented these with Eunomia, Dice, and Irene. These trials had set him on the right road,

[1] The manuscript was later rebound for Mr Evelyn and so made secure for the future.

[2] de Beer, III, 507.

and his final scheme is triumphantly headed 'Localities for the shelves & presses'. In this table the subjects are set out on the left, then follow the classes of names which he proposed to use and the names themselves. Grammar is assigned to Cadmus; Poetry to the nine Muses; Theology to the Graces; Philosophy to the Sages; Military matters to the Furies; Medicine (a little unkindly) to the Fates, Clotho, Lachesis, and Atropos; Jurisprudence to the Judges; unspecified subjects to the Hours, Satyrs, Gods, Goddesses, and the Syren; Politics to the Four Empires; History, including Geography, to the Emperors, Seasons, and Continents; Science to the Elements and the Winds; Mathematics to the Planets and the signs of the Zodiac. The whole table is printed below. The actual names number ninety-five, and even these do not include all that he used. Evelyn was satisfied, and the compilation of the catalogue proceeded. On the fly-leaves of his books he wrote *Catalogo J. Evelyni Inscriptus*, and below is usually written the name of the shelf according to the Scheme. The assignment of the name was not always exactly suitable: thus it

LOCALITIES FOR THE SHELVES AND PRESSES

24 Lit: A. B. C. D. E. F. &c.			
Gram:			Cadmus.
Poet:	9	Muses:	Calliope, Clio, Euterpe, Thalia, Melpomene, Erato, Terpsichore, Polymnia, Urania.
Theol:	3	Graces:	Aglaia, Thalia, Euphrosyne.
Philos:	7	Sapientes:	Cleobulus, Periander, Pittacus, Solon, Bias, Thales, Chilon.
Rei Milit:	3	Furies:	Tisiphone, Megæra, Alecto.
Medic:	3	Parcæ:	Clotho, Lachesis, Atropos.
Jurid:	4 [3]	Judices Imp:	Eacus, Minos, Rhadamanthus.
	3	Horæ:	Eunomia, Dice, Irene.
	3	Satyri:	Silenus, Pan, Bacchus.
	5	Divi:	Hercules, Neptune, Vulcan, Apollo, Mercury.
	3	Deæ:	Juno, Venus, Minerva.
	1	Syren:	Parthenopea.
Polit:	4	Monarches:	Assyrian, Persian, Grecian, Roman.
Histor:	12	Imper Ro:	Jul., Aug., Tiberius, Caligula, Claudius, Nero, Galba, Otho, Vitellius, Vespasian, Titus, Domitian.
	4	Anni Tem:	Ver, Æstus, Autumnus, Hyems.
	4	Mundi par:	Europa, Asia, Africa, America.
Mater:	4	Elements:	Ignis, Aer, Aqua, Terra.
	4	Venti:	Oriens, Occidens, Auster, Nola.
Mathemat:	7	Planeta:	♄ ♃ ♂ ☉ ♀ ☿ ☾
	12	Signa:	♈ ♉ ♊ ♋ ♌ ♍ ♎ ♏ ♐ ♑ ♒ ♓

happened that *De Imitatione Christi* somehow got into Apollo, and the *Book of Common Prayer* rested in Venus. But that did not matter provided the scheme worked, which apparently it did for some years, to Evelyn's satisfaction.

A perusal of the catalogue gives a plain proof of the width of Evelyn's interests and the thoroughness of his way of cultivating them. The analysis of the catalogue below gives the number of books he possessed in the various sections,

ANALYSIS OF EVELYN'S LIBRARY, 1687

	Books	Pamphlets
Libri Theologici Scholastici & Heterodoxi	782	107
Libri Ecclesiast. Gen. Partic. Chronologici, Virorum Illustrium Vitæ &c.	832	15
Libri Poetici	518	112
Libri Philologici Literatores et Miscellanei	148	2
Libri Juridici	231	62
Libri Grammatici Logici Rhetorici Dictionar. Bibliothecarii Epistolae &c.	308	66
Libri Philosophici	204	8
Libri Medici	189	48
Historiae Materiarum & Œconom. Rei Rustici Mechanologici &c.	127	36
Politici et Rei Militaris	276	238
Libri Mathematici Musici &c.	244	97
Farrago Miscellanea & Sched'æ	.	31
Manuscripts	225	.
	4084	822
	4906	

The Manuscripts include bundles of letters. There were also Historical Tables upon pastbord; Chronological Tables; Mr Oughtred's Large Horizontal dials; Mapps & Sea Cards; Charts & Maps; Graphicè, Sculpture & Taille-douce in Books & Rolls; Copy Books; Icones &c.; Prospects, Landscapes &c.; Effigies of Famous Persons.

and although it shows a preponderance on the theological side, it also shows that poetry (including drama)[1] occupied a very large place in his mind, and that all the branches of science, mathematics and philosophy were represented in due proportion. The shortest section, dealing with his special interests in forestry and country affairs, is printed in an appendix to the present work as an example of a portion of his library and his manner of listing it.

It is impossible to specify many individual books among a collection of almost five thousand titles. It may be noted, however, that Evelyn's interests were more contemporary than antiquarian, whatever the subject. There are therefore very

[1] Many of the books in this section were added by John Evelyn jun.

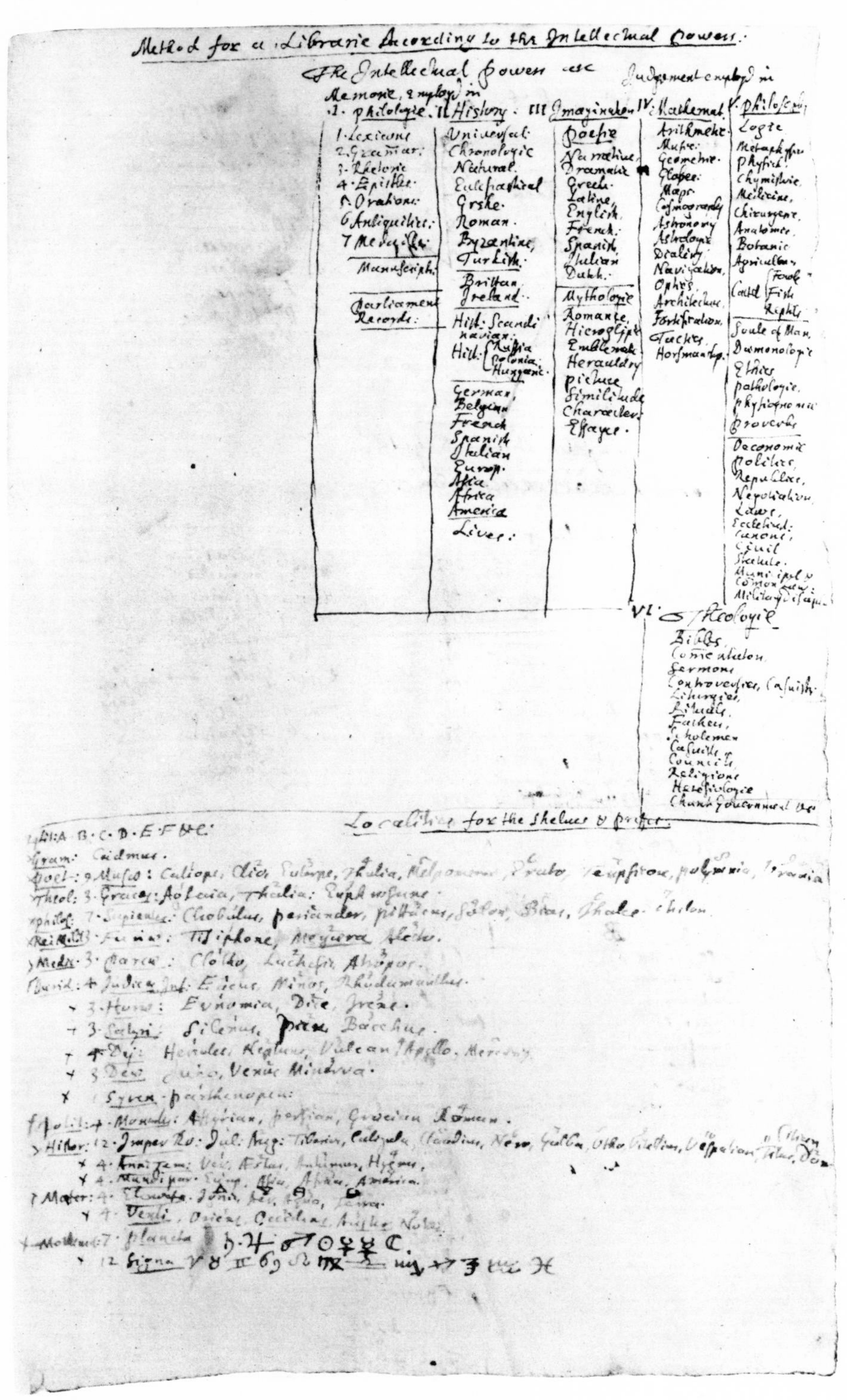

Method for a Librarie According to the Intellectual Powers.

The Intellectual Powers are

Memorie, employed in | Judgement employed in

I. Philologie.
1. Lexicons
2. Grammar.
3. Rhetoric
4. Epistles.
5. Orations.
6 Antiquities.
7 Medals.

Manuscripts.

Parliament Records.

II History.
Universal.
Chronologic
Natural.
Ecclesiastical
Greke.
Roman.
Byzantine,
Turkish.

Brittan.
Ireland.

Hist: Scandinavian.
Hist: Russia, Polonia, Hungarie.

German,
Belgian
French
Spanish
Italian
Europ.
Asia
Africa
America

Lives:

III Imagination
Poesie
Narrative,
Dramatic
Greek.
Latine,
English.
French.
Spanish
Italian
Dutch.

Mythologie
Romance,
Hieroglyph
Emblemata
Herauldry
picture
Similitude
Character.
Essayes.

IV. Mathemat.
Arithmetic.
Music.
Geometrie.
Globes.
Maps.
Cosmography
Astronomy
Astrologie
Dialing
Navigation.
Optics.
Architecture.
Fortification.
Tactics.
Horsmanship.

V. Philosophy
Logic
Metaphysics
Physics.
Chymistrie.
Medicine,
Chirurgerie.
Anatomie.
Botanic
Agriculture
Cattle: Fowle, Fish, Reptils

Soule of Man.
Dæmonologie
Ethics
pathologie.
physiognomie
Proverbs

Oeconomic
Politics,
Republics,
Negotiation.
Laws,
Ecclesiast:
Canonic,
Civil
Statute.
Municipal & Comon Law:
Military Discipline

VI. Theologie
Bibles,
Comentation
Sermons
Controversies, Casuists.
Liturgies,
Rituals,
Fathers,
Scholemen
Casuists
Councils,
Religions
Heresiologie
Church Government &c

Localities for the Shelves & presses.

Alph: A · B · C · D · E · F &c:
Gram: Cadmus.
Poet: 9 Muses: Caliope, Clio, Euterpe, Thalia, Melpomene, Erato, Terpsichore, polymnia, Urania
Theol: 3. Graces: Aglaia, Thalia: Euphrosyne.
Philos: 7. Sapientes: Cleobulus, periander, pittacus, Solon, Bias, Thales, Chilon.
[illegible]: 3 Furies: Tisiphone, Megæra, Alecto.
Medic: 3. Parcæ: Clotho, Lachesis, Atropos.
Jurid: 4 Judices Inf: Eacus, Minos, Rhadamanthus.
3. Horæ: Eunomia, Dice, Irene.
3. Satyri: Silenus, Pan, Bacchus.
4 Dij: Hercules, Neptune, Vulcan, Apollo, Mercury.
3 Deæ: Juno, Venus, Minerva.
1 Syren: parthenope.
Polit: 4. Monarch: Assyrian, persian, Grecian, Roman.
Histor: 12. Imper. Ro: Jul: Aug: Tiberius, Caligula, Claudius, Nero, Galba, Otho, Vitellius, Vespasian, Titus, Domitian
4. Anni Tem: Ver, Æstas, Autumnus, Hyems,
4. Mundi par: Europ, Asia, Africa, America.
Mater: 4. Elementa: Ignis, Aer, Aqua, Terra.
4. Venti: Oriens, Occidens, Auster, Notus.
Mathemat: 7. planeta ♄ ♃ ♂ ☉ ♀ ☿ ☾.
12 Signa ♈ ♉ ♊ ♋ ♌ ♍ ♎ ♏ ♐ ♑ ♒ ♓

PLATE 3

Evelyn's library catalogue, 1687

first leaf verso

Index Capitum

1. Libri Theol.-Schol. &c. p. 1
2. Libri Historici &c. — 49
3. Poetici — 77
4. ~~Philolog.~~ Litterat. Miscellanea — 97
5. Juridici — 109
Gram: Logic. Rhetor. Dict. Bibl. Epistolae — 121
7. Philosophici — 137
8. Medici — 149
9. Historiae Materiarum [Mechan.] — 159
10. Politici et Rei militaris — 167
11. Mathemat. Musici — 183 / 201
Farrag.

Booke & pamphlets stitch'd, Schedae & loose papers under every head. [illegible]

1. Mercurius
2. Apollo:
1. Calliope:
2. Clio:
3. Erato:
4. Thalia:
5. Melpomene:
6. Terpsichore:
7. Euterpe:
8. Polyhymnia:
9. Urania:

Schedae in Loculis

		Cove	pag:
1	Theol:	A	1
2	Histor:	B	49
3	Polit:	C	167
4	Jurid:	D	109
5	Mathemat. Musica	E	183
6	Medic:	F	149
7	Gramat:	G	121
8	Poet:	H	77
9	Philos:	I	137
10	Philolog:	K	97
11	Mater: Rei Rust. Mechan. Oeconom:	L	159
12	Farrag:	M	201
13	Mss. Fragmenta	N	
14	Almanacs	O	
+15	Mss		

In the Closet

Theol: 1. Julius — 2. Augustus
Hist: 3. Tiberius
Polit: 4. Caligula
Math: 5. Claudius — 6. Nero
Medic: 7. Galba — 8. Otho
Gram: 9. Vitellius
Poet: 10. Vespasian — 11. Titus
12. Domitian

1. Thales: philos
2. Bias: philol
3. Solon: Mater
4. Pittacus
5. Periander
7. Cleobulus
6. Chilon
1. Jeane
2. Dice
3. Eunomia: Farrag

A short Method for Catalogue:

Numb.	Author in B	Vol	Impress	Ann	Subject	Place	fig
1	Biblia Sacra &c.	fol.	Roma	1563	Theol:	A	1
2	Bellarminus	fol.	Paris	1633	Theol:	A	6
3	Bodinus	Octav.	Lugd:	1596	Polit:	C	12
4	Bacon Sr Fra:	fol:	Lond:	1620	Philos:	I	20
5	Buxtorf	4°	[illegible]	1643	log.	G	34
6	Barclay	8°	Paris	1614	Polit:	M	15
7	Baluzi	4	Lond	1640	Hist:	B	18

Et sic per totum Alphabetum

Compacti	Numb of Volumes &c.	Pamphlets Coves	
Theol	780	107	A
Hist:	830	16	B
Polit:	327	101	C
Jurid:	231	52	D
Math:	247	45	E
Medic	189	40	F
Gram:	306	56	G
Poet:	518	110	H
Philos:	201	8	I
Philol:	147	2	K
Mater:	127	39	L
Farrag: &c.		31	M
	3703	605	
	605		
Total	4308		

PLATE 4

Evelyn's library catalogue, 1687

first leaf recto

few books of the sixteenth century and none of the fifteenth. His Chaucer is the edition of 1602; his Shakespeare the folio of 1632; his Spenser the edition of 1653; his Donne the octavo of 1650. He seems to have taken special note of the works of the great Dean of St Paul's, and in different parts of the catalogue are found, besides the *Poems*, *Pseudomartyr*, 1610, *Juvenilia*, 1633, *Ignatius*, 1634, *Biathanatos* (1646), and *Letters*, 1651. Among the poetical pamphlets there is one entitled 'Dr Dunn's good-night', which suggests that there may have been a separate printing, not known at the present time, of Elegie XII, or of one of the Epithalamions.

One of the most tantalizing entries in the catalogue is Evelyn's note on a bundle among the manuscripts headed 'Letters from divers Learned men & others to me'. It contained letters from 'Mr. Caly, Mr. Thicknesse, Henshaw, Owen, Dr. Needham, Melington, Burgh, Wase, Barton, Dr. Rand, Thurland, Mr. Boile, Hartlib, Dr. Brown, Tuke, Carter, Dr. Worsley, Sr Rob. Murray, Ab. Cowley, Sr R. Fanshaw, Mr. Creech, Oldenburg, Dr. Casaubon, Mr. Philips, Heath, Sr G. Mackenzie, Sr Ja. Langham, Dr. Glanvill, Sr T. Hanmer, Dr. Stokes, Sr W. Curtius, Mr. Ashmole, Mr. Hooke, Greene, Mr. Flamested, Sr Chr. Wren, Blount, Dr. Grew, Dr. Tyson'. It is to be feared that many of this imposing array have disappeared, though several of them are represented among Evelyn's published correspondence.

It may be surmised that Evelyn ultimately found his gods and goddesses too cumbrous to preside permanently over his shelves and presses, for these class-marks have been erased in some of his books (see facsimile on p. 127). Also he wrote below his other schemes in the catalogue a table headed 'A shorter Method for the Catalogue' as follows:

Numb.	Author in B	Vol.	Impress.	Ann.	Subject	Abac.	fig.
1	Biblia sacra &c:	fol	Roma	1563	Theol.	A	1
2	Bellarminus	fol	Paris	1633	Theol.	A	6
3	Bodinus	8	Lugd	1596	Polit.	C	12
4	Bacon Sr Fra:	fol	Lond:	1620	Philos.	P	20
5	Buridan	4°	Argent	1643	Log.	G	34
6	Barckley	8	Patav	1614	Poet.	M	15
7	Baleus	4	Lond	1640	Hist.	B	18

It is clear that Evelyn took infinite pains over the constitution and arrangement of his own library. He was also solicitous for the instruction of others, and in May 1661 he drew up a scheme for the formation of a library for the use of

DESIGNE FOR A LIBRARY

1 Dictionaries & Bookes Subsidiary

2 Bookes of Naturall Philosophy
- 1 Physici
  - 1 Men
  - 2 Birds
  - 3 Beasts
  - 4 Fishes
  - 5 Insects
  - 6 Monsters
  - 7 Stones metalls Water Earth &c
- 2 Medici
  - 1 Anatomie
  - 2 Chirurgirie
  - 3 Botanie
  - 4 Druggs *Materia Medica*
  - 5 Formes &c
  - 6 Chymistrie
  - 7 Cures

3 Bookes of Arts Liberall
- 1 Arithmetick
- 2 Geometry
  - 1 Architecture
  - 2 Machines
  - 3 Paynting
- 3 Optics
  - 1 Perspective
  - 2 Sceanes &c
- 6 Musick

4 Bookes of Arts Illiberall and purely Mechanick
- 1 Usefull & Vulgar
- 2 Meane
- 3 Servile
- 4 Rusticall
- 5 Female
- 6 Polite
- 7 More Liberall
- 8 Curious
- 9 Exotick
- (1–9: See my Catalogue)
- 10 Modells & Engines belonging to them

5 Bookes treating of the Universe
- 1 Cosmography
- 2 Hydrography
- 3 Geography
- 4 Uranometry
- 5 Astrologie

6 Bookes of
- Oeconomy
  - 1 Georgicks
  - 2 Gardning
- Gymnasticks
  - 1 Fencing
  - 2 Cavalerizzo
- Military
  - 1 Tacticks
  - 2 Fortification

7 Bookes of
- 1 Pneumaticks
- 2 Magick

J Evelyn 1661 22 May

For Sr Robert Murray.

the Royal Society. This appears to have been done at the instigation of Sir Robert Moray, then President of the Society, and is as on the page opposite.[1]

Evelyn's methodical survey of the sciences in this *Designe for a Library* shows his desire for a compendious selection of books which should give the reader all he needed without the necessity for finding his own way through a maze of superfluities. He expressed the same thought many years later in a letter to Pepys dated 2 September 1694: 'What a benefactor were he that were able and willing to give us such a catalogue of authors as were onely, and absolutely, and fully effectual to the attaining of such a competency of practical, usefull, and speculative knowledge too, as one might hope to benefit by within the ordinarie circles of one's life, without being bewildered and quite out of the way when one should be gotten home. I am still perswaded this were not impossible, and that lesse than an hundred authors, studied in proper method, would go a greate way towards this end.'[2] Yet, in spite of this desire for order, Evelyn did not achieve his aim in forming the library of the Royal Society. It was, indeed, at his instigation that in 1667 Henry Howard presented the Society with 'the Library of Arundel House, to dispose thereof as their propriety, desiring only that in case the Society should come to faile, it might return to Arundel House'.[3] The Society thus came to possess a very miscellaneous collection of books and manuscripts, many of which had belonged to Bilibald Pirckheimer and contained his book-plate engraved by Albert Dürer. A later generation, however, with too little regard for Howard's generosity and too much for Evelyn's wish for a short way to knowledge, saw fit to dispose of many of these. The manuscripts were sold to the British Museum in 1830 and 1835, a step which can scarcely be criticized. Evelyn had, indeed, himself suggested to Howard in 1669 that the Society should be allowed to exchange the manuscripts with the University of Oxford 'for Mathematical, Philosophical, and such other Books, as may prove most usefull to the designe and Institution of it'.[4] With less propriety, 'superfluous books from the collection of works in miscellaneous literature' were disposed of in 1872 by open sale.[5] A further selection of 228 lots was sold at Sotheby's on 4 May 1925.

[1] Copied from the manuscript in Evelyn's hand in the archives of the Royal Society (Classified Papers, XVII, i). The manuscript was the subject of a note by W. R. B. Prideaux in *The Antiquary*, n.s. 1912, vol. VIII, pp. 127–9.

[2] *Private Correspondence of Pepys*, ed. Tanner (1926), vol. I, pp. 100–1.

[3] *The Record of the Royal Society*, ed. 3 (London, 1912), p. 233.

[4] de Beer, III, 472.

[5] *The Record of the Royal Society*, p. 234.

Evelyn's solicitude for learning extended also to the improvement of the English language,[1] and to the improvement of the classical texts provided for the instruction of the young. On 27 November 1666 he wrote to the Lord Chancellor Clarendon,

recommending a reformation in the printing of books in England, especially school-books and Greek and Latin authors, they being so incorrectly printed here, and from bad copies, that we export great sums to buy foreign editions. He suggests whether it might not be expedient, 1. That inspection might be had what Text of the Greek and Latin authors should be followed in future impressions; 2. That a Censor be established to take care that our Presses in London be provided with able Correctors, principally for school-books, which are of loose and repeated impressions. 3. That the charge be advanced by the [Stationers'] Company who can easily be re-imbursed by allowance on better editions. The season is now most proper, when this sad calamity has mortified a Company which was exceedingly hauty and difficult to manage to any useful reformation.[2]

Evelyn's catalogue of his own library establishes by itself his claim to the style of Bibliophil, and is one of the many existing testimonies to his extraordinary industry. Besides this catalogue he made many other manuscript volumes in his own hand. Some of these are still in the Collection, as for example *Instructions for the Gardiner at Sayes Court*, and *Memoires for my Grandson*, both of which I have been privileged to transcribe and edit. Others have somehow leaked out into collectors' hands, such as the *Coelum Sanitatis*, formerly in Lord Crewe's library, containing an extravagant account of the manufacture and chemical properties of alcohol, and *A Particular of my Estate*, now in the Houghton Library, Harvard University. More important than these is Evelyn's *Life of Mrs Godolphin*, which he wrote some time after her tragic death at the age of twenty-six in September 1678. This excellent lady, formerly Mrs Blagge, a maid of honour to the Queen, was admired by Evelyn as a paragon of all the virtues. He was more than thirty years her senior, but they had much in common, and they felt for one another a deep, though platonic affection. After her death, following the birth of a son, Francis, Evelyn was charged by the grief-stricken husband with all the funeral arrangements. He was also given much of the responsibility for the upbringing of the son, and wrote her life at considerable length. A manuscript, beautifully written in his own hand, is still extant. Sixteen years after sending it to Lady Sylvius, at whose instigation the book was first written, he amplified it and added a dedicatory letter to the widower, who was now Lord High Treasurer

[1] See below, p. 277, no. 163. [2] *Memoirs*, ed. Bray (1818), vol. II, p. 128.

[3] Sold at Sotheby's, 4 March 1937, lot 686 (Goldschmidt, £58).

of England. Evelyn caused the book to be bound in elaborately tooled morocco with his cipher in the centre of the design (see plate 14), and the whole forms a beautiful and touching tribute to the memory of Mrs Godolphin. It is more fully described on another page (see pp. 247, 250).

Evelyn had a passion, in fact, for making everything into a book. Others in his own hand formerly at Wotton include a book of recipes, beginning with one 'to comfort an over-ridden horse'; a volume of *Loci communes theologici*, an immense folio, quite full; also numerous volumes of religious Offices and pious meditations![1] Another large folio is headed *A substantial and learned digest of common-places*, though the pages have mostly remained blank. Perhaps it was intended for the reception of the 'packets & Bundles of Excerpts of all Subjects intended to have been transcribed into Books and Adversaria, but growing too numerous and most of them superfluous, I left off that thought'.[2] Another collection of miscellaneous papers and notes sold at the Upcott sale in 1846 is now in the British Museum (Add. MS. 15950). He wrote a small volume of rather commonplace poetry and an unfinished tragi-comedy entitled *Thirsander*. These are both in the Evelyn Collection. Another incomplete play attributed to him was sold with the Upcott papers in 1846, and was called *The Originals, A Comedy*. Evelyn read some of his poetry to Pepys, 'though with too much gusto'. The poems, Pepys thought, 'were not transcendant, yet one or two very pretty epigrams, among others, of a lady looking in at a grate, and being pecked at by an eagle that was there'. The reading was interrupted by the entry of Captain Cocke, 'as drunk as a dogg, but could stand, and talk and laugh',[3] and we hear no more literary criticism.

Probably other works by Evelyn existed and have been lost. One such is mentioned by him in a letter to Pepys dated 6 December 1681 as

> that discourse wherein I did attempt to shew how far a gentleman might become very knowing, and to good purpose, by the onely assistance of the modern languages.... There is in it a usefull rescention of good authors, and a method of reading them to advantage; beside some thing in the discourse (after my way) which perhaps would not have displeased you; nor was it without purpose of one day publishing it, not for ostentation, but because 'twas written with a virtuous design of provoking the Court *fopps*, and for incouragement of illustrious persons who have leasure and inclynations to cultivate their minds beyond the farce, 'A *whore* and a *dog*', which (with very little besides) are the confines of their greate understandings.[4]

[1] A list is given by Hiscock, pp. 243–4.

[2] *Memoires for my Grandson* (1926), p. 63.

[3] Pepys, *Diary*, 5 Nov. 1665.

[4] *Private Correspondence of Pepys*, ed. Tanner (1926), vol. II, pp. 16–17.

This work, written for Henry Howard, afterwards Duke of Norfolk, had been lent to a friend and lost.

Even Evelyn's industry could not cope with everything, and he followed the Peireskian model in having an assistant to carry out some of his ideas. This man, Richard Hoare by name, is only twice mentioned in the Diary, though he must have played an important part in Evelyn's life from about 1645 to 1653 when he fell of a fit of an 'Apoplexie'.[1] In 1660 a post was obtained for him in the Prerogative Office under Charles II.[2] Evelyn stated that he was 'an incomparable writer of several hands', and he was certainly much more than this. An example of his penmanship is seen in the title-page to one of his master's catalogues, and at the bottom of this he has signed himself: *Ricardus Hoare. Authoris Bibliothecarius*, *Amanuensis*, *Famulusque*, librarian, scribe, and servant—or secretary, as he would probably now be called. Truly a heaven-sent secretary for a bibliophil, and clearly appreciated by Evelyn to the full. He employed him to design title-pages which were put in place of the original title-pages of books, to transcribe favourite passages, and most of all to make the small illuminated books of devotion and piety in which Mrs Evelyn and Mrs Godolphin were expected to read daily in their closets. Hoare's writing, as seen in a small grammatical *Vade-mecum*, is not specially distinguished, though it is pretty enough for a man who was primarily a servant and factotum. He also illuminated a number of manuscripts of this kind, but his illuminations have mostly been obliterated, water having invaded the cellars at Wotton House where the books were put for safe keeping some years ago.[3]

Hoare accompanied his master during his later residence in France, and when he was not with him he wrote letters reporting all manner of affairs. These are still in the Evelyn Collection, and one is dated:

Paris, 6 July, 1650.

Sr., Your books are working on, and I hope to hand them all bound within this fortnight at furthest. Mr. Salmonet desires you to deliver this note to some stationer, who will marke in the margin which of these Bookes may be had and at what price and upon the return of the note there shall be order taken for payments and sending them hither.

My mistress, thanks be to God, is in good health, and her father [that is, Sir Richard Browne] desires you to add to the note he gave you, the Scipio Amerati, his Genealogies in sheets which you will find in the Study, and 12 pairs of Spectacles of 40 or 50 yeares of Age to

[1] de Beer, III, 84.

[2] de Beer, II, 559.

[3] It seems probable that Hoare was ultimately dismissed for intemperance; see Hiscock, p. 24.

be sent or brought with the other things; he thanks you for your letter of the 2nd July, but saith you forgot to send him word how the stockings fitted the faire Ladys legs at Beauvais. . . .

Sr. I am,

the faithfullest, humblest and
obedientest of your servants,

R.H.

Hoare aided and abetted his master in many bibliophilic ways, notably in connexion with the binding of books. Evelyn evidently had a number of books bound in Paris in 1650, and on 13 July Hoare writes: 'Mr. R. tells me you shall have the stampe of your cipher for your Books this weeke, and if I can possible you shall have a proofe sent you by the next opportunity.' Some three weeks later he writes:

I have in my letter of the 27 July sent you enclosed a proof of that Stamp for your Books which Mr. R. cut for which he asks a round price, and 2 pistolls will but content him, but he is not yet paid, wherefore I desire to know your mind what you will give; which if you count about a pistoll or at the most a pistoll and a half, you will in the opinion of those that know what belong to it, give too much; wherefore you may be pleased in yr next to certifie yr will therein, because I suppose he is not well pleased to stay for his money. . . . The book binder is not so honest I supposed he was for notwithstanding his quotidian promises to me, he has not done a Stich in your Bookes. I beseech you Sr imagine not that it proceeds out of any negligence of mine, for I protest he hath not wanted Persecution. Your Book of Taille-douces I have almost finished, and pasted them there-in, and there is nothing of yr other affairs that goes on anything slowly but yr Books. . . Your lark sings still merrily and the knight's setting dog, parrate & dwarf are in health. I most humbly take my leave.

There are other references to the loss and recovery of books (notably a volume of Ben Jonson which had been re-lent by a borrower, but was ultimately returned to Evelyn's library), to Evelyn's collection of prints, to engravings for his books, and other matters. Later references to bindings are as follows:

London, 10 January, 1653.

For the best of masters, your self.

S^r^, Returning yesterday from Waltham to London I by chance mett with your Book-binder, who told mee he hath beene at Deptford to render you the manuscript, but finding you not at home carried it back with him. He therefore hath desired mee to convey it to you, which I have here inclosed. The price of the binding thereof (of which he professes he cannot abate) amounts to the sum of five shillings, and whether it be worth so much you may easily judge.

London 24 October, 1654

For yr self.

. . . And as for the Dutch Booke binder, I shall endeavour to send him to you some tyme this weeke with the Latin Booke seller, whom I have not as yet spoken with. Your Enchiridion or Manual I am promised shall be neatly covered with good shagreen, but I could not possibly agree about the price because they could not tell what the cover might cost. . . .

Evidently Hoare was careful to protect his master's interest in the matter of expense, and sometimes he even stopped the work until his master's approval had been obtained. His reference to 'the knight's setting dog, parrate & dwarf' calls attention again to Evelyn's father-in-law, Sir Richard Browne, Ambassador in Paris, and so leads to a closer consideration of how Evelyn bound his books. Did he follow Peiresc in lavishing care and expense on their outward adornment, or did he believe with Gabriel Naudé that the insides were more important than the outsides, and so save money on the bindings? The answer is that Evelyn was a great lover of all minor vanities in books, and of none more so than the bindings. Also it is plain that Sir Richard Browne was partly responsible for fostering this pleasant form of extravagance.

The Evelyn Collection at Christ Church contains a large number of books bound in somewhat elaborate and very beautiful gold tooled bindings of calf or morocco. A number of similar volumes have also crept, in one way or another, into the outer world, and have graced the collections of other bibliophils during the last and the present centuries. When, in 1921, I was permitted by the late John Evelyn to investigate the books at Wotton I assumed that Evelyn was responsible for all the fine bindings in the library and that most of them were English. I described them on this basis in a communication to the Bibliographical Society of London, and as a result of this publicity facts came to light which caused me to revise my hastily formed opinions somewhat drastically. In the first place the late G. D. Hobson remarked that it was most unusual in the seventeenth century to use morocco for binding the general run of books in English libraries, this material being reserved for presentation or other special copies. On the other hand a number of book-collectors in France used morocco freely, and Evelyn would certainly have seen some of their books, such as those in the libraries of Sir Kenelm Digby, Habert de Montmor, de Thou, the Mazarin Library, and others, and would have been imbued with a liking for morocco as a binding.

A number of Evelyn's morocco bindings are decorated with a cipher com-

PLATE 5

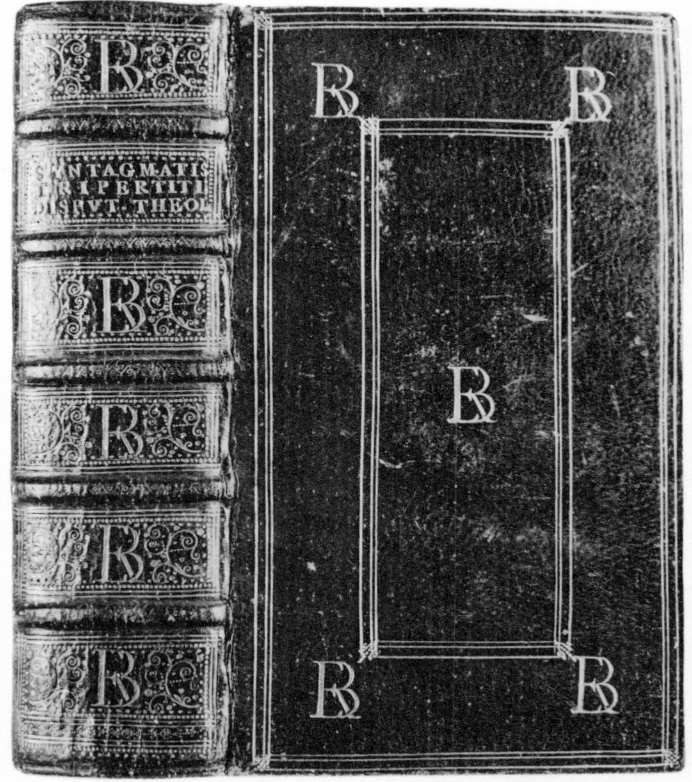

I

2

Bindings done for Sir Richard Browne

posed of the letters E R B, and I fondly supposed this to represent Evelyn and his father-in-law, Sir Richard Browne, expressing their joint book-passion in a pretty way (plate 5, no. 1). So it had to be admitted that all the bindings of this type were done in France exclusively for Sir Richard Browne, who included the initial of his wife, Elizabeth, in his cipher. Another very beautiful type of morocco binding, probably also done for Sir Richard Browne, but without arms or cipher, can be closely matched by a binding from another library known to have been done by the celebrated French binder Clovis Eve.

A third type of binding has another cipher which I took to be actually that of John Evelyn, since it is apparently composed of the initials J E repeated backwards and forwards (plate 5, no. 2). There is another tool sometimes associated with this cipher and shewn in the binding illustrated, which attracted the particular attention of the late Geoffrey Hobson. This is the S *fermé*, the capital letter being closed by a stroke carried down from the head to the tail. Hobson informed me[1] that this symbol, probably signifying *fermesse* or loyalty, had been used on bindings, in embroideries, and even with the signatures in letters since early in the sixteenth century. It was used on books by Peiresc, by Habert de Montmor, and in other libraries, including that of Marie de' Medici, in whose bindings it sometimes occurs as chief *motif*. Hobson had noted fifty examples of its use in French bindings, but it was never, as far as he knew, used by English binders. It seemed clear, therefore, that the binding from Wotton here illustrated is of French workmanship, and it had to be revealed, moreover, that the cipher is again really that of Sir Richard Browne, being composed of two B's, and is not John Evelyn's. Another superb binding on a Book of Common Prayer is in the Clovis Eve style,[2] and in others this style is associated with a heraldic stamp, which first gave the clue to the discovery of the truth.

The simplest of these Browne bindings has the Browne cipher at the corners, and in the centre a plain shield charged with a chief, and surmounted by a vulture.[3] This coat, of a kind usually borne only by ancient families of feudal line, was an augmentation specially granted to Sir Richard Browne by a warrant dated 6 January 1649/50. The late C. G. des Graz pointed out to me that this

[1] See also Hobson's book, *Les reliures à la fanfare, le problème de l'S fermé* (Chiswick Press, London, 1935).

[2] Illustrated with other examples of Evelyn's bindings in the *Transactions of the Bibliographical Society*, vol. XII (September 1931), plate I, no. 2.

[3] *Ibid.* plate II, no. 1.

warrant specifies the addition of *a canton ermine*. The heralds' records would not have been available during the Commonwealth, and they would therefore add the canton lest there should be a prior claimant to the simple coat. Sir Richard Browne seems, however, to have ignored this addition and to have used the arms without the canton on his book-bindings. Soon after the Restoration he applied to have them authorized in this form, and a certificate was issued to him on 24 July 1663 to the effect that the visitation had been searched and no other family found surviving with a right to bear *or a chief sable*. Browne's grounds for wanting the privilege of this augmentation are obscure, unless the reason presently to be suggested is the correct one. The next style of binding (first edition, plate 7) shows the Browne arms with all the quarterings including the augmentation, and a gryphon passant with a chief. The motto above, *Domino potiora*, is Browne's, not Evelyn's. This shield was used again in the more elaborate design tooled on a case made for one of Richard Hoare's small manuscript books.[1] In another type of binding (first edition, plate 7) both the quartered and the plain shields are used, the latter in more than one size. In all these stamps the additional wing at the bottom of the shield is irregular as heraldry, but effective from the point of view of the designer of the stamp. All these, then, are Sir Richard Browne's bindings, since the ambiguous cipher, if associated with arms at all, is only found with the Browne arms.

Nearly all John Evelyn's bindings, on the other hand, carry an unmistakable J E cipher and are usually associated with some part of the Evelyn arms. One of the simplest is a binding of limp black vellum decorated on the spine in gold, probably by Richard Hoare, with a crest, on a wreath a gryphonpassant (first edition, plate 8). The cipher by itself is found in another simple style, or with elaborate tooling in the Clovis Eve style (first edition, plate 8). One binding has a shield only, showing a gryphon passant, and a chief with a martlet for difference. The martlet is the proper and regular sign of a fourth son. John Evelyn was a fourth child, but a second son, and the martlet was derived from the fact that his father had been a fourth son.

In several other bindings the shield is associated with the cipher at the corners, and on the spine the cipher alternates in the panels with the crest, on a wreath a gryphon passant gorged with a ducal coronet. One example is illustrated (plate 7, no. 1).

Another binding (first edition, plate 10) shows the same shield surrounded with

[1] See *Transactions of the Bibliographical Society*, vol. XII (September 1931), plate IV.

PLATE 6

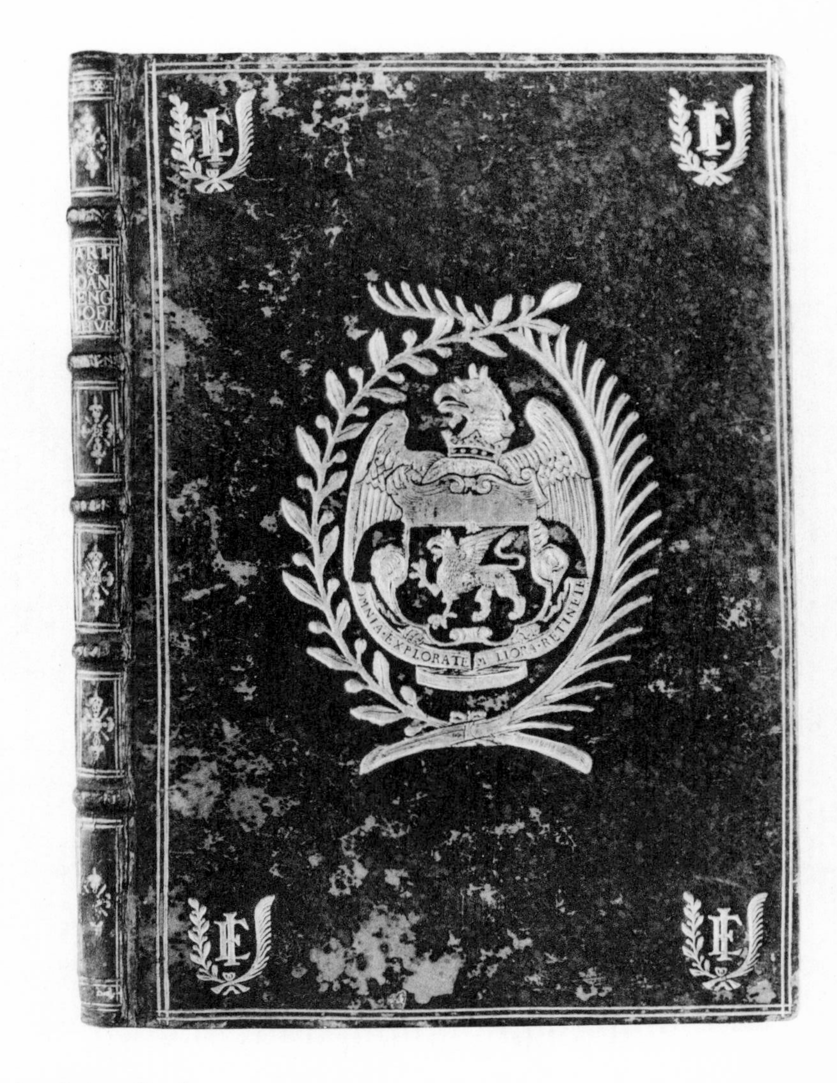

Bindings done for John Evelyn

1 2

PLATE 7

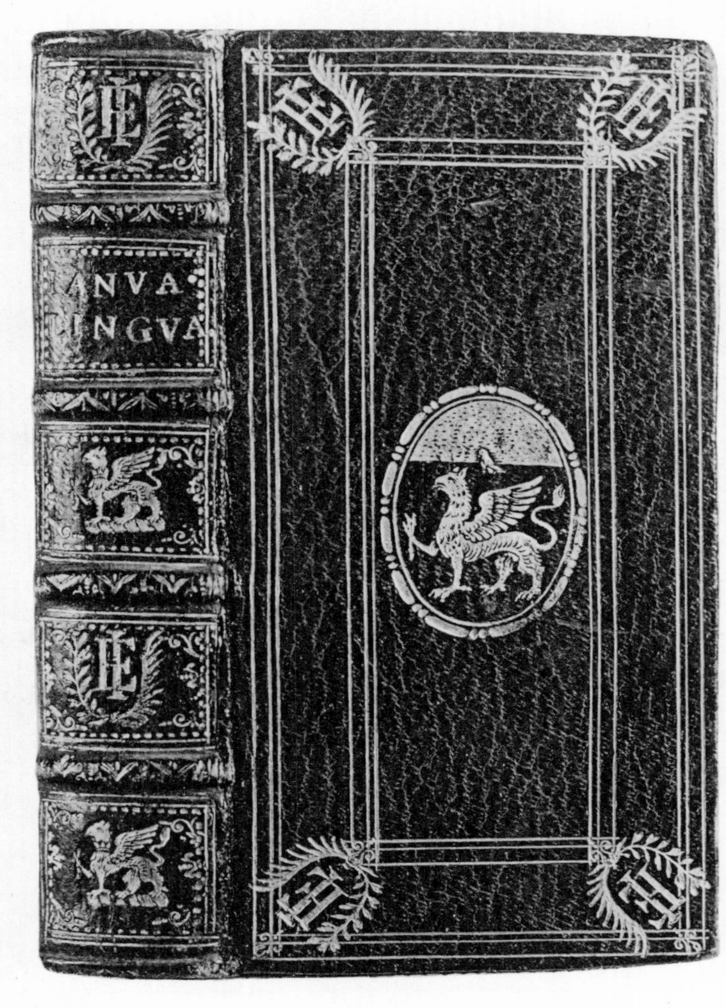

I

2

Bindings done for John Evelyn

a wreath and the second half of Evelyn's motto, *Meliora Retinete*. Both these stamps were further elaborated by associating them with the cipher and the crest (first edition, plate 10). Yet another design shows the shield as before, but with the addition of a gryphon surmounting the shield, wings displayed and gorged with a ducal coronet, and with the complete motto below, the whole being surrounded by palm and bay leaves (plate 6, no. 2). One of the volumes bound in this style touches my heart nearly, for it is a copy of the second edition of Sir Thomas Browne's *Pseudodoxia Epidemica*, 1650, and it shows further signs of Evelyn's favour in that he has enriched it with an elaborately engraved book-plate, in the centre of which Richard Hoare has exercised his penmanship. A similar coat of arms, together with Evelyn's cipher, was also on one occasion made into a heavy brass mounting on a black morocco binding (plate 6, no. 1), producing a very handsome effect. Finally, the cipher was further embellished with oak and bay leaves, and made to do duty instead of the arms (plate 7, no. 2). In the Evelyn Collection is a scrap of paper stamped with impressions of the several binding tools and inscribed by Evelyn: 'Stamps for the Book-binder ingraved by Mr Symonds His Ma[s] Gr. at the Tower 1641.' The craftsman, Thomas Simon (?1623–65), worked at the Mint and was appointed Chief Graver in 1645.

There were further minor variations; these examples, however, are enough to illustrate fully the care that Evelyn and his father-in-law took over their books and to show that the designs were not, as was previously thought, made only for John Evelyn. It is probable from the references in Richard Hoare's letters already quoted (see pp. 22–3) that the stamps for the bindings were made in Paris, and that many of the books were bound there.

A long-standing muddle, in fact, was at last straightened out, though it may be that we do not yet fully understand all the circumstances. Attention may be drawn to the fact that all, or nearly all, these bindings appear to have been made later than January 1649/50, when Browne was granted the augmentation. By that date he and Evelyn were very intimate, and Evelyn had been his son-in-law for more than two years. Perhaps, therefore, the inspiration for all the bindings came from Evelyn, and they were designed by him in the knowledge that the books would eventually come by inheritance to his library. The ambiguous cipher may thus have been a deliberate confusion of R B and J E, which would have the more point from the fact, duly appreciated by the two conspirators, that the Evelyn coat of arms and part of the Browne coat (a gryphon passant and a chief or) were identical except for the tincture, which was gules in the Browne arms and azure for the Evelyn. These tinctures would, of course, not be shown in the book-stamps, and the similarity may have had a great deal to do with Browne's application for an augmentation, the chief being already in the Evelyn arms. The inconspicuous martlet for difference was the *only* difference, apart from the additional quarterings in the Browne arms. Browne and Evelyn must have had much to talk about, and have derived a great deal of fun from the designing and cutting of the stamps. Their innocent mystification was effective for nearly 300 years, but in the end the martlet revealed it to an observant eye.[1] Anyone who was deceived by these bindings was in good company. The Browne bindings were regarded as Evelyn's by collectors and connoisseurs such as Lord Ashburnham, John Pearson, and Gordon Duff, and there is one formerly attributed to Evelyn in the Bodleian.

We know how many books Evelyn possessed, and it would be pleasant to form, if we could, a mental picture of how he disposed them in his library. His house at Sayes Court, Deptford, has long since disappeared, and at Wotton House in Surrey, to which he moved only in 1699 after the death of his brother George, and seven years before his own death, many later alterations were made. Some years ago I was allowed to edit a small unpublished manuscript by Evelyn, *Memoires for my Grandson*, in which in his old age he gave careful instructions for the administration of the house and estate soon to pass to his heir. I commented there upon the admirable fussiness of the author, which led him to record so many intimate details of life in a country house, details that might have seemed too trivial to many another. In this work Evelyn wrote at some length of the library and the books it should contain, together with its equipment.

> In my judgement [he wrote] most of the trifling Books should be weeded out to give place to better till it were thro'ly purged. Be sure to keepe an exact Catalogue of your Books and another Booke with the names to whom you lend any. Also you should take Care of the presses, standishes, and instruments belonging to writing, Desks, stamps, Seales, Skrew-presses, All the Tooles belonging to the Binding of Bookes, Cyfers, Coats of Arms, stamp letters, figures, Gilding tooles, Glew-pots, Cizers, Knives, &c. of all which you have store. Velume, paper, &c. pen-knives, erasers, wax, &c. This of Book-binding some gentlemen have been very expert in & exercis'd now and then themselves.

From this we may infer that Evelyn at one time possessed all the equipment for binding and kept his own binder, as recommended by Peiresc, or had even

[1] Dr Esmond de Beer first drew my attention to this point.

dabbled in the craft himself. But none of his appliances survived at Wotton, and it is probable that all the tools which he must have had specially cut were kept by a binder in London and have long since disappeared.

In writing of Evelyn's manuscripts and books formerly at Wotton and elsewhere I have made no mention of his chief claim to the gratitude of posterity, that is, the pains he took to record his daily doings in his Diary. The several manuscripts of this give a full account of his life from 1640 to 1706, and run to more than half a million words. About two thirds of it were transcribed at the beginning of the last century, and were printed under the editorship of William Bray and William Upcott in 1818. Revised texts were printed in 1819, 1827, and 1850, but according to modern standards of text and scholarship no adequate edition had yet been published, nor had any attempt been made to present the text in full. It was in 1921 when the late A. T. Bartholomew and I determined to make an attempt on the stronghold at Wotton, with the object of bringing the famous Diary out into the light of day. For more than fifty years the manuscript had been shrouded in mystery, and no scholar had been allowed access to it for any adequate revision of the text. The reason for this negative attitude which was maintained at Wotton for so long was said to be distrust of scholars engendered by William Upcott's depredations when he was allowed to work among the Evelyn archives at the beginning of the last century. Upcott was a collector as well as a scholar, and it is certainly remarkable how many of John Evelyn's papers and manuscripts were to be found among his collections when they were sold at Sotheby's in 1846. It seems to be fairly clear, however, that Upcott acquired his materials by fair means, and not by foul. For it is related that the Lady Evelyn who was in possession in 1814 did not take her responsibilities very seriously, and on finding that Upcott was interested in 'old handwritings' immediately produced packets and basketfuls of papers and begged Upcott to accept them. Actually she was using some of them to be cut up for dress patterns, so that Upcott is to be regarded (as are most collectors) in the light of a benefactor rather than a malefactor. At least there was reason to hope that the cloud of suspicion might have lifted a hundred years later, in 1921. As related elsewhere (see p. 268) the manuscript of the Diary was soon afterwards deposited for several years at the Bodleian Library in order that an accurate transcript might be made, and eventually the whole text was printed at Oxford under the editorship of Dr Esmond de Beer. It was a little disappointing to find that, as the years passed, Evelyn developed a tendency to fill the pages of his Diary with sermon notes of ever increasing length. There is, however, plenty of justification for a proper presentation of the Diary as Evelyn wrote it, omitting nothing and modernizing nothing.

Sir Godfrey Kneller's portrait of Evelyn formerly at Wotton was painted in 1689 for Pepys,[1] when he was sixty-five years old (plate 8). He holds a finely bound copy of *Sylva*, his great work on forestry, in his hand, and in his sensitive, intelligent face we may read something of what he felt, suffered and enjoyed during the troubled years through which he lived. His sense of duty impelled him to take a part in public affairs. His passion for horticulture earned him contemporary fame. Books formed the background of his life, and it is this congenial picture that the present volume has attempted to portray. In the Bibliography that follows it will be found that he published his first book in 1649 and his last in 1699. He produced no further books after his eightieth year, though his output during half a century testifies not only to his industry but also to the remarkable fecundity and diversity of his mind. 'Something of a bore'[2] he may have been at times, yet his figure viewed from a distance of some three centuries takes on an aura of sympathy and understanding, at least for those who have enough in common with him to sympathize and understand.

[1] de Beer, IV, 644.

[2] See *The Common Reader*, by Virginia Woolf (London, 1925), pp. 110–20, for an acute analysis of Evelyn's character. This was first printed in *The Times Literary Supplement*, 28 October 1920.

PLATE 8

JOHN EVELYN AET. 65
by Sir Godfrey Kneller

JOHN EVELYN

A BIBLIOGRAPHY OF HIS WRITINGS

OF LIBERTY AND SERVITUDE

1649

EXTRACT of the *Royall Privilege.*

BY the grace and Privilege of the King, bearing date the 20th of *January*, 1643 and signed *CONRAT*, it is permitted unto the *Sieur de la Mothe le Vayer substitut du Procurer Generall* of His Majesty, to cause to be printed a booke of his Composition, intituled, *OF LIBERTY, AND SERVITUDE*; for, and during the space of ten yeares. And defences unto all *Printers* or *Booksellers*, either to imprint or sell it, without consent of the said *Sieur de la Mothe*, or those unto whom he shall give leave, under paine of two thousand liures of *Amende*, as in the same *Privilege* more at large it is contained.

OF

OF

LIBERTY

AND

SERVITUDE.

Translated out of the French into the English *Tongue*.

And Dedicated to

Geo: Evelyn, Esquire.

VIRG. Eclog. I.

Melib. *Et quæ tanta fuit Romam tibi causa videndi?*

Tit. *Libertas: quæ sera, tamen respexit Inertem.*

London, Printed for *M. Meighen*, and *G. Bedell*, and are to be sold at their shop at the middle Temple-gate. 1649.

Imprimatur and title-page of no. 1

PREFACE

EVELYN'S first book was published in January 1648/9, when he was lodging in his father-in-law's house at Sayes Court. He noted in his diary: '21st. Was publish'd my translation of Liberty and Servitude, for the Preface of which I was severely threatned.' On the title-page of his own copy of the book he made the further note in pencil: 'I was like to be call'd in question by the Rebels for this booke being publish'd a few days before his Majesty's decollation.'

The treatise had been published at Paris by the Sieur de La Mothe le Vayer in 1643 under the title *De la Liberté et de la Servitude*. Evelyn's dedication of his translation to his elder brother George is dated Paris, 25 March 1647, and he there stated that the book was one 'which (in pursuite of other Bookes to entertain my time withall) it was my chance to encounter amongst the stationers at Paris'. He signed himself *Phileleutheros*, and in his brief preface, *To Him that reads*, he expressed himself freely in condemnation of the lack of freedom under the usurpers and in praise of the government 'under wch. we our selves have lived, during the Reign of our most gratious Soveraignes *Halcion daies*'. Ten days after the publication of the book King Charles was beheaded, so that the translator of this treatise might well have been called in question. It may be supposed, however, that the Regicides were too fully occupied to pay serious attention to the then almost unknown translator of so obscure a little book. Probably few copies were distributed and it is now exceedingly scarce, so that only six copies are known to me at the present time. It was still being advertised, however, in the publisher's lists with other books by Evelyn in 1656 and 1658.[1] Evelyn's own copy was in Bindley's library and was bought by Upcott for seven guineas in 1823; after being also in the libraries of G. W. Taylor and R. S. Turner it is now in the Pierpont Morgan Library, New York.

The author of the Latin lines on A11 was Alexander Ross, 1591–1654, well known as a tedious writer of prose and verse, and also as a critic of Sir Thomas Browne in *Medicus Medicatus*, 1645, and *Arcana Microcosmi*, 1651.

The book was reprinted in *Miscellaneous Writings*, 1825, pp. 1–38.

[1] It is in Bedell and Collins' list at the end of T. Goff's *Three Excellent Tragedies*, 1656, and Dr R. Steward's *Three Sermons*, 1658.

1 OF LIBERTY AND SERVITUDE [W. L 302] 12° 1649

Title, within ornamental border: Of Liberty and Servitude. Translated out of the French into the English Tongue. And Dedicated to Geo: Evelyn, Esquire. [*quotation between rules*]

Virg. Eclog. 1.
Melib. *Et quæ tanta fuit Romam tibi causa videndi?*
Tit. *Libertas: quæ sera, tamen respexit Inertem.*

London, Printed for M. Meighen, and G. Bedell, and are to be sold at their shop at the middle Temple-gate. 1649.

Collation: A–F^{12} G^{6}; 78 leaves.

Contents: A1*a* blank; A1*b Extract of the Royall Privilege*; A2 title; A3*a*–A6*b The Authors Epistle*, addressed to *Cardinal Mazarin* by *De la Mothe le Vayer*; A7*a*–A8*b The Translators Epistle, to George Evelyn of Wotton*, signed *Phileleutheros*; A9*a*–A10*b To Him that reads*; A11*a In Nobilissimi, Doctissimiq; D. Translationem Alexandri Rosæi hexastichon*; A11*b*–A12*a* contents; A12*b* blank; B1*a*–*b The Proem*; B2*a*–G6*b* (pp. 1–130) text. *Errata*, 9 lines, at bottom of G6*b*.

Copies: BLO (275.0.16), BM (8005.aa.25), K; CLC, HCL, PML.[1]

[1] Evelyn's copy with signature, motto and pencil notes on the title-page.

THE STATE OF FRANCE

1652

PREFACE

THE STATE OF FRANCE is dated on the last page from 'Paris, this 15 of Febr. 1652. Stilo novo'. It appears to have originated in conversations held by Evelyn with an unnamed friend after he had been travelling abroad, his friend afterwards suggesting that the substance of their conversations be committed to paper. The book is not mentioned in the Diary, and thirty years after its publication Evelyn seems even to have forgotten its existence, for he did not include it in the list of his works sent to Dr Plot in 1682. Nothing, in fact, is known about the book beyond what may be gleaned from the Prefatory Letter with which it begins. In this Evelyn reminds his friend of how the idea of the book was started, and he goes on with a brief disquisition on travelling in general, its objects and pleasures. In the course of it he introduces a juvenile poem of his own, an '*Ode* against *Travell*' and in favour of the delights of home, written many years before at Naples. The treatise itself consists for the most part of a somewhat dry account of the French monarchy, court, army, constitution, etc., and the manner of their government under Louis XIV. It becomes somewhat more enlivening towards the end, where Evelyn describes the people of France, their habits and their persons, and this part of the book contains some telling phrases, as when he says of French women that they, 'after twenty, presently strike forty in their faces' (p. 101).

The State of France is one of the prettiest of Evelyn's books, and exhibits in some copies a pleasant personal touch on the title-page in the shape of an engraved vignette of the author's monogram entwined with oak and bay leaves. This little plate was used again seven years later in some copies of *The Golden Book* (see no. 13), but it does not appear elsewhere. In each case it is possible that those copies with the engraved vignette were specially printed for the author to give to his friends, but the evidence on this point is very scanty (see p. 57). *The State of France* with either title-page is uncommon at the present time.

The book was reprinted in *Miscellaneous Writings*, 1825, pp. 39–95. The description of Paris, pp. 107–14, was reprinted in the *Diary*, ed. de Beer, 1955, III, 637–9.

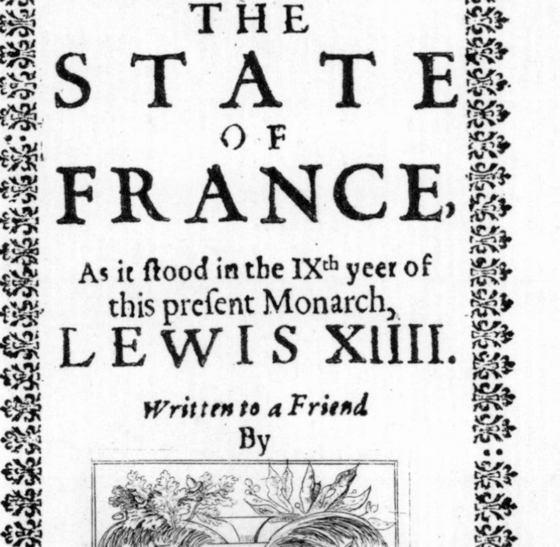

THE
STATE
OF
FRANCE,

As it ſtood in the IXth yeer of
this preſent Monarch,
LEWIS XIIII.

Written to a Friend
By

LONDON, Printed by *T.M.* for *M.M.*
G.Bedell & *T.Collins.* at the middle
Temple gate, *Fleetſtreet.* 1652.

PLATE 9

Title-page of no. 3

THE 743
STATE
OF
FRANCE,

As it ſtood in the IXth yeer of
this preſent Monarch,
LEWIS XIIII.

Written to a Friend
By

J. E.

July 18

LONDON, Printed by *T.M.* for *M.M.*
G.Bedell & *T.Collins.* at the middle
Temple gate, *Fleetſtreet.* 1652.

Title-page of no. 2

2 THE STATE OF FRANCE [first issue? W. E 3514] 12° 1652

Title, in red and black, within ornamental border: The State of France, As it stood in the IXth yeer of this present Monarch, Lewis XIIII. Written to a Friend By J. E. [*ornaments between rules*]
London, Printed by T. M. for M. M. G Bedell & T Collins, at the middle Temple gate, Fleetstreet. 1652.

Collation: A–G^{12}; 84 leaves.

Contents: A1 blank; A2 title; A3*a*–B12*a* *A Prefatory Letter* (*errata*, 16 ll., on B12*a*); B12*b* blank; C1*a*–G11*b* (pp. 1–118) *The State of France*; G12 blank.

Copy: BM (E.1328.2).

3 THE STATE OF FRANCE [second issue? W. E 3515] 12° 1652

Title, in red and black, within ornamental border: The State of France [etc., as in no. 2]...By [J. E., *monogram in engraved vignette*] [*rule*]
London, Printed by T. M. for M. M. G. Bedell & T. Collins, at the middle Temple gate, Fleetstreet. 1652.

Collation, contents: As in no. 2.

Note: There is nothing to show whether this or the other issue was printed first, the books being identical except for the title-page.

Copies: BLO (Linc.8°.C.83),[1] CCE, K, VAF; CLC, HCL (2).

[1] From the library of Dr Thomas Barlow, Bodley's Librarian and Bishop of Lincoln, mentioned many times in Evelyn's *Diary*.

LUCRETIUS

1656

PREFACE

IN June 1656 Evelyn wrote in his Diary: '12th Was publish'd my Essay on Lucretius, with innumerable errata by the negligence of Mr Triplet[1] who undertook the correction of the press in my absence. Little of the Epicurean philosophy was then known amongst us.' The inclusion of these unnecessary defects in his text aroused the greatest indignation in Evelyn's mind, and on a fly-leaf of his own copy of the book, still preserved in the Evelyn Collection, he made a note of the facts. Beneath his usual motto, *Meliora Retinete*, he added another:

''Tis Easier not to like then to doe the like,'

and then the following statement: 'Never was book so abominably misused by printer, never copy so negligently surveid by one who undertooke to looke over the proofes with all exactnesse & care, namely Dr Triplet, well knowne for his abillitie, & who pretended to oblige me in my absence, & readily offer'd himselfe. This good yet I receiv'd by it, that publishing it vainely its ill successe at the printers discourag'd me from troubling the world with the rest.'

Evelyn evidently felt that Dr Triplet's negligence cast a slur on his own scholarship, and the memory rankled for many years. In a letter to Meric Casaubon written nearly twenty years later, after excusing himself on the ground that he 'was very young & therefore very rash, or ambitious when [he] adventur'd upon that knotty piece', he makes still more bitter remarks than before upon the iniquities of his 'friend'.[2] The manuscript of the five remaining books, he added, 'still lies buried in the dust of my study, where 'tis like to be for ever buried'.[3]

Lucretius had not been turned into English before, and it was not without some misgivings that Evelyn gave it to the world. Jeremy Taylor wrote to him with mild reproof in April 1656,[4] while the book was still printing, and Evelyn replied, 'my animadversions upon it will I hope provide against all the ill consequences and totaly acquit me either of glory or impiety'.[5] When Thomas

[1] Thomas Triplet (*c.* 1603–70), probably at this time a schoolmaster at Hayes, Middlesex; later D.D. Oxon, and prebendary of Westminster.

[2] Wheatley, III, 398.

[3] The MS of Books III–VI was ultimately excavated, with many other prizes from among the Evelyn papers, by William Upcott, and was sold with his collections at Sotheby's, 22 June 1846, lot 117. It is described as wholly in Evelyn's hand, bound in blue morocco, 4to. It was probably bought then for the Evelyn library, and is now at Christ Church. There is also a volume in limp vellum containing notes on Books III–VI. Book II is not accounted for in these MSS.

[4] Wheatley, III, 213.

[5] Wheatley, III, 215.

Creech published his translation of Lucretius twenty-six years later Evelyn generously contributed some lines in commendation, 'To Mr Creech, On His accurate Version of Lucretius', in which he tells how he, like Columbus, had only *discovered* the unknown land, leaving it for his successor to *win* it.[1]

Evelyn prefaced his volume with a brief justification of his aims. He then fortified his resolution with commendations from his father-in-law, Sir Richard Browne, from Waller and Fanshaw, and from the Oxford scholar Christopher Wase. The Latin and English texts of the First Book occupy only seventy pages, so that the publisher, Bedell, in his notice to the reader on F8 *b*, stated that the Animadversions following were printed partly with the object of enlarging the volume, although their author had desired that they should be totally suppressed lest they should 'importune the Learned'—a somewhat disingenuous plea in view of what Evelyn had written in his correspondence with Jeremy Taylor. These notes occupy over a hundred pages, and are concluded with a copy of the epitaph from the tomb of Gassendus, 'who for being so great an Assertor of Epicurus's Institution deserves highly to be remembred by Posterity'.

The allegorical frontispiece, designed by Mrs Mary Evelyn and engraved by Hollar, is of more interest than beauty. It was based in its main features on the engraved frontispiece used in the first French translation of Lucretius by Marolles, Paris, 1650 (C. A. Gordon, *Bibliography of Lucretius*, 1962, no. 301). It may be supposed that the head of the poet in the wreathed medallion bears more than a chance resemblance to the profile of the translator. This was, indeed, noticed by Mrs Lucy Hutchinson, another contemporary translator of Lucretius.[2]

The book is not uncommon, though it is difficult to find a satisfactory copy owing to the size of the frontispiece, which has usually been cut by the binder. In spite of its shortcomings Evelyn distributed a few copies to his friends. One has an inscription to Edward Luttrell (*fl.* 1670–1710), one of the earliest mezzotint engravers. Another is inscribed on the title-page: 'For my Bro. R. Offley', and has many manuscript corrections by Evelyn in the text. George Evelyn had married Sir Robert Offley's daughter, widow of Sir George Cotton. Jeremy Taylor thanked Evelyn for a copy in a letter dated 16 July 1656.[3]

No part of the book has ever been reprinted.

[1] See no. 129.

[2] See *Memoirs of the Life of Col. Hutchinson*, ed. C. H. Firth (London, 1906), p. 45. In the dedication of her translation of Lucretius Mrs Hutchinson wrote, 'a masculine wit hath thought it worth printing his head in a laurel crown for the version of one of these books'.

[3] Wheatley, III, 216. In another letter, dated 15 Nov. 1656, now in my collection, Taylor urged Evelyn to continue his translation.

4 LUCRETIUS [W. L 3446] 8° 1656

Title in red and black, within double lines: An Essay on the First Book of T. Lucretius Carus De Rerum Natura. [*rule*] Interpreted and Made English Verse by J. Evelyn Esq; [*quotation between rules*]

Ovid, Amor, lib. 1. Eleg. 15.
Carmina sublimis tunc sunt peritura Lucreti,
Exitio terras cum dabit una dies.

London: Printed for Gabriel Bedle, and Thomas Collins, and are to be sold at their shop at the Middle-Temple-Gate in Fleetstreet. 1656.

Collation: A–M⁸; 96 leaves.

Contents: A1 frontispiece; A2 title; A3*a*–A8*b* *The Interpreter to Him that Reads*; B1*a*–*b* (pp. 1–2) lines *On my Son Evelyns Translation*, signed *Richard Brown, Knight and Baronet*; B2*a*–*b* (pp. 3–4) lines *To his Worthy Friend Master Evelyn*, signed *Edmund Waller*; B3*a* (p. 5) Latin lines signed *Christopherus Wasi*; B3*b*–B5*a* (pp. 6–9) letter to Evelyn signed *Richard Fanshawe, Tankersley, 27 Decem.*, 1653; B5*b*–6*a* (pp. 10–11) *The Argument*; B6*b*–F8*a* (pp. 12–79) *De Rerum Natura, Lib. I*, Latin and English on opposite pages; F8*b* (p. 80) *The Stationer to the Reader*, signed *G. Bedell*; G1*a*–M5*a* (pp. 97–185) *Animadversions*; M5*b* note on the epitaph following; M6*a*–*b* epitaph on Gassendus; M7*a* *Errata*, 27 lines; M7*b*–M8*a* *Books printed for Ga: Bedell and Tho: Collins*; M8*b* blank.

Frontispiece: On A1*b*, line-engraving, plate-mark 15·5 × 10·5 cm. Five allegorical figures surrounding a medallion bust of the poet. On a pedestal below the bust is inscribed: *T. Lucretius Carus. De Rerum Natura Lib. i Interpreted by J. E.*; the rim of an amphora at the base of the pedestal is inscribed *Mary Evelyn inv.*, and the bottom of the engraving, *W. Hollar fec.* Below is the imprint: *London Printed for G: Bedell and T: Collins at Middle Temple Gate. A°* 1656. The plate-mark is almost the same size as the trimmed page, and the front edge of the print has often been removed by the binder.

Note: The pagination omits pp. 81–96. The collation and the catchword on p. 80 show that nothing has been cancelled.

Copies: BLO (Art. B.S. 8°. L. 17), BM (E. 1572. 2), CCE,[1] K,[2] ULC (L. 12. 36); CLC (2),[3] CH, HCL (2).[4]

[1] Evelyn's copy with motto, inscription and corrections.

[2] An uncropped copy from the Heber and Britwell Court libraries.

[3] One inscribed to R. Offley.

[4] One inscribed to Edward Luttrell.

T. LUCRETIUS CARUS. De Rerum Natura Lib. I. Interpreted by J.E.

W. Hollar fecit

London. Printed for G: Bedell. and T. Collins. at Middle Temple Gate. A° 1656.

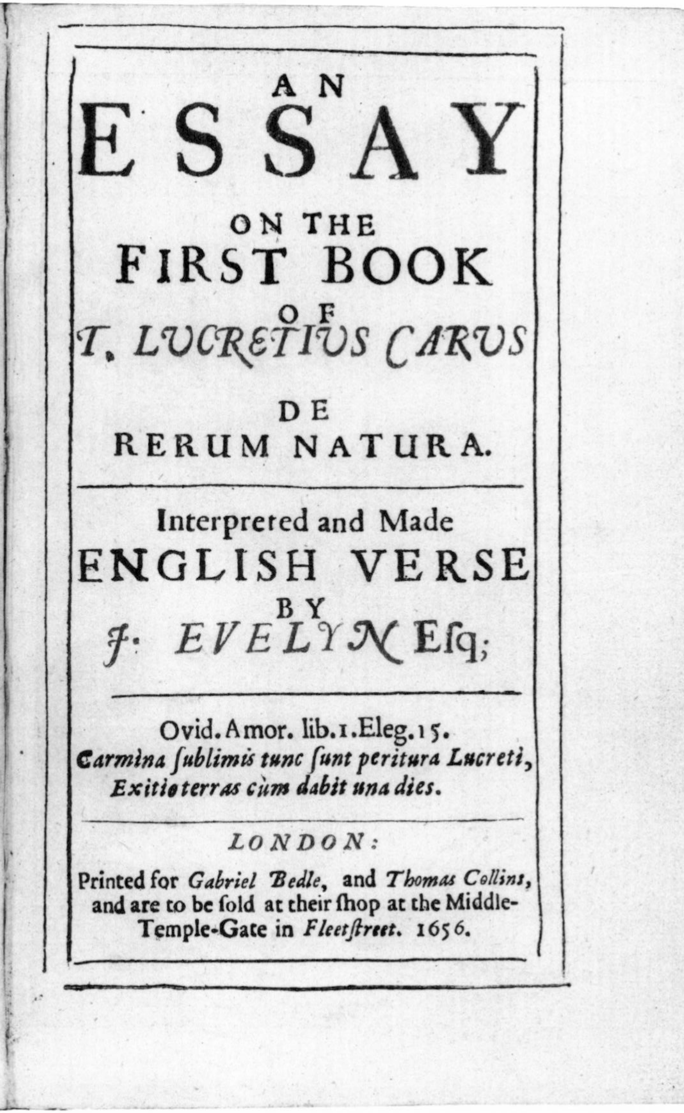

AN
ESSAY
ON THE
FIRST BOOK
OF
T. LUCRETIUS CARUS
DE
RERUM NATURA.

Interpreted and Made
ENGLISH VERSE
BY
J. EVELYN Esq;

Ovid. Amor. lib. 1. Eleg. 15.
Carmina ſublimis tunc ſunt peritura Lucreti,
Exitio terras cùm dabit una dies.

LONDON:

Printed for *Gabriel Bedle*, and *Thomas Collins*, and are to be ſold at their ſhop at the Middle-Temple-Gate in *Fleetſtreet*. 1656.

PLATE 10

Frontispiece and title-page of no. 4

THE FRENCH GARDINER

1658

PREFACE

THOMAS HENSHAW (1618–1700) had already known Evelyn for some time when they met at Pisa in October 1644.[1] They travelled together for more than a year afterwards, and Henshaw was thenceforward to be reckoned among Evelyn's closest friends. He owed the offices he held under Charles II partly to Evelyn's activity on his behalf, and he is frequently mentioned in the Diary. He was one of the original Fellows of the Royal Society and was secretary from 1668 to 1672, when he was succeeded by Evelyn. To this friend Evelyn stated that he owed the idea of translating *Le Jardinier François*,[2] of Mons. Nicolas de Bonnefons, and thus he was embarked upon his first essay in gardening literature. *The French Gardiner* was the result, and according to the Diary it was published on 6 December 1658, being 'the first and best of the kind that introduc'd the use of the olitorie garden to any purpose'.[3] Evelyn here first introduced into English the word 'olitorie', meaning 'kitchen' garden. In the *Epistle Dedicatory* to Henshaw Evelyn explains that the treatise he has translated deals excellently with 'the *soyle*, the *situation*, and the *planting*', but that his real desire was, out of his own experience, 'to introduce the least known (though not the least delicious) *appendices* to Gardens; and such as are not the *Names* only, but the *Descriptions*, *Plots*, *Materials*, and *wayes of contriving the* Ground for *Parterrs*, *Grotts*, *Fountains*; the proportions of *Walks*, *Perspectives*, *Rocks*, *Aviaries*, *Vivaries*, *Apiaries*, *Pots*, *Conservatories*, *Piscina's*, *Groves*, *Crypta's*, *Cabinets*, *Eccho's*, *Statues*, and other ornaments of a *Vigna*, &c. without which the best Garden is without life, and very defective. Together with a Treatise of *Flowers*, and *Evergreens*; especially the *Palisades* and *Contr-Espaliers* of *Alaternus*, which most incomparable *Verdure*, together with the right culture of it, for beauty and sence, I might glory to have been the first *propagator* in England'.

1 de Beer, II, 179.

2 *Le Iardinier François, Qui enseigne a cultiver les Arbres, & Herbes Potageres; Auec la maniere de conseruer les Fruicts, & faire toutes sortes de Confitures, Conserues, & Massepans. Dedié aux Dames. A Paris, Chez Pierre Des-Hayes, rue de la Harpe, aux Gands Couronnez, prés la Roze Rouge. M.DC.LI. Auec Priuilege du Roy.* 12°. The *Epistre aux Dames* is signed *R. D. C. D. W. B. D. N.* There is a frontispiece and three other plates designed and engraved by F. Chauveau (BM, 725.a.48; G. L. Keynes). Evelyn himself seems to have possessed only the edition of 1656 (according to his library catalogue compiled in 1687), and probably this was the text that he translated.

3 Wheatley, II, 105.

Here Evelyn, the hortulan virtuoso, is speaking from his heart. He had already been engaged for five years in laying out his hundred acres at Sayes Court, and we must for ever regret the circumstances which hindered 'the birth and maturity of that *Embryo*'. This *Epistle* appeared only in the first edition of the book, being rewritten, with omission of the more personal passages, for the second and later editions. The first edition is also the only one to give any indication of the author of the original French treatise. Mons. de Bonnefons is, it is true, hidden under the initials R. D. C. D. W. B. D. N.,[1] which, being arranged backwards, are scarcely explicit, but even these were afterwards omitted. Evelyn affects the pseudonym of *Philocepos* on the title-page, but appends his initials to the *Epistle Dedicatory*. His name appeared in full on the title-page of the second and later editions. In the notice *To the Reader* he explains what portions of the original work have been omitted, these consisting chiefly of instructions in cooking (*French* cooking!). Translating these he did not think fit employment for him, for 'though', he explains, 'I have some experience in the Garden, and more divertisement, yet I have none in the Shambles,' and so it is dismissed.

The engraved frontispiece and three plates were copied by A. Hertochs from the plates in the first French edition by F. Chauveau, and they form charming embellishments to the volume, though they show signs of wear after the first edition. This fact might suggest that the first edition was a large one, yet it is now a very rare book, and the first two issues, with their odd title-pages, were described in 1937 for the first time. The second edition of 1669 is enlarged by the addition of *The English Vineyard Vindicated* by John Rose, which had been published separately under Evelyn's auspices in 1666 (see no. 80), and of ten pages by Evelyn himself, headed 'The Vintage', giving 'Directions concerning Making and Ordering of Wines'. Three more editions, published in 1672, 1675, and 1691, are similar to the second.

The dedicatory *Epistles* and the address *To the Reader* were reprinted in *Miscellaneous Writings*, 1825, pp. 975–100, where are also engraved copies by P. Audinet of the frontispiece and first plate.

[1] I.e. Nicolas de Bonnefons.

5 THE FRENCH GARDINER [first edition, first issue. W. B 3597]
12° 1658

Title: The French Gardiner: Instructing How to Cultivate all sorts of Fruit-Trees, and Herbs for the Garden: Together With directions to dry and conserve them in their Natural; Six times printed in France, and once in Holland. An accomplished Piece, First written by R. D. C. D. W. B. D. N. And now Transplanted into English by Philocepos. Exceedingly illustrated by Sculptures. [*rule*]
London, Printed by J. C. for John Crooke at the Ship in S^t^. Pauls Church-yard. 1658.

Collation: A–M[12] N[8] O[4] P[2], 1 l. inserted; 159 leaves.

Contents: A1 title; A2*a*–A4*a* dedication to *Thomas Henshaw, Esquire,* signed *J. E.*; A4*b*–A5*b* *To the Reader*; A6*a*–N8*b* (pp. 1–294) text; O1*a*–P2*a* *The Table*; P2*b* blank. *Errata,* 27 lines, on leaf inserted at the end.

Illustrations: i. Frontispiece. Prospect of a garden with allegorical additions. Signed *A. Hertochs fecit.*
ii. Facing p. 1. The cultivation of a walled garden. Signed *A. Hertochs fecit.*
iii. Facing p. 135. Prospect of a garden with landscape behind. Unsigned.
iv. Facing p. 263. Cooking and conserving fruits. Signed ÆH*s*.
The plate-marks measure about 12 × 7·5 cm.

Copies: K; HCL.

6 THE FRENCH GARDINER [first edition, second issue. W. B 3598]
12° 1658

Title: The French Gardiner: Instructing How to Cultivate all sorts of Fruit-Trees, and Herbs for the Garden: Together With directions to dry and conserve them in their Natural; Three times printed in France, and once in Holland. An accomplished Piece, First written by R. D. C. D. W. B. D. N. And now Transplanted into English by Philocepos. [*rule*]
London, Printed by J. C. for John Crooke at the Ship in S^t^. Pauls Church-yard. 1658.

Collation: A–M[12] N[8] O–P[4]; 160 leaves.

Contents: A1 title; A2*a*–A4*a* dedication to *Thomas Henshaw, Esquire,* signed *J. E.*; A4*b*–A5*b* *To the Reader*; A6*a*–N8*b* (pp. 1–294) text; O1*a*–P2*a* *The Table*; P2*b*–P4*b* *Books printed for John Crooke.*

Illustrations: As in no. 5, except that ii faces A5*b* in the copy collated.

The French

GARDINER:

INSTRUCTING

How to Cultivate all ſorts of

FRUIT-TREES,

AND

HERBS for the GARDEN:

TOGETHER

With directions to *dry* and *conſerve* them in their *Natural*;

Six times printed in France, *and once in* Holland.

An accompliſhed Piece,

Firſt written by R. D. C. D. W. B. D. N.

And now

Tranſplanted into Engliſh by

PHILOCEPOS.

Exceedingly illuſtrated by Sculptures.

LONDON,

Printed by *J. C.* for *John Crooke* at the *Ship* in S[t]. *Pauls* Church-yard. 1658.

Title-page of no. 5

KJE

The French

GARDINER:

INSTRUCTING

How to Cultivate all sorts of

FRUIT-TREES,

AND

HERBS for the GARDEN:

TOGETHER

With directions to *dry* and *conserve* them in their *Natural*;

Three times printed in France, *and once in* Holland.

An accomplished Piece,

First written by R. D. C. D. W. B. D. N.

And now

Transplanted into English by

PHILOCEPOS.

LONDON,

Printed by *J. C.* for *John Crooke* at the *Ship* in St. *Pauls* Church-yard. 1658.

Title-page of no. 6

Note: The only copy of this issue that has come to my notice is in the Huntington Library, and it was collated for me there by Mr C. K. Edmonds. Since it contains the list of Crooke's books at the end as in no. 7, it is presumably the second issue, and not the first. The mistake on the title-page, *Three times printed* for *Six times printed*, resulted in its cancellation and reprinting as in no. 7. This copy does not contain the *errata*.

Copy: CH (from the Britwell Court library).

7 THE FRENCH GARDINER [first edition, third issue. W. B 3599] 12° 1658

Title: The French Gardiner: Instructing How to Cultivate all sorts of Fruit-Trees, and Herbs for the Garden: Together With directions to dry and conserve them in their Natural; [*rule*] Six times printed in France, and once in Holland. [*rule*] An accomplished Piece, [*rule*] First written by R. D. C. D. W. B. D. N. And now transplanted into Euglish [*sic*] by Philocepos. [*rule*] Illustrated with Sculptures. [*rule*]

London, Printed for John Crooke at the Ship in S^{t}. Pauls Church-yard. 1658.

Collation: A–M^{12} N^{8} O–P^{4}, 1 leaf cancelled, 2 leaves inserted; 161 leaves.

Contents: A1 cancelled; title-page and *errata* on a gathering of 2 ll. inserted before A2; A2*a*–A4*a* dedication to *Thomas Henshaw Esquire*, signed *J. E.*; A4*b*–A5*b* *To the Reader*; A6*a*–N8*b* (pp. 1–294) text; O1*a*–P2*a* *The Table*; P2*b*–P4*b* *Books printed for John Crooke.*

Illustrations: As in no. 5.

Note: The title-page of no. 6 has been cancelled and two leaves, with a new title-page and the *errata* as before, have been substituted. The rest of the book is printed from the same type as no. 5, with the addition of matter to sig. P, which is enlarged to four leaves.

Copies: BM (E. 1890), K, ULC (Adams. 8. 65. 29); CH, CLC, HCL (Arnold Arboretum).

8 THE FRENCH GARDINER [second edition. W. B 3600] 8° 1669

Title: The French Gardiner:... Natural; An accomplished Piece, Written Oorginally in French, and now Transplanted into English, [*rule*] By John Evelyn Esq; Fellow of the Royal Society. [*rule*] Illustrated with Sculptures. [*rule*] Whereunto is annexed, The English Vineyard Vindicated by John Rose, now Gardiner to his Majesty: with a Tract of the making and ordering of Wines in France. [*rule*]

London, Printed by J. M. for John Crooke, and are to be sold at his Shop in Duck-Lane. 1669.

The French

GARDINER:

INSTRUCTING

How to Cultivate all ſorts of

FRUIT-TREES,

AND

HERBS for the GARDEN:

TOGETHER

With directions to *dry* and *conſerve* them in their *Natural*;

Six times printed in France, *and once in* Holland.

An accompliſhed Piece,

First written by R. D. C. D. W. B. D. N.

And now tranſplanted into Engliſh by

PHILOCEPOS.

Illustrated with Sculptures.

London, Printed for *John Crooke* at the *Ship* in S^t^. *Pauls* Church-yard. 1658.

Title-page of no. 7

Collation: A–T⁸ A–D⁸; 184 leaves.

Contents: A1 blank; A2 title; A3*a*–A4*a* dedication to *Thomas Henshaw Esquire*; A4*b*–A5*b* *To the Reader*; A6*a*–T8*b* (pp. 1–294) *The French Gardiner*; A1 sub-title to *The English Vineyard Vindicated by John Rose*; A2*a*–A3*b* dedication by Rose to the King; A4*a*–A6*b* *The Preface* signed *Philocepos*; A6*b* blank; A7*a*–C2*a* (pp. 13–35) *The English Vineyard Vindicated*; C2*b* *To the Reader*; C3*a* blank; C3*b* address to *Mr. Rose* signed *J. Evelyn*; C4*a*–C8*b* (pp. 39–48) *The Vintage* by Evelyn; D1*a*–D8*b* *The Table.*

Sub-title: The English Vineyard Vindicated by John Rose Gard'ner to His Majesty, at His Royal Garden in St. James's. Formerly Gard'ner to her Grace the Dutchess of Somerset. With an Address, where the best Plants are to be had at easie Rates. [*rule*]
London, Printed by J. M. for John Crook, and are to be sold at his Shop in Duck-lane, 1669.

Illustrations: i–iv as in the first edition.
v. Folding plate facing p. 26 of *The English Vineyard,* as in the first edition (see no. 80) with *Chap: 5:* added at the lower right-hand corner.

Copies: BLO (12 Θ.1572), K, VAF; CH, HCL (Arnold Arboretum).

9 THE FRENCH GARDINER [third edition. W. B 3601] 8° 1672

Title: The French Gardiner:...Natural:...English, By John Evelyn Esq; Fellow of the Royal Society. [*rule*] The third Edition illustrated with Sculptures. [*rule*] Whereunto...France. [*rule*]
London, Printed by S. S. for Benj: Tooke at the Ship in St. Pauls Church-yard, 1672.

Collation, contents, illustrations: As in no. 8.

Sub-title on A1*:* The English Vineyard Vindicated by John Rose...[*rule*]
London, Printed by S. S. for B. Teuke, and are to be sold at the Ship in St. Pauls Church Yard, 1672.

Note: A line-for-line reprint of no. 8, though wholly reset.

Copies: BM (969.a.17; lacks *The English Vineyard*), K; CLC, HCL.

10 THE FRENCH GARDINER [fourth edition. W. B 3602] 8° 1675

Title: The French Gardiner:...Natural. An Accomplished Piece, Written Originally in French, and now Translated into English. By John Evelyn Esquire, Fellow of the Royal Society. [*rule*] The third Edition illustrated with Sculptures. [*rule*] Whereunto is annexed, the English Vineyard Vindicated... France. [*rule*]

London, Printed by T. R. & N. T. for B. Tooke, and are to be sold at the Ship in St. Pauls Church-yard. 1675.

Collation, contents, illustrations: As in no. 8.

Sub-title on A1: The English Vineyard Vindicated by John Rose,... [*rule*]
London, Printed by T. R. & N. T. for B. Tooke, and are to be sold at the Ship in St. Pauls Church-yard. 1675.

Note: Called on the title-page *The third Edition,* though actually it is the fourth, the type having been entirely reset.

Copies: BLO (2, Art.8°.S.50; Douce.E.47), K, ULC (Hhh.295); CLC, HCL (Arnold Arboretum).

11 THE FRENCH GARDINER [fifth edition. W. B 3603] 12° 1691

Title within double lines: The French Gardiner; Instructing How to cultivate all Sorts of Fruit-Trees & Herbs for the Garden. Together With Directions to Dry and Conserve them in their Natural. An Accomplished Piece. [*rule*] Written Originally in French, and now Translated into English, By John Evelin Esq; Fellow of the Royal Society. [*rule*] The Fourth Edition, illustrated with Sculptures. [*rule*] Whereunto is annexed, the English Vineyard Vindicated; by J. Rose, now Gardiner to His Majesty: With a Tract of the Making and Ordering of Wines in France. [*rule*]
London, Printed by T. B. for B. Took, and are to be sold by J. Taylor at the Ship in St. Paul's Church-Yard, 1691.

CollLtion: A–L[12]; 132 leaves.

Contents: A1 title; A2 dedication to *Thomas Henshaw, Esq.*; A3 *To the Reader*; A4*a*–K3*a* (pp. 1–215) *The French Gardiner*; K3*b* blank; K4 sub-title to *The English Vineyard*; K5*a*–K6*a* dedication to the King; K6*b*–K7*b* *The Preface* signed *Philocepos*; K8*a*–L4*b* (pp. 1–18) *The English Vineyard*; L5*a* (p. 19) *To the Reader*, and to *Mr. Rose* by *J. Evelyn*; L5*b*–L8*b* (pp. 20–26) *The Vintage* by Evelyn; L10*a*–L12*b* *The Table.*

Sub-title on K4: The English Vineyard, Vindicated;... [*rule*]
London, Printed by T. B. for B. Took, and are to be sold by John Taylor at the Ship in St. Paul's Church-Yard, 1691.

Illustrations: As in no. 8, facing title, pp. 1, 97, 191, and 11 of the second treatise.

Note: Called on the title-page *The Fourth Edition,* but actually the fifth. The pagination of the second treatise is very erratic.

Copies: BLO (Art.8°.G.162), BM (449.a.38), K; CLC, HCL (Arnold Arboretum).

THE GOLDEN BOOK

1659

PREFACE

IN July 1652 Evelyn entered in his Diary: '24th. My first child, a sonn, was born precisely at one o'clock,' and in September: '2nd. Mr Owen, the sequestered divine of Eltham, christened my sonn by the name of Richard.' Five years later came one of the greatest sorrows of his life when his son Richard died on 27 January 1657/8. Under this date in his Diary is a long and affecting passage describing the death and attainments of this remarkable little boy. 'After six fits of a quartan ague with which it pleased God to visite him, died my deare Son Richard, to our inexpressible griefe and affliction, 5 yeares [5 months] and 3 days old onely, but at that tender age a prodigy for witt and understanding; for beauty of body a very angel; for endowment of mind of incredible and rare hopes.'[1] Evelyn adds many particulars of the reasons for these hopes, and ends with an account of the boy's burial at Deptford on 30 January, when rings were distributed among the relations and neighbours who attended, with the motto *Dominus abstulit.* On 14 February he wrote a letter of much feeling to his father-in-law Sir Richard Browne[2] telling him of his loss, and on the next day, 15 February, less than three weeks after the death of Richard, Evelyn also lost his youngest son, an infant of seven weeks. During the succeeding months he found some consolation in translating St John Chrysostom's *Golden Book Concerning the Education of Children*, a work which had been lately discovered in a MS in the Cardinal's Library at Paris and had been printed in 1656.[3] Evelyn's translation was soon printed, and was published, according to the Diary, on 16 September 1658,[4] although the book is dated on the title-page 1659. He prefaced his book with an *Epistle Dedicatory* to his brothers George and Richard Evelyn. The greater part of it is occupied with an account of the boy Richard and his extraordinary attainments, to some extent in the same words as in the Diary entry but in more detail. Near the end Evelyn wrote, 'But my tears mingle so fast with my ink that I am forced to break off here, and be silent,' and the reader cannot help sharing in his grief, so strongly does his affection shine. The *Epistle* is followed by a Latin Epitaph on Richard Evelyn by Christopher Wase.[5] John Aubrey visited Surrey in his perambulations and recorded the monuments to be seen in the Evelyn Chapel in Wotton Church. In his *Natural History and*

[1] Wheatley, II, 96.
[2] Wheatley, III, 244.
[3] *Advertisement to the Reader.*
[4] de Beer, III, 220.
[5] See *Miscellaneous Writings* (1825), p. 112.

Antiquities of Surrey, vol. IV (1718), pp. 137–42, will be found a copy of the epitaph on Richard's tomb with a long quotation from the *Golden Book*. The account of Richard and the epitaph are also reprinted in Clement Barksdale's *Memorials of Worthy Persons: Two Decades* (London, 1661), pp. 76–85.

Largely owing to the subject and to the occasion of its production *The Golden Book* is perhaps the most personal and attractive of all Evelyn's publications, and, with *The State of France*, it is the prettiest. It is extremely uncommon in any form, but is nevertheless found in two different states. In one the title-page is wholly typographical, in the other the author's initials are conveyed in the same monogram, engraved as a vignette, as was used for the title-page of *The State of France*. The two issues are otherwise printed from the same type, so that the change in the title-page was made while the book was in the press. It is not possible to say which issue preceded the other, though the fact that several of the copies that I have seen with the vignette have an *errata* slip pasted onto the last leaf may mean that this one is the later of the two. It has been suggested that the vignette was used for the copies presented by Evelyn to his friends, but I do not know of conclusive evidence for this. He must undoubtedly have given away many copies to those who had known his boy, though few of them can now be identified. One was given, for example, to Dr Jeremy Taylor, who had already, a few days after Richard's death, written Evelyn a letter[1] of great beauty grieving with him 'in the loss of that pretty person, your strangely hopeful boy'. Taylor acknowledged the book in a letter dated 4 June 1659: 'Sir, I received your two little bookes, & am very much pleased with the golden booke of St Chrysostom, on which your epistle hath put a black enamel, & made a pretty monument for your dearest, strangest miracle of a boy; & when I read it, I could not choose but observe St Paul's rule, *flebam cum flentibus*. I paid a teare at the hearse of that sweet child. Your other little Enchiridion is an emanation of an ingenuous spirit; & there are in it observations, the like of which are seldom made by young travellers.'[2] This companion volume was probably *The State of France*.

The Golden Book has only been reprinted in the *Miscellaneous Writings* (1825), pp. 103–40.

[1] Wheatley, III, 245, dated 17 Feb. 1657/8.

[2] Wheatley, III, 257.

12 THE GOLDEN BOOK [first issue? W. C 3978] 12° 1659

Title, in red and black: The Golden Book of St. John Chrysostom, Concerning the Education of Children. Translated out of the Greek by J. E. Esq; [*ornaments between rules*]
London, Printed by D. M. for G. Bedel and T. Collins, at the Middle Temple Gate in Fleetstreet, 1659.

Collation: A^{12} a^{12} $B–E^{12}$; 72 leaves.

Contents: A1–A2 blank; A3 title; A4*a*–a9*b* *The Epistle Dedicatory To my Most Imcomparable* [*sic*] *Brothers George & Richard Evelyn,* signed *J. E.*; a10*a* *Epitaphium. R. Evelyn, I.F.*; a10*b* blank; a11 *To the Reader*; a12 blank; B1*a*–E9*b* (pp. 1–90) text; E10*a*–E12*b* notes.

Note: The page number on p. 9 is omitted in some copies; the pagination is otherwise correct.

Copies: BLO (Linc. 8°. A. 125),[1] BM (E. 1931), K; CH.

13 THE GOLDEN BOOK [second issue? W. C 3979] 12° 1659

Title, in red and black: The Golden Book [etc. as in no. 12]... by [J. E., *monogram in engraved vignette*] Esq; [*rule*]
London, [etc. as in no. 12]..., 1659.

Collation, contents: As in no. 12.

Insertion: An errata slip of eight lines has been pasted onto the last leaf in some copies.

Copies: CCE (2), K; CLC, HCL.

[1] Presentation copy to Dr Thomas Barlow.

THE
GOLDEN BOOK
OF
S^t. John Chrysostom,
Concerning the
EDUCATION
OF
CHILDREN.

Translated out of the Greek

BY

Esq;

LONDON, Printed by *D.M.* for *G. Bedel* and *T. Collins*, at the Middle Temple Gate in Fleetstreet, 1659.

PLATE II

Title-page of no. 13

THE
GOLDEN BOOK
OF
S^t. John Chrysostom,
Concerning the
EDUCATION
OF
CHILDREN.

Translated out of the Greek

BY

J. E. Esq;

LONDON, Printed by *D.M.* for *G. Bedel* and *T. Collins*, at the Middle Temple Gate in Fleetstreet, 1659.

Title-page of no. 12

A CHARACTER OF ENGLAND

1659

PREFACE

EVELYN'S *Character of England* was published anonymously in 1659. There has been some confusion about this date, as it was stated by Upcott in the *Miscellaneous Writings* (pp. ix and 141) to have been first printed in 1651. There is no discoverable evidence for this statement, all the three editions that are known having 1659 on their title-pages. Evelyn made no reference to the work in the Diary, and it does not seem to have occupied much place in his mind as he did not mention it in the list of his works sent to Dr Plot in 1682/3. He may have regarded it as a *jeu d'esprit* scarcely worthy of being recorded. Direct evidence of the actual date of publication is to be found in a letter to Evelyn from Jeremy Taylor dated 10 Feb. 1659/60, in answer to a letter of 2 December 1659. 'Your Character', Taylor wrote, 'hath a great part of a worthy reward, that it is translated into a language in which it is likely to be read by very many *beaux esprits*.'[1] This follows a reference to the *Apology for the Royal Party*, 1659, and presumably indicates a gift to Taylor of a copy of *A Character of England*. The sentence might also be taken to mean that the work had been translated into French, though nothing is known of any such rendering. More probably Taylor was misled by Evelyn's address *To the Reader*, wherein he pretended that he had 'first chanced upon this severe piece' in French, and was minded 'to suppress the publication of our shame.... But upon second and more impartial thoughts [he was] tempted to make it speak English, and give it liberty, not to reproach, but to instruct our Nation.'

Evelyn's *Character*, as described on the title-page, is in the form of a letter addressed to 'a Noble Man of France' by a friend who had recently travelled in England, and it is interesting to notice which of the national characteristics Evelyn thought most worthy of chastisement. His complaints begin immediately upon arrival at Dover, where he complains of the incivility shown to foreigners. He next meets with unpleasant familiarity from the host at his inn at Rochester, and is offended by having garbage thrown at him by children in the streets of the metropolis. London he finds to be 'a City consisting of a wooden, northern, and inartificiall congestion of Houses', with narrow streets and without fountains or running water. He admires St Paul's and the Banqueting-house at Whitehall, but is disgusted at the meanness of their surroundings, and above all at the de-

[1] Wheatley, III, 276.

filement of St Paul's itself, which he says was now being 'converted into raskally warehouses'. At this he exclaims, 'how lothsome a Golgotha', and it leads him on to describing the methods of worship in English churches; he then returns to complaints about the inconveniences of London and of the 'cloud of Sea-coal', a theme to which he reverted several years later in his *Fumifugium*. He has much to say of the national practice of drinking in *Ale-houses*, and of the vile manners of the ladies, and describes a drunken brawl about nothing which he had witnessed in the *withdrawing Roome* of a country house. He is displeased with the women for being '*much* affected with *Gaudry*', and for 'there being nothing more frequent than to see an ancient *Ladie* wear colours'. He dislikes English social manners at dances, at dinners, in *Hide-park*, and in the *Spring Garden*. He is very difficult to please.

The true first edition of *A Character of England*, containing 42 leaves with 71 numbered pages, is an exceedingly rare book, and only one copy is recorded here.[1] It was very soon reset and reprinted on 36 leaves with 66 numbered pages, and this is also very uncommon. Meanwhile the anonymity of the tract seems to have been well preserved, and an indignant reply entitled *Gallus Castratus* was published under the date 1659. This was dedicated 'To the Illustrious Starres of Glory, the Incomparable Beauties of the English Nation', and was appended to a counterblast, also anonymous, called *A Character of France*.

This publication prompted Evelyn to re-issue the greater part of the second edition of his tract in a new form which he called 'the third edition'. The title-page of most of the copies of the second edition was cancelled and a section of 12 leaves, with a new title-page followed by a reply to *Gallus Castratus*, was put in its place. *Characters* were in fashion in the seventeenth century, and Nath. Brooke, the publisher of *A Character of France*, was responsible also for *The Character of Spain*, 12°, 1660, and *The Character of Italy*, 12°, 1660. Included in a list of books advertised at the end of the latter is a second edition of *A Character of France* containing, besides *Gallus Castratus*, 'a fresh Whip for the Mounsieur, in answer to his letter, in vindication to his Madam'. This work, in continuation of the controversy, has so far eluded me. A fourth edition was published in 1700.

[1] In 1937 I knew of three copies: one had been in a bookseller's catalogue in 1916; another was sold with the Britwell Court library, 1 April 1924, lot 302; the third was in the library of the late Marquess of Crewe in a binding with an elaborate panel containing the arms of the Stationers' Company stamped in gold on the covers. I do not know the present location of any of these.

A
CHARACTER
OF
FRANCE.

To which is added,
Gallus Castratus.
OR AN
ANSWER
TO A LATE
Slanderous Pamphlet,
CALLED
The Character of England.

Si talia nefanda & facinora quis non Democritus?

LONDON,
Printed for *Nath: Brooke* at
the *Angel* in *Cornhill*, 1659.

Gallus Castratus.
AN
ANSWER
TO A
Slanderous Pamphlet,
Called the
CHARACTER
OF
ENGLAND.

Si talia nefanda & facinora quis non Democritus.

LONDON,
Printed for *Nath. Brooke* at
the *Angel* in *Cornhill*, 1659.

Collation: A^4 B–D^{12} E^8; pp. [viii], 45, [3], 38, 1 l. blank.
Copies: BM (901.a.23), K.

Evelyn's criticism of his countrymen was carried a step further by Samuel de Sorbière's *Relation d'un voyage en Angleterre, ou sont touchees plusieurs choses, qui regardent l'estat des sciences, et de la religion*, published at Paris and translated in 1664, but Evelyn did not think it incumbent upon him to second Sorbière in his attack. In fact he did the opposite, and on 31 October 1664 he wrote a long letter[1] concerning 'this disingenuous Traveller' to Dr Thomas Sprat, in which he exposed the facts of Sorbière's shady origin and history. Sprat had recently completed a reply to the *Voyage en Angleterre* which was published in the following year as:

[1] Wheatley, III, 294.

Observations on Monsieur de Sorbier's Voyage into England. Written to Dr. Wren, Professor of Astronomy in Oxford. By Thomas Sprat, Fellow of the Royal Society. London, Printed for John Martyn, and James Allestry, Printers to the Royal Society. 1665. A^2 $B–V^8$.

The letter is dated at the end 1 August 1664, so that Sprat can hardly have been indebted to Evelyn for any substantial assistance, as has often been stated.

Evelyn's *A Character of England* was reprinted by Sir Walter Scott in the second edition of the *Somers Collection of Tracts*, vol. VII, London, 1812, 4°, pp. 176–87. Scott was unaware of the authorship, but expressed a doubt as to whether the piece were really translated from the French, and stated that it had been 'found useful to the commentators on dramatic authors, as throwing light upon the private life at the period'. It is also in the *Harleian Miscellany*, 1808, vol. x, and in Evelyn's *Miscellaneous Writings*, 1825, pp. 141–67.

A manuscript copy of the *Character of England* was offered by Messrs George Sexton Ltd. of Brighton in their cat. 51, March 1958. It was bound in contemporary sheep with clasps and had Evelyn's motto, *Meliora Retinete*, on the fly-leaf. The script appeared to be somewhat juvenile and was perhaps written by one of the author's family. At the end was a prescription: 'To stuff birds.' This MS is now in the Houghton Library, at Harvard University.

14 A CHARACTER OF ENGLAND [W. E 3485] 12° 1659

Title: A Character of England, As it was lately present-ed in a Letter, to a Noble Man of France. [*ornaments between rules*]
Londons Printed for Jo. Crooke, and are to be sold at the Ship in St. Paul's-yard, 1659.

Collation: A–C[12] D[6]; 42 leaves.

A
CHARACTER
OF
ENGLAND,

As it was lately preſent-
ed in a Letter, to a
Noble Man of
FRANCE.

LONDONs
Printed for *Jo. Crooke*, and
are to be ſold at the Ship
in St. *Paul's*-yard,
1659.

A
CHARACTER
OF
E N G L *A* N *D*.

As it was lately preſent-
ted in a Letter, to a
Noble Man of
FRANCE.

LONDON,
Printed for *Jo. Crooke*, and
are to be ſold at the Ship
in St. *Paul's*-yard,
1659.

Title-pages of nos. 14 and 15

Contents: A1 blank; A2 title; A3*a*–A5*b* *To the Reader*; A6*a*–D5*b* (pp. 1–72) text; D6 blank.

Note: In the copies examined (1937) a lowercase s has been used instead of a comma after *London* on the title-page (see facsimile). Page 63 is erroneously numbered 62, so that the pagination is thrown out after this, pp. 63–72 being numbered 62–71.

Copy: HCL.

15 A CHARACTER OF ENGLAND [second edition. W. E 3486]

12° 1659

Title: A Character of England. As it was lately present-ted in a Letter, to a Noble Man of France. [*ornaments between rules*]
London, Printed for Jo. Crooke, and are to be sold at the Ship in St. Paul's-yard, 1659.

Collation: A–C[12]; 36 leaves.

Contents: A1 title; A2*a*–A3*b* *To the Reader*; A4*a*–C12*b* (pp. 1–66) text.

Note: A reprint of the preceding edition on fewer pages. In the four copies I have examined the word *present-ted* is so printed on the title-page. The title-page and the whole of the text have been reset.

Copies: BLO (2, Wood. 582 (3), Douce. A. 32); BM (292. a. 43), K;[1] HCL.[2]

16 A CHARACTER OF ENGLAND [third edition W. E 3487]

12° 1659

Title: A Character of England, As it was lately present-ed in a Letter, to a Noble Man of France. With Reflections upon Gallus Castratus. [*rule*] The third Edition. [*rule*]
London, Printed for John Crooke and are to be sold at the Ship in St. Paul's Church-yard, 1659.

Collation: a[12] A–C[12] (A1 cancelled); 47 leaves.

Contents: a1 blank; a2 title; a3*a*–a11*a* *A Letter in Vindication of this Character, against the sordid reproaches of Gallus Castratus*, dated 24 *June*, 1659; a11*b*–a12*b* blank; [A1, title of previous edition, usually cancelled]; A2*a*–A3*b* *To the Reader*; A4*a*–C12*b* (pp. 1–66) text.

Note: This consists of the unsold sheets of no. 15 to which a new section, a, has been prefixed; the original title-page, A1, has usually been cancelled, so that the book appears to lack a leaf

[1] From the library of Alfred Cock, and bought by a previous owner at 'Pickering's sale', i.e. in 1854.

[2] From the library of H. B. Wheatley.

before *To the Reader*. In one of the copies recorded below the original title-page remains in position. In this the word *present-ed*, previously misprinted, has been corrected.

Copies: BLO (5, Douce. A. 26, 335, H. 11; Linc. 8°. B356; Lister. I. 90 (4)), K (4),[1] ULC (R. 6. 78), VAF; CLC, HCL.

A
CHARACTER
OF
ENGLAND,
As it was lately present-
ed in a Letter, to a
Noble Man of
FRANCE.
With Reflections upon
Gallus Castratus.

The third Edition.

LONDON,
Printed for *John Crooke* and
are to be sold at the Ship
in St. *Paul's* Church-
yard, 1659.

Title-page of no. 16

[1] i. bound in contemporary sheep as above; ii. bound in nineteenth-century calf, with original title-page in position, from the libraries of Harrison Ainsworth and James Crossley; iii. bound in eighteenth-century calf with *A Perfect Description of the People and Country of Scotland*, Lond. 1659, and *A Brief Character of the Low-Countries*, Lond. 1659; iv. bound in seventeenth-century calf with *A Brief Character Of the Low-Countries*, Lond., 1660, *The Character of Italy*, Lond., 1660, and *The Character of Spain*, Lond., 1660, from the Heber Library, 7th part, 1835.

16*a* A CHARACTER OF ENGLAND [fourth edition. Not in W.]

8° 1700

Title within double lines: A journey to England. With some Account of the Manners and Customs of that Nation. [*rule*] Written at the Command of a Nobleman in France. Made English. [*rule*] London. Printed, and Sold by A. Baldwin, near the Oxford-Arms-Inn in Warwick-Lane. 1700.

Collation: A–E⁴ F²; 22 leaves.

Contents: A1 half-title; A2 title; A3*a–b* *To the Reader*; A4*a–b* *Contents:* B1*a*–F2*a* (pp. 1–35) text; F2*b* blank.

Copy: BM (T.1860(3)).

AN APOLOGY
FOR THE ROYAL PARTY
1659

PREFACE

UNDER the date 7 November 1659 Evelyn made the following entry in his Diary: 'Was publish'd my bold Apologie for the King in this time of danger, when it was capital to speak or write in favour of him. It was twice printed, so universaly it took.'[1] Evelyn's memory was at fault as to the date, for the Thomason copy of the second edition, one of a collection of pamphlets each of which was dated by its owner as received, bears the date *Nov. 4*. Evelyn had never been a militant royalist, though at this time he was ready to run considerable risks, as his pamphlet bears witness. It was entitled *An Apologie for the Royal Party*, and is in the form of a letter *To a Person of the Late Councel of State*;[2] it is dated at the end *27 Octob. 1659*, so that the printing appears to have occupied less than a week. It contains an eloquent and outspoken attack upon the parliamentary party, and the depth of the author's feelings has conferred upon his style an effectiveness which is sometimes lacking in his writings. The title-page states that the *Apologie* also contains *A Touch At the Pretended Plea for the Army*. This refers to another tract as follows:

Title within double lines: The Army's Plea for Their present Practice: Tendered to the consideration of all ingenuous and impartial men. [*double rule*] Printed and published by special command. [*double rule*] London, Printed by Henry Hills, Printer to the Army, dwelling in Aldersgate Street next door to the Peacock. 1659. A–D4. (*Copies:* BM (2, E.1000.24 and 104.a.25); K.)

This pamphlet, according to a note on one of the BM copies, was published on 24 October, three days before Evelyn completed his answer.

Evelyn soon afterwards engaged in a persistent attempt to induce Colonel Henry Morley, then Lieutenant of the Tower, to declare for the King, and in a contemporary account of his negotiations it is stated that 'Mr Evelyn gave him some visits to attemper his affection by degrees to a confidence in him, & then by consequence to ingage him in his designes; and to induce him the more powerfully thereunto, he put into his hands an excellent and unanswerable hardy treatise by him written and several times reprinted, intituled *An Apology for the Royall Party*, which he back'd with so good Arguments and dextrous Addresses

[1] de Beer, III, 235.

[2] This *Person* is to be identified with Colonel Morley himself.

in the prosecution of them, that, after some private discourse, the Colonel was so well inclin'd, as to recommend to him the procurement of his Majestie's Grace for him, his Brother-in-law Mr. Fagg, and one or two more of his Relations'.[1] This was included in Baker's *Chronicle of the Kings of England* when it was edited by Edward Phillips in 1665. Phillips added an account of a letter written by Evelyn to Col. Morley, and gave him great credit for the influence which he brought to bear. The narrative was drawn up by Sir Thomas Clarges, who sent a draft to Evelyn himself. This was still among the papers at Wotton in 1818 and was printed by Upcott.[2] It carried an endorsement by Evelyn, who stated that his letter 'was not rightly copied', and that there 'was too much said concerning me'. It was improved, he added, in Phillips's second impression (1665). The account by Clarges is further confirmed by an inscription written by Evelyn himself on the title-page of a copy of the last issue of the pamphlet in my collection. The inscription is as follows:

> 'Delivered to Coll. Morley a few daies after his contest wth Lambert in the palace yard by J. Evelyn.'

The 'contest with Lambert' took place on 12 or 13 October, when Morley, pistol in hand, refused to allow Lambert at the head of his troops to pass through the Palace Yard.[3]

In his Diary Evelyn stated that the pamphlet was 'twice printed', and in the list of his works sent to Dr Plot in 1682/3 he wrote that there were 'three editions'. Further than this, he added on the title-page of my copy, above the inscription already quoted, the words 'three tymes printed'. In spite of these statements the pamphlet is now extremely scarce in any form, though actually they underestimate the number of printings. Among the copies examined, I have identified four printings, comprising two editions with three variants of the second setting. In the fourth and last issue two leaves have been cancelled and reprinted in order to omit one paragraph from p. 7 and to make other minor alterations. The new settings of the two leaves A4 and B1 are printed together in one gathering, while A1 and B4 are left as detached leaves, their fellows having

1 Sir Richard Baker's *Chronicle of the Kings of England* (1665), p. 736.

2 *Memoirs* (1818), II, 121; Wheatley, III, 177.

3 For a full study of Evelyn's relations with Col. Morley see E. S. de Beer, *Sussex Archaeological Collections* (1937), LXXVIII, 177–83, and A. H. Nethercot, *Huntington Library Quarterly* (1937–8), I, 439–46.

been removed. Two of these four issues are at present known in only one copy each. All of them were distinguished in 1937 for the first time.

The *Apology for the Royal Party* was reprinted in the *Miscellaneous Writings*, 1825, pp. 169–92, with numerous footnotes added, the text being that of the amended (fourth) issue. It was not printed again until 1951.

17 APOLOGIE FOR THE ROYAL PARTY [first edition. W. E 3481]
4° 1659

Title: An Apologie for the Royal Party: Written in a Letter to a Person of the late Councel of State. [*rule*] By a Lover of Peace and of his Country. [*rule*] With A Touch At the Pretended Plea for the Army [*ornaments between rules*] *Anno Dom.* MDCLIX.

Collation: A–B4; 8 leaves.

Contents: A1 title; A2*a*–B4*b* (pp. 1–14) text, dated at the end 27 *Octob.* 1659.

Note: This is the only issue of the pamphlet with the spelling *Apologie* for *Apology* on the title-page. The text also contains many minor errors which were corrected when it was reset. It is probably the true first edition, though known at present only in two copies, one of them preserved among the Godwin Pamphlets in the Bodleian Library.

Copy: BLO (G.P.1787 (11)), VAF.

18 APOLOGY FOR THE ROYAL PARTY [second edition, first issue. W. E 3482] 4° 1659

Title: An Apology for the Royal Party: Written in a Letter To a Person of the Late Councel of State. [*rule*] By a Lover of Peace and of his Country. [*rule*] With A Touch At the Pretended Plea for the Army. [*ornaments between rules*] *Anno Dom.* MDCLIX.

Collation, contents: As in no. 17.

Note: The title-page and the whole of the text have been reset. Many minor errors have been corrected, and others introduced. The signature on A3 is misprinted A2.

Copies: BLO (G.P.1118 (33)), BM (E.763 (11)), K, VAF; HCL.

19 APOLOGY FOR THE ROYAL PARTY [second edition, second issue. W. E 3483] 4° 1659

Title: An Apology for the Royal Party...[etc., as in no. 18].

Collation, contents: As in no. 17.

Note: The first section except for the title-page and A4 verso (p. 6) has been reset, and some misprints have been corrected, including the alteration of the misprinted signature on A3 (A2 for A3).

Copy: BLO (Wood.632 (32)).

AN

APOLOGIE

FOR THE

ROYAL PARTY:

Written in a

LETTER

To a Perſon of the late

COUNCEL of STATE.

By a Lover of Peace and of his Country.

WITH

A TOUCH

At the Pretended

PLEA FOR THE ARMY

Anno Dom. *MDCLIX.*

Title-page of no. 17

AN

APOLOGY

FOR THE

ROYAL PARTY:

Written in a

LETTER

To a Perſon of the Late

COUNCEL of STATE.

By a Lover of Peace and of his Country.

WITH

A TOUCH

At the Pretended

PLEA FOR THE ARMY.

Anno Dom. MDCLIX.

Title-page of no. 18

20 APOLOGY FOR THE ROYAL PARTY [second edition, third issue. W. E 3484] 4° 1659

Title: An Apology...[etc. as in no. 18].

Collation, contents: As in no. 17.

Cancels: Although the collation appears to be the same as before, the make-up of the pamphlet is different. Two leaves, A4 and B1 (pp. 5–8), have been cancelled and reprinted on a gathering of two leaves, so that A1 and B4 are detached leaves.

Note: In the reprinting of the cancelled leaves a paragraph on p. 7, 'But now he comes next ...and imprisoned with them', has been omitted, and the rest of the text has been expanded accordingly.

Copy: K (stitched in a contemporary paper wrapper and with an inscription in Evelyn's hand on the title-page).

20*a* APOLOGY FOR THE ROYAL PARTY & A PANEGYRIC 8° 1951

The Augustan Reprint Society John Evelyn An Apologie for the Royal Party (1659); and A Panegyric to Charles the Second (1661) With an Introduction by Geoffrey Keynes Publication Number 28 Los Angeles William Andrews Clark Memorial Library University of California 1951

21 cm, pp. [ii], iv, [2], 14, 16, [2].

Note: The two tracts are messily printed in reduced facsimile from copies in my collection.

THE LATE NEWS FROM BRUXELS UNMASKED

1660

PREFACE

IN March 1660 Marchamont Needham, the notorious journalist, pamphleteer, turncoat, and physician,[1] attacked the exiled King in a tract entitled:

> *News from Brussels. In A Letter from a neer attendant on His Majesties Person To a Person of Honour here. Which casually became thus publique.* [rule] *Printed in the Year*, 1660. A4, pp. 1–8. Dated at the end *Brussels, S. V. March* 10. 1659. (*Copies:* CCE, K.)

At this time, from February to April, Evelyn was very ill with 'a kind of double tertian', and was almost given up by his three doctors, Wetherborn, Needham,[2] and Claud. He records in his Diary: 'During this sicknesse...I writ and printed a letter, in defence of his Majesty, against a wicked forg'd paper, pretended to be sent from Bruxells to defame his Majesties person and vertues, and render him odious, now when every body was in hope and expectation of the General and Parliament recalling him, and establishing the Government on its antient and right basis. The doing this towards the decline of my sicknesse, and setting up long in my bed, had caus'd a small relapse, out of which it yet pleased God also to free me, so as by the 14th I was able to go into the country, which I did to my sweete and native aire at Wotton.'[3] Three weeks later Evelyn had his reward, Charles II being proclaimed in London on 8 May. The *Late News from Bruxels Unmasked* is anonymous, though the printer's name is given, the risks attending the publication of a royalist tract being less than they had been six months before. The tract is mentioned with strong approval in Phillips's edition of Baker's *Chronicle of the Kings of England*, 1665, p. 762, where he writes of Needham's letter that 'this Hydra was dextrously cut off by Mr Evelyn in a Reply which was printed, to the intire satisfaction of all that read it'.

Evelyn's piece is now exceedingly scarce, and the British Museum acquired a copy only in 1930. It has been reprinted only in *Miscellaneous Writings*, 1825, pp. 195–204. A few indelicate words are omitted, and the text of Needham's 'letter' is given in a footnote.

[1] One of his most interesting works is an attack on the College of Physicians entitled *Medela Medicinæ. A Plea for the Free Profession, and a Renovation of the Art of Physick. London*, 1665, 8°. He practised physic from about 1660 until his death in 1678 (*D.N.B.*).

[2] Probably Sir John Wedderburn and Jasper Needham, F.R.S.

[3] de Beer, III, 243–4.

21 LATE NEWS FROM BRUXELS UNMASKED [W. E 3503] 4° 1660

Title: The Late News or Message from Bruxels Unmasked, and His Majesty Vindicated, From The Base Calumny and Scandal therein fixed on Him. [*rule*] London, Printed for Richard Lowndes at the White Lion in St. Paul's Church-yard. 1660.

Collation: A4; 4 leaves.

Contents: A1 title; A2*a*–A4*b* (pp. 1–6) text.

Copies: BLO (2, Wood.608.(3); Linc.9.6 (4)[1]), BM (1200.f.3), CCE, K; CLC, HCL.

[1] Dr Thomas Barlow's copy.

The Late News

OR

MESSAGE

FROM

BRUXELS

Unmasked,

AND

HIS MAJESTY Vindicated,

FROM

The Base CALUMNY and SCANDAL therein fixed on Him.

LONDON,

Printed for *Richard Lowndes* at the *White Lion* in St. *Paul's Church-yard*. 1660.

Title-page of no. 21 (reduced)

THE MANNER OF ORDERING FRUIT-TREES

1660

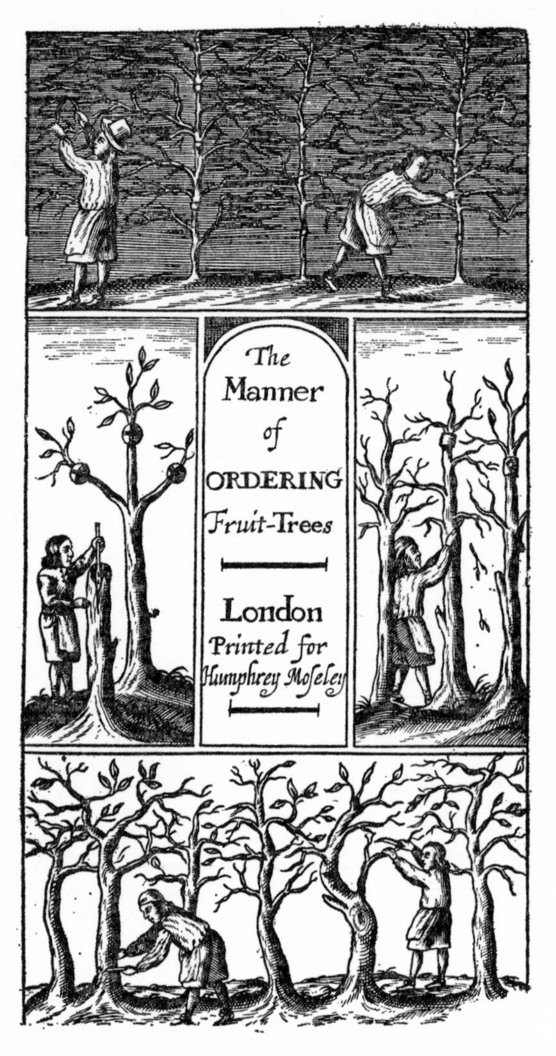

Henry Sheafield

The Manner OF ORDERING Fruit-Trees.

By the SIEUR
LE GENDRE,
Curate of *HENONVILLE.*

Wherein is treated of *Nurseries, Wall-Fruits*, Hedges of *Fruit-Trees, Dwarf-Trees, High-Standers*, &c.

Written originally in *French*, and translated faithfully into *English*, at the request of severall Persons of Honour.

A Piece so highly approved of in France, that it hath been divers times printed there.

LONDON,
Printed for *Humphrey Moseley*, at the Prince's Armes in S. *Paul's* Church-yard. 1660.

PREFACE

ON 26 October 1672 Dr John Beale, F.R.S., horticulturist and Rector of Yeovil, wrote to Robert Boyle: 'And because I have seen your fair and large walls, I recommend to you and for your man, the Sieur Le Gendre's manner of ordering fruit trees... 1660, written with the greatest judgment that ever I saw any, after about fifty years' experience, and a full knowledge of all the best gardeners in Europe, translated (as I guess from the style) by Mr. Evelyn. It is of less bulk than the French Gardiner, translated by Mr. Evelyn.'[1]

The passage was noticed by F. E. Budd, who became convinced that Beale's guess was right and wrote an article in justification of his opinion.[2] Budd rested his case largely on parallels between the Le Gendre and Evelyn's fully authenticated translation of *The French Gardiner*, vocabulary and style providing good evidence of Evelyn's responsibility for both translations. According to the catalogue of his library (see p. 300). Evelyn possessed a marked copy of *La manière de cultiver les arbres fruitiers Par le Sieur Le Gendre Curé d'Henonville. Seconde édition. A Paris MDCLIII.* The volume was removed from Wotton by Upcott in January 1814, according to a note on the fly-leaf, and is now in the British Museum (class-mark: 7077.aa.22). The first edition was published in 1652 and a third in 1661. The translation was made from the second edition. The fact that Evelyn did not mention the book in his Diary or elsewhere does not make the attribution less probable, since there are other instances of fully authenticated books against which the same objection could be raised. It seems reasonable, therefore, to admit *The Manner of Ordering Fruit-Trees* to the Evelyn canon.

The book, with its attractive frontispiece of pruning and grafting operations, is concise and practical, and its instructions admirably clear. The text is divided into eleven chapters with a short section of 'A principall Advice concerning all Trees' added at the end; this explains that 'no man can have fair plants, unless he love them', an opinion which Evelyn would be likely to endorse. It seems to have been used up, for it is now very scarce. No part of it has ever been reprinted.

[1] Boyle's *Works*, 1740, vol. v, p. 499.

[2] *Review of English Studies* (1938), XIV, 285–97.

21*a* THE MANNER OF ORDERING FRUIT-TREES [W. L 943A]
12° 1660

Title: The Manner of Ordering Fruit-Trees. By the Sieur Le Gendre, Curate of Henonville. Wherein is treated of Nurseries, Wall-Fruits, Hedges of Fruit-Trees, Dwarf-Trees, High-Standers, &c. Written originally in French, and translated faithfully into English, at the request of severall Persons of Honour. A Piece so highly approved of in France, that it hath been divers times printed there. [*rule*]
London, Printed for Humphrey Moseley, at the Prince's Armes in S. Paul's Church-yard. 1660.

Collation: A^6 a^{12} B–G^{12} H^6; 96 leaves.

Contents: A1 title; A2*a*–A5*b* dedication to *John Lewis de Faucon, Knight*; A6*a*–a12*a The Preface*; a12*b* blank; B1*a*–H5*b* (pp. 1–154) text; H6 blank.

Frontispiece: Inserted, platemark *c.* 14 ×7·5 cm, with illustrations of men pruning and grafting fruit-trees and central legend: *The Manner of Ordering Fruit-Trees London Printed for Humphrey Moseley.*

Copies: K, R; CH, HCL.

PANEGYRIC TO CHARLES II

1661

PREFACE

As a devout Royalist, Evelyn felt deeply stirred by the return of Charles II to England in 1660. He had played some part in the restoration of the monarchy, and so, with his literary instincts, naturally took his place among those who wished to present the King with an address on the occasion of his Coronation. This took place on 23 April 1661 and on the following day Evelyn recorded in his diary: 'I presented his Matie with his Panegyric in the Privie Chamber, which he was pleas'd to accept most graciously; I gave copies to the Lord Chancellor and most of the noblemen who came to me for it.'[1] This private distribution of his piece resulted in its almost complete disappearance. Evelyn possessed a copy in 1687 according to his library catalogue compiled in that year, but it afterwards disappeared and no copy survived in any other library that was accessible, so that it could not be included in the *Miscellaneous Writings*, 1825. Afterwards it was erroneously identified by Upcott and by Wheatley[2] with the anonymous piece:

> *A Poem upon his Maiesties Coronation the* 23. *of April* 1661. *Being St Georges day*. . . *London, Printed for Gabriel Bedel and Thomas Collins, near the Middle-Temple-Gate*: 1661. f° A–C².

A manuscript copy of this *Poem* was made by Bray or Upcott and is now among the Evelyn papers in the British Museum (Add. MS. 15950). Upcott's mistake was not put right until a copy of the true *Panegyric*, with Evelyn's name on the title-page, was acquired by the British Museum in May 1927.[3] It was then seen that it was not a poem, but an eloquent and extravagant prose composition, in which Evelyn attributed to Charles II every conceivable virtue and all wisdom. This eulogy, written in all sincerity, was to be somewhat falsified by the actual trend of events, and it must have caused Evelyn some distress if he ever read it again in later years.

In 1935 a second copy of the *Panegyric* was acquired by Bernard Quaritch from a Berlin dealer bound up in a volume of later folio tracts, and this is now in my collection. It will be noticed that the date on the title-page has been misprinted XXXIII for XXIII; the first figure has been deleted in my copy.

[1] de Beer, III, 284. [2] Wheatley, II, 130.

[3] This copy was sold with the Britwell Court library at Sotheby's, 31 March 1927, lot 713, £70. It is probably to be identified with one offered by Messrs Robson & Co., cat. 97, July 1916.

The *Panegyric* was not reprinted until 1951 (see no. 22*a*).

Under the date 22 December 1660 Evelyn wrote in his Diary: 'The Princesse gave my Wife an extraordinary complement, & gracious acceptance, for the *Character* she had presented her the day before, & which was afterwards printed.' This was Mrs Evelyn's *The Picture of the Princesse Henrietta*, another piece of fulsome prose describing Henrietta Anne, Duchess of Orleans, sister to the King. Upcott and Wheatley (II, 121) identified this piece with Evelyn's *Character of England*, but this had been printed nearly a year before the date of this entry. Mrs Evelyn's *Character* was printed as a folio broadsheet signed M. E., a copy of which is now in the Evelyn Collection. The younger Evelyn followed suit in 1685 with a *Congratulatory Poem* addressed to James II (see p. 293).

A

PANEGYRIC

TO

Charles the Second,

PRESENTED

TO HIS MAJESTIE

The xxxiii. of *APRIL*, being the Day

OF HIS

CORONATION.

MDCLXI.

By *JOHN EVELYN*, Esqnire·

LONDON,

Printed for *John Crooke*, and are to be sold at the Ship in St. *Paul's* Church-Yard.

Title-page of no. 22 (reduced)

22 PANEGYRIC TO CHARLES II [W. E 3506] f° 1661

Title: A Panegyric to Charles the Second, presented to His Majestie The XXXIII. of April, being the Day of His Coronation. MDCLXI. [*rule*] By John Evelyn, Esquire. [*a crown between rules*]
London, Printed for John Crooke, and are to be sold at the Ship in St. Paul's Church-Yard.

Collation: A–D²; 8 leaves.

Contents: A1 title; A2*a*–D2*b* (pp. 3–16) *A Panegyric.*

Note: In my copy XXXIII on the title-page has been altered to XXIII, and two corrections have been made in the text in Evelyn's hand as follows:

p. 6, line 18, *Family* altered to *Firmament.*

p. 8, line 16 from bottom, *suffer* altered to *surfeit.*

These corrections do not appear in the BM copy.

Copies: BM (C.57.g.33), CCE, GLL, K; CLC, HCL.

22*a* PANEGYRIC TO CHARLES II 8° 1951

Note: Printed in reduced facsimile with *An Apologie for the Royal Party*; see no. 20*a*.

FUMIFUGIUM

1661

PREFACE

ONE day in 1660 or 1661 Evelyn was walking in the King's palace at Whitehall, when he saw 'that a presumptuous Smoake issuing from one or two Tunnels near Northumberland-House, and not far from Scotland-yard, did so invade the Court; that all the Roomes, Galleries and Places about it were fill'd and infested with it'.[1] He had often noticed this nuisance before, but his indignation was especially kindled by the trouble it must procure to the King's Majesty and the 'hazzard to [His Health]'. The result was one of his better-known books, *Fumifugium*, presented to the King on 13 September 1661, and published by his special command.[2] On 1 October Evelyn accompanied the King in one of his 'yaachts', which was being matched against one of the Duke of York's, and at dinner the King 'was pleased to discourse to me about my book inveighing against the nuisance of the smoke of London, and proposing expedients how, by removing those particulars I mention'd, it might be reform'd; commanding me to prepare a bill against the next session of Parliament, being as he said resolv'd to have something done in it'.[3] This plan was taken a step further, for Evelyn records that on 11 January 1661/2 'I receiv'd of Sir Peter Ball, the Queene's Attorney, a draught of an Act against the nuisance of the smoke of London to be reform'd by removing severall trades which are the cause of it, and indanger the health of the King and his people. It was to have been offer'd to the Parliament as his Majesty commanded.'[4] But Charles II was not a Mussolini, and at this point the matter seems to have been dropped, for nothing more was heard of it.

In his *Address to the Reader* Evelyn 'deplores with indignation' that London, 'which from Wood might be rendred Brick, and from Brick made Stone and Marble,...should wrap her stately head in Clowds of Smoake and Sulphur, so full of Stink and Darknesse'.[5] He deplores also the narrow streets, the bad paving, the leaking spouts and gutters, and 'the Deformity of so frequent Wharfes and Magazines of Wood, Coale, Boards, and other course Materials, most of them imploying the Places of the Noblest aspect for the situation of Palaces towards the goodly River, when they might with far lesse Disgrace be removed to the Bank-side'.[6] This, he wrote later, 'was look'd on as a prophecy'

[1] *Fumifugium*, A2.
[2] de Beer, III, 295.
[3] *Ibid.* 297.
[4] *Ibid.* 310.
[5] *Fumifugium*, a1.
[6] *Fumifugium*, a2.

when, in September 1666, London was blazing and 'the coale and wood wharfes and magazines of oyle, rosin, &c. did infinite mischiefe'.[1]

The greater part of *Fumifugium* is occupied by a review of the iniquities of 'the Hellish and dismall Cloud of SEA-COAL' which perpetually enveloped London, so that gardens and orchards in the Strand and Barbican had never been observed to be so fruitful as in the year (1644) when Newcastle was besieged and blocked up. It is remarked as a climax that in ordinary times the dirt which settled on the hands, faces and linen of the fair ladies resulted in a prodigious waste of almond-powder and soap.

Evelyn's suggested remedies were two. First he proposed to banish various trades such as brewers, dyers, soap- and salt-boilers, and lime-burners to a distance of several miles from London, for he did not attach much importance to the effect of 'the Culinary fires', which, in any case, could be greatly reformed by 'charking'. Secondly he advocated the extensive planting of fragrant and odoriferous trees, shrubs, and flowers in the neighbourhood of London, particularly on the low ground to the east and south-west. These were to be plantations of a hundred and fifty feet deep, and between them wide 'Beds and Bordures of Pinks, Carnations, Clove, Stock-gilly-flower, Primroses, Auriculas, Violets, not forgetting the White, which are in flower twice a year, April and August: Cowslips, Lillies, Narcissus, Strawberries, whose very leaves as well as fruit, emit a Cardiaque, and most refreshing Halitus: also Parietaria Lutea, Musk, Lemmon, and Mastick, Thyme: Spike, Cammomile, Balm, Mint, Marjoram, Pempernel, and Serpillum, &c. which upon the least pressure and cutting, breathe out and betray their ravishing odors'.[2] The imagination faints in the delicious contemplation of Evelyn's London dream.

The first edition of *Fumifugium* is now somewhat rare, though there were two issues, first distinguished in 1937, one containing some corrections. It was still of interest in 1772, for in that year, the nuisance of London smoke being still unabated, it was reprinted with a preface and additional footnotes by the antiquary Samuel Pegge the elder (1704–96). It was abstracted in the *Journal of Science, Literature, and the Arts*, vol. XII (1822), p. 243, and was next reprinted in the *Miscellaneous Writings* (1825), pp. 207–42, with additional notes. It was twice printed in 1930, when the controversy over the Chelsea power station had again brought up the question of smoke disposal, in 1933 for the National Smoke Abatement Society, and lastly in 1961 for the National Society for Clean Air.

[1] de Beer, III, 456.

[2] *Fumifugium*, p. 24.

23 FUMIFUGIUM [first issue. W. E 3488] 4° 1661

Title: Fumifugium: or The Inconveniencie of the Aer and Smoak of London Dissipated. Together With some Remedies humbly proposed By J. E. Esq; To His Sacred Majestie, and To the Parliament now Assembled. [*rule*] Published by His Majesties Command. [*quotation between rules*]

Lucret. l. 5.
Carbonúmque gravis vis, atque odor insinuatur
Quam facile in cerebrum? ——

London, Printed by W. Godbid for Gabriel Bedel, and Thomas Collins, and are to be sold at their Shop at the Middle Temple Gate neer Temple-Bar. M.DC.LXI.

Collation: A^4 a^2 B–D^4 E^2; 20 leaves.

Contents: A1 title; A2*a*–A4*a* *Epistle Dedicatory to the King*; A4*b* blank; a1*a*–a2*b* *To the Reader*, dated 1. *May*. 1661; B1*a*–E1*b* (pp. 1–26) text; E2 blank.

Note: The page numeral on p. 24 is misprinted 14. The signature on D2 is misprinted C2, the text on this page being in black letter, with which the compositor was probably unfamiliar. The words *Nation* and *Maritime* on p. 18 are misprinted as *Mation* and *Naritime*. In some copies these errors have been corrected. The reference to Lucretius should be VI. 802–3.

Copies: BLO (Wood.D.27.(5)), BM (1170.h.4), CCE,[1] GLL (with errors corrected), K (2, one with errors corrected), VAF; CLC, HCL (with errors corrected by hand).

24 FUMIFUGIUM [second issue. W. E 3489] 4° 1661

Title: Fumifugium: [etc., as in no. 23]...now Assembled. [quotation between rules as in no. 23]

London, [etc. as in no. 23]...M.DC.LXI.

Collation, contents: As in no. 23.

Note: In this issue the line on the title-page, *Published by His Majesties Command*, has been omitted. The page numeral on p. 24 has not been corrected, but the signature C 2 has been altered to D2, and the misprints on p. 18 have been put right.

Copy: BM (101.i.15); HCL.

[1] Evelyn's copy with some corrections by him in the text.

FUMIFUGIUM:

OR

The Inconveniencie of the AER

AND

SMOAK of LONDON

DISSIPATED.

TOGETHER

With ſome REMEDIES humbly

PROPOSED

By *J. E.* Eſq;

To His Sacred MAJESTIE,

AND

To the PARLIAMENT now Aſſembled.

Publiſhed by His Majeſties Command.

Lucret. l. 5.

Carbonúmque gravis vis, atque odor inſinuatur
Quam facile in cerebrum? ——

LONDON,
Printed by *W. Godbid* for *Gabriel Bedel*, and *Thomas Collins*,
and are to be ſold at their Shop at the *Middle Temple* Gate
neer *Temple-Bar.* *M. DC. LXI.*

Title-page of no. 23

25 FUMIFUGIUM 4° 1772

Title: Fumifugium:...[etc. as in no. 23]

Reprinted for B. White, at Horace's Head, in Fleet-street. MDCCLXXII.

Collation: A–G[4] [H][2]; 30 leaves.

Contents: A1 title; A2*a*–A4*b* (pp. iii–viii) *Preface by the Editor*, dated *March* 16, 1772; B1*a*–B3*a* (pp. 1–5) *The Epistle Dedicatory*; B3*b* blank; B4*a*–C1*b* (pp. 7–10) *To the Reader*; C2*a*–[H]1*a* (pp. 11–49) *Fumifugium*; [H]1*b* blank; [H]2*a* books printed for B. White; [H]2*b* blank.

Note: Edited by the antiquary Samuel Pegge the elder (1704–96), with a preface and additional notes.

Copies: BM (577.h.10(2)), K, ULC (Hh.13.80[4]); CLC, HCL.

26 FUMIFUGIUM 4° [1930]

Fumifugium:...[etc. as in no. 23 without the imprint]. 17 × 15 cm., pp. [ii], 49, [5]. Issued in ¼ canvas and boards with paper jacket.

Note: Printed at the Swan Press in Baskerville type. Limited to 100 numbered copies on hand-made paper and 10 on Japanese vellum. With a note by Joan Evans, on the penultimate leaf, and a bibliographical note on the verso of the title. There is no place or date of publication. The text is printed from the edition of 1772, and contains Pegge's footnotes, though his preface is omitted.

27 FUMIFUGIUM 8° 1930

Fumifugium by John Evelyn, of Balliol College, Oxford, in 1661. Now re-issued as an Old Ashmolean Reprint in the year of the refacing of the Old Ashmolean Museum, which, like 'Fumifugium', was dedicated to King Charles II, founder of the Royal Society. Oxford, 1930.

19 cm., pp. [iv], vii, 49, [3]. (Old Ashmolean Reprints, VIII.) Issued in green cloth, printed paper jacket.

Note: Printed by the Replica Process from the edition of 1772.

28 FUMIFUGIUM 8° 1933

Fumifugium: Or the Inconvenience of the Aer and Smoake of London Dissipated by John Evelyn [*woodcut of London Bridge*] First Published in 1661 and Reprinted with an Introduction by Rose Macaulay for the National Smoke Abatement Society 1933

21.5 cm., pp. 42, [2]. Issued in drab cloth, with paper label on front cover.

Note: The text and notes are from the edition of 1772, and the preface is printed at the end. There is a woodcut portrait of Evelyn on p. 6, and a note on the then existing position of the smoke problem on p. 42.

8a FUMIFUGIUM 8° 1961

Fumifugium. . . by John Evelyn First Published in 1661 and Reprinted by the National Society for Clean Air 1961

21·3 cm, pp. 41, [3]. With a woodcut portrait. Issued in green cloth.

NARRATIVE OF THE ENCOUNTER BETWEEN THE FRENCH AND SPANISH AMBASSADORS

1661

PREFACE

UNDER the date 1 October 1661 Evelyn relates how he sailed with the King in 'one of his yaachts' from Greenwich to Gravesend and back. After conversation about *Fumifugium* and the improvement of gardens and buildings in England the King 'then commanded me to draw up the matter of fact happening at the bloudy encounter which then had newly happen'd betweene the French and Spanish Ambass^{rs} neere the Tower, contending for precedency, at the reception of the Sweeds Ambassador'.[1] Accordingly the next day Evelyn gathered evidence from the officers of the Tower and others and duly 'drew up a Narrative in vindication of his Ma^{ty} and the carriage of his officers and standers by'.[1] Soon afterwards he was summoned to the King's cabinet, and read to him what he had written, being interrupted in the middle by Mr Secretary Morice with a large paper 'of extraordinary importance'. The reading was finally accomplished 'to his Ma^{tys} greate satisfaction; and after I had inserted one or two more clauses, in which his Ma^{ty} instructed me, commanded that it should that night be sent to the Post-house, directed to the Lord Ambass^{r} at Paris (the Earle of St Alban's) and then at leasure to prepare him a copy which he would publish. This I did, and immediately sent my papers to the Secretary of State, with his Ma^{tys} expresse command of dispatching them that night for France.' On the next evening the King 'espying me came to me from a greate crowde of noblemen standing neere the fire, and ask'd me if I had don; and told me he fear'd it might be a little too sharp, on second thoughts, for he had that morning spoken with the French Ambass^{r}, who it seemes had palliated the matter and was very tame, and therefore directed me where I should soften a period or two before it was publish'd (as afterwards it was)'.[2]

Thus, according to Evelyn's statement, his *Narrative* was published, which may or may not imply that it was printed; up to the present time no example of any such pamphlet has ever been seen or described. It is not mentioned in Evelyn's catalogue of his own library, though a manuscript copy was preserved among the papers at Wotton, and was printed with the *Memoirs* in 1818, vol. II, part I, pp. 349–55.[3] Another version in Evelyn's hand is in the Public Record Office (*Calendar of State Papers Domestic*, 1661–2, p. 105). For the present, therefore, the *Narrative* can only be tentatively included here as a conjectural

[1] de Beer, III, 297. [2] *Ibid.* 300. [3] Wheatley, II, 485–91.

publication, in the hope that it may one day come to light. It should be noted, however, that it was printed soon afterwards in a shorter version with a concluding paragraph referring to the settlement of the precedence question between France and Spain in April 1662. This is in Edward Phillips's edition (the fourth) of Sir Richard Baker's *Chronicle of the Kings of England*, London, fo., 1665, pp. 799–800.[1] It is there stated that 'we have here thought meet to insert from [Mr Evelyn's] more sedulous and ample Collection [the Narrative] as it was by him presented to his Majestie in this following relation'. Evelyn was familiar with this work,[2] and it is possible that it was this form of publication to which he afterwards referred in his Diary.

The longer version was afterwards printed in the *Biographia Britannica*,[3] where it is stated: 'The title of it ran thus "The Manner of the Encounter, between the French and Spanish Ambassadors, at the Landing of the Swedish Ambassador".' The difference in the title suggests the possibility of a source other than Baker's *Chronicle*, but no details are given. In the Public Record Office (*Calendar of State Papers Domestic*, 1661, XLII, no. 50) there is a printed pamphlet consisting of title-page and five pages of text entitled *A True Relation of The manner of the dangerous Dispute, and bloody Conflict betwixt the Spaniards and the French*, &c. [W. T 3000], but this is written in a different manner and is certainly not by Evelyn.

[1] 5th edition, 1670, p. 751. My attention was drawn to this by Dr Esmond de Beer.

[2] See p. 71.

[3] *Biog. Brit.* 2nd ed. 1793, vol. v, pp. 613–14.

29 NARRATIVE OF THE ENCOUNTER [?4° 1661]

Narrative of the Encounter between the French and Spanish Ambassadors at the Landing of the Swedish Ambassador.

Note: A conjectural publication. No copy has yet been recorded.

NAUDÉ'S INSTRUCTIONS

1661

PREFACE

GABRIEL NAUDÉ (1600–53), the great French librarian, first published his *Advis pour dresser une bibliothèque* at Paris in 1627. A second issue was printed in the same year, and a revised edition was published in 1644.[1] Evelyn was living in Paris in that year and it was perhaps this later edition that he obtained and read. Writing to Dr Godolphin, Provost of Eton, on 8 February 1697/8, he said, ''Tis now neere fifty yeares past since Gabr. Naudæus publish'd directions concerning librarys and their furniture, which I had translated; minding to reprint it, as what I conceiv'd might not be unseasonable whilst auctions were become so frequent among us, and gentlemen every where storing themselves with bookes at those learned marts.'[2] This probably refers to a projected second edition of his translation, and Evelyn added in his letter to Dr Godolphin, '& because it was so very thinne a volume, I thought of annexing a sheete or two of Medals, as an appendant not improper'. He went on to explain that this appendant became so bulky that the project was abandoned. The book was not actually printed until 1661, though the translation had been made some years before that date, as is indicated in a letter to Dr Barlow printed on the last leaf. It appears that the work had been 'long since' accepted by Barlow, and Evelyn had hoped it might be printed at Oxford. The copy, however, was mislaid and nothing further was done until Evelyn arranged for its publication in London in 1661.

Evelyn dedicated the book to Lord Chancellor Clarendon, and records in his Diary under the date 16 November 1661, 'I presented my Translation of Naudaus concerning Liberaries to my Lord Chancellor, but it was miserably false printed.'[3] His reasons for making his rather fulsome address to Lord Clarendon he gave at some length in a letter to Samuel Pepys written on 12 August 1689: 'Yes, he was a greate lover of books, & furnish'd a very ample library, writ himself an elegant style, favour'd & promoted the designe of the Royal Society; and it was for this, and in particular for his being very kind to me both abroad & at home, that I sent Naudæus to him in a dedicatory Addresse, of which I am not so much asham'd as of the Translation. There be some, who not displeas'd with the style of that Epistle, are angrie at the application. But they do

[1] Copies of both are in the BM: 1627, 619.c.3; 1644, 271.a.11.

[2] Wheatley, IV, 16.

[3] de Beer, III, 303–4.

not consider that greate persons, & such as are in place to doe greate & noble things, whatever their other defects may be, are to be panegyrized into the culture of those vertues, without which 'tis to be suppos'd they had never ariv'd to a power of being able to encourage them. *Qui monet ut facias*—you remember the sequel. And 'tis a justifiable figure; nor is it properly adulation, but a civilitie due to their characters.'[1]

The dedication has a further interest in that it contains the first reference in print to the Royal Society, this name having then happily occurred to Evelyn to denote the new 'philosophic assembly' of which he was an original member. This reference gave much satisfaction, and Evelyn added in his Diary under the date 3 December 1661, 'By universal suffrage of our philosophic assembly an order was made and register'd that I should receive their public thanks for the honourable mention I made of them by the name of Royal Society in my Epistle dedicatory to the Lord Chancellor before my Traduction of Naudeus. Too great an honor for a trifle.'[2] The Society was not actually incorporated by Royal Warrant until 1662.

Pepys received a copy of the book in 1665 and he mentions in his Diary under the date 5 October, 'I abroad to the office and thence to the Duke of Albemarle, all my way reading a book of Mr Evelyn's translating and sending me as a present, about directions for gathering a Library; but the book is above my reach, but his epistle to my Lord Chancellor is a very fine piece.'[3] If Pepys was dissatisfied with the book, Evelyn was disgusted, and he added in the letter to Pepys already quoted, 'As for the Translation, it has ben so insufferably abus'd at the presse, that the shame any uncorrected copy should come abroad has made me suppresse as many as I could light on, not without purpose of publishing a new edition, and which now perhaps might be more seasonable, since the humor of exposing books *sub hastâ* is become so epidemical, that it may possibly afford some direction to gentlemen who are making collections out of them. Besides, the first impression is I heare prety well worne out, and I should be very unfortunate if it should miscarry twice, or meete with such another accident as happen'd, it seemes, to the blotted manuscript at Oxford: the circumstances whereof I will not now trouble you withall.'[4] In the same year, 1689, as that in which he was writing to Pepys, he had also taken his own copy of the *Instructions*, containing his signature and motto, and despatched it to his friend Dr Godolphin.[5]

[1] Wheatley, III, 446. [2] de Beer, III, 306. [3] Wheatley's *Pepys*, V, 97–8. [4] Wheatley, III, 446.

[5] This may have been the only copy he possessed, for although there are two copies now in the Evelyn Collection, neither contains his signature, and they were probably acquired by one of his more recent successors.

At the top of the fly-leaf facing the title-page he had written, 'full of errors & corrected[?]', but these words he now deleted, adding the following explanation: '*For my worthy Friend Dr Godolphin.*

Sr, This Trifle (which you tell me you met with in some Catalogue of an *Auction*) was printed during my absence from Lond: (now neere 28 yeares since) by a very imperfect copy, my owne having ben lost in the printing-house at *Oxford*, & is so extreamly deform'd thro' the Corrector's negligence, that I have don all I am able to suppresse the vending of it. It is yet a very usefull discourse, and upon that account I presented it to some such Friends as you are, who will pardon the *Errata* & deplore the common calamitie incident to writers & Translators of Books, which is (unlesse they attend on the presse like slaves) to be at the mercy of sotts & drunkards, that can neither print sense nor English, nor indeede any other language, tho' it lie never so plainely before them. Witnesse the first Booke of Lucretius, which I made an Essay on almost 30 yeares past, where the Latine *é regione* (and from an incomparable *Plantine* Edition) was abus'd in some hundreds of places, it not being possible for me to imagine *Dr Triplet* (who was the sole *superviser*, and offer'd me his service) should take no more care. And this little pamphlet has been so miserably treated by them, that the wounds are Incurable.'[1]

Evelyn told both his correspondents that he had tried to suppress the book as far as he was able. Perhaps it is owing to his efforts that the book is somewhat scarce at the present day, though it is probable that only a small edition was printed. Some attempt was made to remedy the typographical shortcomings, for a leaf of *errata* was inserted in some copies at the end. Evelyn's copy, which he gave to Dr Godolphin, has the mistakes corrected, and also a copy given to Sir Thomas Pope Blount,[2] but neither of these contains the leaf of *errata*. In Dr Godolphin's copy Evelyn also wrote at the end, on p. 94:

> *Plurima quidem restant hisce non minora sphalmata, sive a me, sive ab ipso Typographo commissa, quibus ignoscat amicissimus Doctor.*[3]

He had thought of publishing a second edition, as he told Pepys, but never did so, and the book was not reprinted until 1903 (see next entry).

[1] This was in 1825 in the possession of S. W. Singer of Boxhill, and the letter to Dr Godolphin was printed by Upcott in the *Miscellaneous Writings* (1825), p. xii. The book is now in the Bibliotheca Lindesiana and was described by the late Earl of Crawford and Balcarres in a paper to the Bibliographical Society on 21 December 1931. See *The Library*, March 1932.

[2] Britwell Court library, Sotheby's, 17 March 1926, lot 204.

[3] For a reproduction see *The Library*, *loc. cit.*

30 NAUDÉ'S INSTRUCTIONS [W. N 247] 8° 1661

Title, within double lines: Instructions Concerning Erecting of a Library: Presented to My Lord The President De Mesme. [*rule*] By Gabriel Naudeus, P. And now Interpreted by Jo. Evelyn, Esquire. [*rule*]
London, Printed for G. Bedle, and T. Collins at the Middle-Temple Gate, and J. Crook in St. Pauls Church-yard, 1661.

Collation: A–G8; 56 leaves.

Conts: A1 title; A2*a*–A7*a* dedication *To the...Earl of Clarendon, Viscount Cornbery,... Lord High Chancellour of England,...*signed *J. Evelyn*; A7*b* *To the Reader* [by Gabr. Naudeus]; A8*a* *A Tale of the principal Matters*; A8*b* Latin lines addressed to Gabr. Naudeus by J. C. Frey, M.D.; B1*a*–G7*b* (pp. 1–94) text; G8 (pp. 95–6) *The Copy of a Letter sent to...Dr. Barlow, D.D. Provost of Queens Colledge, and late Proto-Bibliothecary of the Bodleian Library in Oxford,* signed *J. Evelyn.*

Insertion: An *errata* leaf of 32 lines, slightly shorter than the leaves of the book, has been inserted at the end of some copies.

Copies: BL,[1] BLO (3, Linc·8°.B.385;[2] Wood.68 (3); Mason.A.A.252), BM (619.c.4), CCE (2), K, VAF; CLC, HCL, PML.

31 Instructions Concerning Erecting of a Library: Presented to My Lord The President De Mesme. [*rule*] By Gabriel Naudeus, P. And now Interpreted by Jo. Evelyn, Esquire. [*rule*]
Cambridge, Printed for Houghton, Mifflin & Company, at the Riverside Press, 1903.
18 cm, pp. [ii], xxxii, 160, [6], last 2 ll. blank.

Note: Four hundred and nineteen copies were printed in red and black on MBM hand-made paper in February 1903. The typography was designed by Bruce Rogers, whose thistle device appears on the verso of the colophon. The type used is the Brimmer fount. Bound in quarter stamped calf, and marbled paper boards. The Introduction (pp. iii–vii) is by John Cotton Dana. It explains that Evelyn's translation has been followed exactly, except that a few obvious typographical errors have been corrected. The publishers also issued a prospectus (4 pp.) printed in the same style and on the same paper as the book.

[1] Evelyn's copy with motto, corrections and inscription to Dr Godolphin.

[2] Presentation copy to Dr Thomas Barlow.

INSTRUCTIONS
Concerning Erecting of a
LIBRARY:
Presented to My LORD
The PRESIDENT
De MESME.

BY
GABRIEL NAUDEUS, P.

And now Interpreted
BY
Jo. EVELYN, Esquire.

LONDON,
Printed for *G. Bedle*, and *T. Collins*, at the Middle-Temple Gate, and *J. Crook* in St. *Pauls* Church-yard, *1661*.

Title-page of no. 30

TYRANNUS

1661

PREFACE

ENGLISH addiction to French fashions was one of Evelyn's favourite themes, and in 1661 he amused himself by mildly scourging the affectation of wearing Frenchified clothes. He recorded in his Diary[1] that, on 7 December 'I presented my little trifle of Sumptuary Laws, intitl'd Tyrannus'. In this 'gentle Satyr', as he called it, he 'indulg'd himself the liberty of a Prevaricator', and was evidently pleased with his prowess in this style of writing. The King, who himself favoured these fashions, might not have been best pleased with Evelyn's satire. He had many courtiers of the kind of whom Evelyn wrote: 'It was a fine silken thing which I spied walking th' other day through *Westminster-Hall*, that had as much Ribbon on him as would have plundered six shops, and set up twenty Country Pedlers. All his Body was dres't like a May-Pole, or a *Tom-a Bedlam's* Cap. A fregat newly rigg'd kept not half such a clatter in a storme, as this Puppets Streamers did when the Wind was in his Shrouds; the Motion was Wonderfull to behold, and the Colours were Red, Orange, and Blew, of a well gum'd Sattin, which argu'd a happy fancy.'[2] Evelyn estimated that no less than two millions of treasure had been dissipated in a short time in gold and silver lace, and suggested that such extravagance should be controlled by the King through the provision of Sumptuary Laws which should be the envy and pattern of all other monarchs. He pleaded for rational clothes of plain materials, and five years later was able to preen himself on having influenced the King in the right direction, writing in his Diary under the date 18 October 1666: 'To Court. It being the first time his Ma^ty^ put himself solemnly into the Eastern fashion of vest, changeing doublet, stiff-collar, bands and cloake, into a comely mode, after the Persian mode, with girdle or shash, and shoe strings and garters into bouckles, of which some were set with precious stones, resolving never to alter it, and to leave the French mode, which had hitherto obtain'd to our greate expence and reproach. Upon which divers courtiers and gentlemen gave his Ma^ty^ gold by way of wager that he would not persist in this resolution. I had sometime before presented an invectique against that unconstancy, and our so much affecting the French fashion, to his Majesty, in which I tooke occasion to describe the comelinesse and usefulnesse of the Persian clothing, in the very same manner his Ma^ty^ now clad himselfe. This pamphlet I intitl'd Tyrannus, or

[1] de Beer, III, 306.

[2] *Tyrannus*, pp. 11–12.

the Mode, and gave it to the King to reade. I do not impute to this discourse the change which soone happen'd, but it was an identity that I could not but take notice of.'[1]

The King, however, certainly lost his wager, and it may be doubted whether *Tyrannus* can have circulated widely or have carried much weight. It is an exceedingly scarce book at the present time; one of the few accessible copies is in the Bodleian Library. This copy was formerly in the collection of James Bindley who wrote in it: 'I never saw another copy of this curious Tract. This, which is corrected throughout by the Author (Mr Evelyn) with his own hand for a second edition, was bought at an auction at Paterson's, at Essex House, near forty years ago.' Evelyn evidently intended to reprint his book, and wrote on the title-page, *The Second Edition, enlarged* (see no. 32). The corrected copy was printed by William Bray in the first edition of Evelyn's *Memoirs*, 1818, vol. II, pp. 320–32, and was reproduced in facsimile in 1951 (see no. 32*a*). I am able to record only four complete copies and have seen one other, an untrimmed copy, which was formerly in the possession of the bookseller, P. J. Dobell.

[1] de Beer, III, 464–5.

32 TYRANNUS [W. E 3519] 8° 1661

Title: Tyrannus Or the Mode: in a Discourse of Sumptuary Lawes. [*rule*]

Nec affectatæ sordes, nec exquisitæ munditiæ.

[*ornament between rules*]

London, Printed for G. Bedel, and T. Collins, at the Middle-Temple Gate, and J. Crook at the Ship in St. Pauls Church-yard. 1661.

Collation: A–B^8; 16 leaves.

Contents: A1 title; A2*a*–B7*b* (pp. 3–30) text; B8*a–b* *To Him that Reades*, signed *I.E.*

Note: The leaf *To Him that Reades* is sometimes found inserted after the title-page, but dissection of a copy (lacking the title-page) now in Princeton University Library has proved that the leaf is conjugate with B1, and was therefore imposed as B8.

Copies: BLO (Mason.A.A.393),[1] BM (C.113.a.15), CCE (title-page and seven leaves only), K; HCL, PUL (title-page in facsimile).

32*a* TYRANNUS 8° 1951

Tyrannus or The Mode By John Evelyn Edited from the edition of 1661 by J. L. Nevinson Oxford Published for the Luttrell Society by Basil Blackwell MCMLI

18·5 cm, pp. [ii, blank], xxiv, [2], 30, [4, blank]. Issued in stiff printed paper wrappers.

Note: This edition is a facsimile of the BLO copy of no. 32, with an illuminating introduction by the editor.

[1] Evelyn's copy corrected for a second edition.

TYRANNUS
Or the
MODE:
IN A
DISCOURSE
OF
SUMPTUARY LAWES.

The Second Edition enlarg'd.

~~*Nec affectatæ sordes, nec exquisitæ munditiæ.*~~

Gratius Falisc: Cyneg:
Sed Lubricus err
Mos, et ab expertis festinat usibus om

LONDON,

Printed for *G. Bedel*, and *T. Collins*, at the Middle-Temple Gate, and *J. Crook* at the Ship in St. *Pauls* Church-yard. 1661.

Title-page of the Bodleian copy of no. 32

SCULPTURA

1662

PREFACE

EVELYN wrote in his Diary under the date 16 January 1660/1, 'I went to the Philosophic Club, where was examin'd the Torricellian experiment. I presented my Circle of Mechanical Trades, and had recommended to me the publishing what I had written of Chalcography.'[1] This Circle of Mechanical Trades indicates that Evelyn with his usual all-embracing zeal designed to write a technical history, the contents of which are to be found summarized by his own hand in a manuscript preserved by the Royal Society. It bears the same date as the entry in the Diary, and is no doubt the actual document that he presented. It is headed *History of Arts Illiberal and Mechanical*, and classifies these arts into eight groups. How much of the whole *History* was ever written is not known, and probably it was one of the many grandiose schemes that Evelyn conceived but never finished; but he forthwith set about printing that portion dealing with copperplate engraving, and eighteen months later, in 1662, he was able to record in his Diary: '[June] 10th. I returned to London, and presented my History of Chalcographie (dedicated to Mr Boyle) to our Society.'[2] This was the book better known since as *Sculptura, or the History and Art of Chalcography and Engraving in Copper*, 1662.

Meanwhile a new interest had come to Evelyn in this connexion, for he states that on 21 February 1660/1 'Prince Rupert first shewed me how to grave in mezzo tinto'.[3] Long afterwards he added in his Diary under the date 13 March 1660/1: 'This afternoone Prince Rupert shew'd me with his owne hands the new way of graving call'd mezzo tinto, which afterwards by his permission I publish'd in my History of Chalcography; this set so many artists on worke that they soone arriv'd to that perfection it is since come, emulating the tenderest miniatures.'[4] This new manner of engraving was advertised on the title-page of *Sculptura*, but actually the four pages devoted to it convey nothing at all beyond the mere announcement of its discovery, and the author left it 'thus Ænigmatical', as he says at the end, lest the method be prostituted at too cheap a rate. Evelyn has been taken severely to task by a recent editor, C. F. Bell, for ascribing the invention of mezzotint to Prince Rupert. There can be no doubt that he made the statement in good faith, and that it would have been corrected had he ever published a

[1] de Beer, III, 268.
[2] *Ibid.* 325.
[3] *Ibid.* 271.
[4] *Ibid.* 274.

second edition of *Sculptura*. References in his letters show that he contemplated a revision, and, although this was never published, he regarded a chapter of a much later work *Numismata, A Discourse of Medals*, 1697, as embodying his afterthoughts.[1] Here (on p. 283) he correctly ascribes the invention of mezzotint to 'the late Melanochalcographer N. de Seigen',[2] that is, Ludwig von Siegen, an officer in the service of the Landgrave of Hesse-Cassel, and gives the date of the invention as 1648, though other authorities have ascribed it to 1643. Probably he was the first historian to set this down, and he did, moreover, actually write a full account of mezzotinting, intending to present it to the Royal Society. This remained in manuscript, and was still in existence about 1740, when an account of it, with extracts, was printed in an English edition of Bayle's *General Dictionary*.[3] It is not known to exist at the present time, but while a search was being made for it by Prof. A. H. Church in the archives of the Royal Society, another interesting discovery was made. At the end of *Sculptura* Evelyn announced in an *Advertisement* that he had prepared a technical account of printing from engraved plates, but that he withheld it, as he believed a similar account was to appear in a work by William Faithorne. Evelyn's chapter[4] remained unprinted, therefore, until it was transcribed from the Register Book of the Royal Society and printed in 1906 as Part II of *Sculptura* in C. F. Bell's edition (see no. 38).

Faithorne's work was in fact published in the same year as *Sculptura*, and is as follows:

The Art of Graveing and Etching... Published by Willm. Faithorne. And Sold at his shop next to ye Signe of ye: Drake, without Temple Barr. 1662.
Engraved title-page, A–D8 text, 10 engraved plates. (BM: 679.b.34 (2).)

This work so well supplied the deficiency in Evelyn's book that the two were often bound up together, as is exemplified by all three copies in the library of the British Museum. Evelyn's own copy of *The Art of Graveing and Etching*, with his signature on the title-page, was sold at Hodgson's on 19 January 1933 (lot 481) and was afterwards offered for sale by Tregaskis (March 1933; £37. 10*s*.).

[1] Ch. viii, 'Of Heads and Effigies in Prints and Taille-douce'.

[2] This was first noticed by Howard C. Levis, and recorded in his *Extracts from the Diaries and Correspondence of Evelyn and Pepys relating to Engraving* (1915), p. 31.

[3] Translated by Bernard, Birch, and Lockman, 1734–41, vol. I, p. 131; quoted by C. F. Bell in his edition of *Sculptura* (1906).

[4] 'The Construction of the Rowling Press, and manner how to work off the Plates.' There is a copy in the BM (Sloane MS 243, fols. 127*b*–141*b*); see also nos. 124 and 131.

Sculptura is of interest, then, as containing the first *announcement* of the art of mezzotint, and the body of the book constitutes the first history of engraving published in England. It is, however, a dull, if useful, compilation of names and authorities, and does not make good reading at the present time. In fact, by far the most interesting thing in the volume is the mezzotint of the head of the Executioner specially scraped by Prince Rupert for Evelyn's book. The Prince had made at Frankfurt in 1658 a large plate of the Executioner of St John the Baptist, after Spagnoletto or one of his school,[1] and he now copied the head, reducing it in size by about one tenth. This print has been the prey of collectors of mezzotints and is missing from many copies of the book. When present it enhances the price of the volume quite out of proportion to its rarity or intrinsic value. Sometimes the original print has been replaced by Houston's copy made for the second edition of 1755, which is a good one though the highlights on the head and face are not quite identical. The prints may be further distinguished by the paper, which is thicker in the copy, and by the measurements of the plate-marks, as follows: 1662, size 132 × 166 mm; 1755, size 129 × 163 mm.

The allegorical frontispiece, designed by Evelyn himself and engraved by Hertochs, is painfully banal. Evelyn has taken the seated figure of a girl, representing the Graphic Arts, from the engraved title-page of the first volume of the edition of Vasari's *Lives* published at Bologna in 1647. The design drawn by Conini and engraved by Bloemarts has not been improved by the translation. The engraved vignette on the title-page of *Sculptura* recalls that used some years earlier in *The State of France* and *The Golden Book*, though it is a new design embodying Evelyn's crest and motto, *Meliora Retinete*, as well as the monogram.

The book is dedicated to Robert Boyle, at whose 'reiterated instances' Evelyn had written the treatise. The dedication is followed by 'An Account of Signor Giacomo Favi by Monsieur Sorbiere', which might seem irrelevant did it not describe Favi's virtuosity, which rivalled Evelyn's own, and his intention of compiling and publishing a 'Compleate Cycle and History of Trades', a huge undertaking corresponding to Evelyn's projected *History of the Arts Illiberal and Mechanical* already mentioned.

Evelyn's *Sculptura* is not a rare book at the present time, and no doubt he presented many copies to friends. One of these is now in the Pierpont Morgan

[1] The original picture is now in the Old Pinakothek in Munich. There is a print from Prince Rupert's large plate in the Royal Library at Windsor.

Library and was given to Sir Thomas (then Dr) Browne of Norwich. It is inscribed on the fly-leaf:

For my honor'd Friend
Dr: Browne.
From his most humble
Servant
JEvelyn:

The author's own copy was preserved at Wotton (now at Christ Church), so that his grandson, Sir John Evelyn, was able to communicate to John Payne, the publisher, the corrections and additions which Evelyn had made in the margins.[1] Payne was thus enabled to insert these marginalia in his second edition of 1755 (see no. 34). As frontispiece to this edition Worlidge made an etching after the portrait of Evelyn engraved by Nanteuil in 1650, the mezzotint being copied, as already mentioned, by Richard Houston. The book does not seem to have found a ready sale, and the sheets were three times furnished with a new title-page, being re-issued in 1759 and 1765 by T. Jeffreys, who falsely described the book as 'third edition', and finally in 1769 by the first John Murray, who reverted to the correct description.

Sculptura was next reprinted in the *Miscellaneous Writings* (1825), pp. 243–336, the mezzotint being copied by William Say. The technique of this plate is very much smoother than that of the earlier versions and it could not be mistaken for them. *Sculptura* was reprinted for the last time by the Clarendon Press in 1906, the mezzotint being reproduced in photogravure.

[1] He also wrote opposite the title-page: 'I ever intended a second and much improv'd edition of this Historie.'

33 SCULPTURA [W. E 3513] 8° 1662

Title: Sculptura: or the History, and Art of Chalcography and Engraving in Copper. With An ample enumeration of the most renowned Masters, and their Works. To which is annexed A new manner of Engraving, or Mezzo Tinto, communicated by his Highness Prince Rupert to the Authour of this Treatise. [*engraved vignette*]

XXXI. Exod. XXXV.
Implevi eum Spiritu Dei, Sapientia, & Intelligentia,
& Scientia in omni opere, &c. [*rule*]

London, Printed by J. C. for G. Beedle, and T. Collins, at the Middle-Temple Gate, and J. Crook in St. Pauls Church-yard. 1662.

Collation: A^8 b^8 B–K^8 L^4; 92 leaves.

Contents: A1 title; A2*a*–A4*b* dedication to *Robert Boyle Esq.*, dated *Sayes-Court*, 5. *April*, 1662; A5*a*–b1*b An Account of Signor Giacomo Favi by Monsieur Sorbiere*; b2*a*–b8*a A Table*, with *Errata*, 11 lines, at bottom of b8*a*; b8*b* list of *Authors, and Books consulted*; B1*a*–L2*b* (pp. 1–148) *Sculptura*; L3*a*–L4*a An Advertisement*; L4*b* blank.

Engravings: i. Frontispiece, inserted facing title-page. Line engraving, 12·7 × 8.8 cm. A seated female figure with instruments for engraving at her side supports on her knee a tablet inscribed: *History of Chalcography by J. E.* Signed at the lower corners: *J. E. inve:*, *AH scu.*, i.e. designed by John Evelyn, engraved by A. Hertochs. The plate-mark measures 14 × 9·3 cm.

ii. Vignette on title-page. Line engraving, 3·2 × 5·7 cm., containing Evelyn's monogram, crest, and motto, *Meliora Retinete*, entwined with oak, bay, and palm.

iii. On p. 121. Line engraving, 13·4 × 8·2 cm. Two diagrams in illustration of the text.

iv. Folding plate inserted between K8 and L1 to face p. 145. Mezzotint by Prince Rupert, 13·2 × 16·6 cm., representing the head of Spagnoletto's Executioner of St John the Baptist, signed *R P f* at top right-hand corner.

Note: The page numeral is omitted on p. 121, which is occupied by engraving no. iii. The pagination and signatures are correct throughout.

Copies: BLO (3, Linc.8°.G.119;[1] Ashm.B.8; Lister.I.41 (2)), BM (3, 679.b.34 (1); 52.c.24 (1); 1044.a.12(1)), CCE, K, ULC (3, Syn.7.66.66; Sel.5.136; SSS.32.36), VAF; CLC, CH, HCL (2), PML.[2]

[1] Dr Thomas Barlow's copy.

[2] Presentation copy inscribed to Sir Thomas Browne.

SCULPTURA:
OR THE
HISTORY, and ART
OF
CHALCOGRAPHY
AND
Engraving in Copper.
WITH

An ample enumeration of the most renowned Masters, and their Works.

To which is annexed

A new manner of Engraving, or *Mezzo Tinto*, communicated by his Highness *Prince Rupert* to the Authour of this Treatise.

XXXI. EXOD. XXXV.

Implevi eum Spiritu Dei, Sapientia, & Intelligentia, & Scientia in omni Opere, &c.

LONDON,

Printed by *J. C.* for *G. Beedle*, and *T. Collins*, at the Middle-Temple Gate, and *J. Crook* in St. *Pauls* Church-yard. 1662.

PLATE 12

Title-page of no. 33

34 SCULPTURA [second edition] 8° 1755

Title: Sculptura; or, the History and Art of Chalcography, and Engraving in Copper: with An ample Enumeration of the most renowned Masters and their Works. To which is annexed, A New Manner of Engraving, or Mezzotinto, Communicated by His Highness Prince Rupert to the Author of this Treatise, John Evelyn, Esq; The Second Edition. Containing some corrections and Additions taken from the Margin of the Author's printed Copy; an Etching of his Head, by Mr. Worlidge; an exact copy of the Mezzotinto done by Prince Rupert, by Mr. Houston; a Translation of all the Greek and Latin Passages; and Memoirs of the Author's Life.

Implevi eum Spiritu Dei, sapientia, et intelligentia, et scientia in omni opere, ad excogitandum quicquid fabrefieri potest ex auro, et argento, et ære, marmore, et gemmis, et diversitate lignorum.

EXODUS, *cap.* XXXI, *et cap.* XXXV.

London: Printed for J. Payne, at Pope's Head, in Pater-Noster Row. M.DCC.LV.

Collation: [A]^{2} a–b^{8} c^{2} B–I^{8} K^{2} L^{4}; 90 leaves.

Contents: [A]1 title; [A]2 dedication to Sir John Evelyn, Bart.; a1 sub-title to *The Life of John Evelyn Esq*; a2*a*–b8*b* (pp. iii–xxxii) *The Life*; c1*a*–c2*a* (pp. xxxiii–xxxv) *Corrections and Additions from the Author's Printed Copy*; c2*b* (p. xxxvi) *Errata*, 5 lines, and *Directions to the Binder*; B1*a*–K1*a* (pp. 1–129) text of the first edition; K1*b* blank; K2*a*–L4*b* (pp. 131–40) *The Contents.*

Engravings: i. Frontispiece. Head of Evelyn etched by Worlidge after Nanteuil. Signed *Thos Worlidge Fecit 1753*. Plate-mark 14 × 9·5 cm.

ii. Facing p. 108. Diagrams, as in ed. 1 reversed. Plate-mark 14·5 × 9·3 cm.

iii. Facing p. 128. Mezzotint of the Executioner's Head, by Houston after Prince Rupert. Plate-mark 12·9 × 16·3 cm.

Note: The Memoir is unsigned, but it was probably written by, or under the direction of, John Payne, the publisher. Payne had some literary pretensions, being a member of Dr Johnson's club which met in Ivy Lane, and was the publisher of *The Adventurer* and *The Idler* (see Plomer's *Dictionary of Booksellers and Printers*, 1726–75, p. 194).

Copies: BLO (2, B.S. 8°.C.239; Douce.E.110), BM (564.a.18), K (in original wrappers untrimmed); CH, CLC, HCL.

35 SCULPTURA ['third edition'] 8° 1759

Title: Sculptura...[etc. as in no. 34] The Third Edition. [etc. as in no. 34]. London, Printed for T. Jeffreys, at Charing-Cross. MDCCLIX. Price Five Shillings Bound.

Collation, contents, engravings: As in no. 34.

Note: The sheets of no. 34 with a cancel title.

Copies: BLO (1713.e.2), K; CH.

36 SCULPTURA ['third edition'] 8° 1765

Title: Sculptura...[etc. as in no. 34] The Third Edition. [etc. as in no. 34]. London, Printed for T. Jeffreys, at Charing-Cross. MDCCLXV. Price Five Shillings Bound.

Collation, contents, engravings: As in no. 34.

Note: The sheets of no. 34 with a cancel title.

Copy: K.

37 SCULPTURA ['second edition'] 8° 1769

Title: Sculptura...[etc. as in no. 34] The Second Edition [etc. as in no. 34]. London: Printed for J. Murray, (Successor to Mr. Sandby) N°. 32, Fleet-Street. M.DCC.LXIX.

Collation, contents, engravings: As in no. 34.

Note: The sheets of no. 34 with a cancel title.

Copies: BLO (Mason.A.A.343), K; CLC, HCL.

38 SCULPTURA ed. C. F. Bell 8° 1906

Evelyn's Sculptura With the unpublished Second Part Edited by C. F. Bell [*device*] At the Clarendon Press MCMVI

19 cm, pp. xxiv, [xxxii], 151, [1], viii, 32. Tudor and Stuart Library. Issued in limp parchment.

Note: There is a general introduction by the editor, and an introduction to Part II by A. H. Church. There are three reproductions in half-tone inserted and one in the text on p. 121. The Executioner's Head is reproduced in photogravure.

MYSTERY OF JESUITISM

1664

PREFACE

THE *Lettres Provinciales* were published by Blaise Pascal in 1656 under the name of Louis de Montalte. They were soon afterwards translated into English and printed for the publisher, R. Royston, under the title *The Mysterie of Jesuitism* in 1657. The book was reprinted with additions in 1658 and 1679, and a second volume, entitled *A Further Discovery of the Mystery of Jesuitism*, containing various pieces by other authors, was also printed in 1658. No translator's name appeared in any of these, and it has often been stated that they were done by Evelyn. There is, however, no evidence connecting them with him,[1] and the translator remains unknown. On the other hand a third volume on the same subject was fully acknowledged by Evelyn and is described below under the title: Μυστήριον τῆς Ἀνομίας *That is, Another Part Of The Mystery of Jesuitism; or The New Heresie of the Jesuites, Publickly maintained At Paris... Together with The Imaginary Heresie, in three Letters,... London,...* 1664.

On 23 November 1664 Evelyn wrote in a letter to his friend Robert Boyle, 'If my book of architecture do not fall into your hands at Oxon, it will come with my apology, when I see you at London; as well as another part of the Mystery of Jesuitism, which (with some other papers concerning that iniquity) I have translated, and am now printing at Royston's, but without my name—so little credit there is in these days in doing any thing for the interest of religion.'[2] The printing proceeded during December, and on 2 January 1664/5 Evelyn noted in his Diary, 'This day was publish'd by me that part of The Mysterie of Jesuitism translated and collected by me, tho' without my name, containing the Imaginarie Heresy with 4 letters and other pieces.'[3] On the same day he wrote to Lord Cornbury, son of Lord Chancellor Clarendon, 'I came to present your Lordship with your owne booke [*in the margin*, The other part of the Mystery of Jesuitism translated and published by me]: I left it with my Lord your father, because I would not suffer it to be publiq till he had first seene it, who, on your Lp's score, has so just a title to it. The particulars which you will find added after the 4th letter are extracted out of severall curious papers and passages lying by me, which for being very apposite to your controversy, I thought fit to annex, in danger otherwise to have never been produced.'[4] It seems, therefore, that

[1] See Miss Ruth Clark's *Strangers and Sojourners at Port Royal* (Cambridge, 1932), p. 102.

[2] Wheatley, III, 290. [3] de Beer, III, 393. [4] Wheatley, II, 174–5.

Evelyn had undertaken the translation at Cornbury's instigation, though it was from Sir Robert Moray[1] that he received the copy in French from which he worked. *The Epistle Dedicatory* prefixed to the translation is addressed, 'To my most honoured *Friend* from whom I received the *Copy*', and that this friend was Moray was noted by Evelyn in his own copy of the book now in the Evelyn Collection. On 25 January 1664/5 Evelyn wrote in his Diary, 'This night being at White-Hall, his Ma^ty came to me standing in the withdrawing roome, and gave me thanks for publishing The Mysterie of Jesuitism, which he said he had carried two days in his pocket, read it, and encourag'd me; at which I did not a little wonder; I suppose Sr Robt Morray had given it to him.'[2]

It will be noticed that the title-page of the book mentions *The Imaginary Heresie, in three Letters*, whereas Evelyn mentions '4 letters' in his Diary. This is explained by examination of the make-up of the book.

Antoine Arnauld had published in 1662 a short piece entitled *Nouvelle Hérésie des Jésuites*, and this was immediately translated into English as *The New Heresie of the Jesuits*.[3] Evelyn either did not know of this translation or ignored it, and made another translation, which was the first piece printed in his book (pp. 1–48). Then follows *The Imaginary Heresie* in letters one to three (pp. 49–206) translated from the *Lettres de l'hérésie imaginaire* by Pierre Nicole, and some copies of the book are completed by several minor papers (pp. 207–54). The third of the *Imaginaires* had appeared on 15 April 1664,[4] and presumably the three were all that were known to Evelyn when he was engaged on the translation in November. Copies of the completed book were in fact published in the following January containing three *Imaginaires* only. Meanwhile, however, a fourth had been published by Nicole on 19 June 1664,[4] and this seems not to have come to Evelyn's notice until the last moment. He then interrupted the issue of the book, and a translation of the fourth *Imaginaire* on 40 unnumbered pages was inserted in the unsold copies, a note being added on the last page, 'This Fourth Letter not arriving till some time after the Three first were printed,

[1] Sir Robert Murray or Moray (d. 1673) had been knighted by Charles I in 1643 and had worked on his behalf. In addition to his political activities he was learned in the natural sciences and was one of the founders of the Royal Society in 1661 (*D.N.B.*).

[2] de Beer, III, 397.

[3] *The New Heresie of the Jesuits: Publickly maintained at Paris in the Colledge of Clermont, by Conclusions, Printed* 12 *Decemb.* 1661...*Translated out of the French Original*...*London Printed in the Year of our Lord* 1662. 4°. (BM: 3938.aaa.61 (1).)

[4] See Ruth Clark, *op. cit.* p. 107.

and the Papers following them ready to be publish'd, must excuse the interruption of the numbers of the ensuing Pages.' As will be seen from the facsimile of the title-page of Evelyn's copy, he has altered *three* to *foure* with his pen and has added *Translated by J. Evelyn*. The number remained uncorrected, however, on the title-page of the book as published, and copies may contain three *Imaginaires* or four according to when they were issued. Of three copies in my collection, all in contemporary bindings and quite untouched, one has the fourth *Imaginaire* and two are without it. The British Museum copy given by Evelyn to Sir Henry Herbert contains it.

Evelyn included the book in the list of his works sent to Dr Plot, and though he did not refer to it again in his Diary, his interest in the subject remained very active, and he soon afterwards published a second book on the Jesuits which was described for the first time in 1937 (see no. 79). It is stated[1] that another book, *The Jesuits' Morals*, was translated by Dr Ezrael Tonge at Evelyn's desire. Evelyn did refer to Tonge in his Diary[2] as the translator of the book, but he made no claim to any part in it for himself. In the *Miscellaneous Writings*, p. 500, the book referred to is stated in error to be *The Moral Practice of the Jesuits*, the translator of which is unknown.

Evelyn's book is now difficult to find, though it is possible that it is sometimes overlooked, as there is nothing in it to suggest any connexion with him. The engraving of Loyola inserted in the volume had already been used by the same publisher in the second English edition of *Les Provinciales*, 1658. *The Epistle Dedicatory* to Sir Robert Moray was reprinted in *Miscellaneous Writings*, 1825, p. 499. The rest of the book has not been reprinted.

[1] Wheatley, II, 344.

[2] de Beer, IV, 154.

Catalogo Evelyni inscriptus:

Meliora Retinete.

1664

Μυστήριον τῆς Ἀνομίας.

That is,

ANOTHER PART OF

The Mystery of Jesuitism;

OR

The new *Heresie* of the *Jesuites*,

Publickly maintained
At PARIS, in the *College* of CLERMONT,
the XII of *December* MDCLXI.

Declar'd to all the *Bishops* of *France*.

According to the *Copy* printed at *Paris*.

Together with

The Imaginary Heresie,
in ~~three~~ foure LETTERS,

With divers other *Particulars* relating to this Abominable *Mysterie*.

Never before published in *English*.

Translated by J. Evelyn:

LONDON,
Printed by *James Flesher*, for *Richard Royston*,
Bookseller to His most Sacred MAJESTY, 1664.

Fly-leaf and title-page of Evelyn's copy of no. 39

39 MYSTERY OF JESUITISM [W. A 3729] 8° 1664

Title, within double lines: Μυστήριον τῆς 'Ανομίας. That is, Another Part Of The Mystery of Jesuitism; or The new Heresie of the Jesuites, Publickly maintained At Paris, in the College of Clermont, the XII of December MDCLXI. Declar'd to all the Bishops of France. According to the Copy printed at Paris. Together with The Imaginary Heresie, in three Letters, With divers other Particulars relating to this Abominable Mysterie. Never before published in English. [*rule*]
London, Printed by James Flesher, for Richard Royston, Bookseller to His most Sacred Majesty, 1664.

Collation: A^8 B–R^8, 132 leaves, with Oo^8 Ooo^8 $Oooo^4$, 20 leaves, inserted in some copies after O7.

Contents: A1 blank; A2 title; A3*a*–A4*b* *The Epistle Dedicatory*, dated 21 Sept. 1664; B1*a*–D8*b* (pp. 1–48) *The New Heresie*, with *An Advertisement to the Reader* on D8*b*; E1*a*–O7*b* (pp. 49–206) *The Imaginary Heresie, The First, Second* and *Third Letters*; O8*a*–R7*b* (pp. 207–54) minor papers; R8 blank. Inserted in some copies between O7 and O8 is Oo1*a*–Oooo4*b* (unnumbered) *The Fourth Letter*.

Illustration: Inserted after A4 is an engraving representing Ignatius Loyola in the centre, flanked by Lessius, Molina, Vasquez, and Escobar. The plate-mark measures 13·5 × 16 cm.

Note: As explained in the preface *The Fourth Letter* of *The Imaginary Heresie* was printed after the publication of the book had begun, so that some copies do not contain the unnumbered leaves Oo–Oooo. When these leaves were inserted after O7, the succeeding leaf, O8, was detached and so may be loose in the binding.

Copies: BLO (2, Linc. 8°. A. 44; Linc. 8°. B. 22),[1] BM (C. 53. bb. 20),[2] CCE, K (3, two without the inserted leaves), ULC (8. 38. 46), VAF; CLC, HCL (2, one without the inserted leaves).

[1] Both Dr Thomas Barlow's copies.

[2] With presentation inscription to Sir Henry Herbert.

SYLVA

1664

PREFACE

EVELYN'S contemporary fame rested chiefly on his achievements as a gardener and afforester, and he is still well known as the author of *Sylva*, a book which nobody in recent times has read. For many years much of the woodlands of England had been carelessly despoiled, and no effort was made to redress the destruction by planting of trees. Evelyn always felt the greatest affection for the woods of Wotton, where he was born, and from these he transferred his interest to woods and trees in general. He obtained practical experience in planting trees both at Wotton and on his estate at Sayes Court, and this culminated on 15 October 1662, when he delivered to the Royal Society a 'Discourse concerning Forest-Trees'.[1] After the Restoration wood suitable for shipbuilding was in great demand, but was difficult to obtain. The Royal Society was requested to investigate the subject, and in turn asked Evelyn to provide the necessary material. His Discourse delivered in 1662 was approved, and in 1664 an order was issued by the Royal Society that it should be printed by their official printers, John Martyn and John Allestry. *Sylva* thus came to possess the distinction of being the first official production of the Royal Society. Evelyn presented a copy of his book to the Society on 16 February 1663/4, and on the next day gave copies to the King, the Lord Treasurer, and the Lord Chancellor.[2] Ten days later, on 26 February, he received special thanks from the King in person, and again on 27 October,[3] so that the book brought him an immediate access of royal favour. It was also quickly bought up by the public, an edition of over a thousand copies being sold in less than two years, and Evelyn was assured by the booksellers that this was 'a very extraordinary thing in volumes of this bulk'. He felt a pardonable pride in his work and boasted to the King in the dedication of the second edition of 1670 that it had been 'the sole Occasion of furnishing your almost exhausted Dominions with more than two Millions of Timber-Trees; besides infinite Others, which have been Propagated within the three Nations, at the Instigation and by the Direction of this Work'. When, after much importunity from all sides, he was induced to revise the work for a third edition, published in 1679, he began to regret that the book had been given to the printers for their own benefit. He heard that 'nere £500 has been already gotten by it', though characteristically he did not want this gain to be

[1] de Beer, III, 340. [2] *Ibid.* 369. [3] *Ibid.* 386–7.

in his own pocket. It was the benefit of the Royal Society that he desired, 'but', he regretfully concludes, 'we are not yet œconomists'.[1] The demand for a fourth edition in 1690 was the occasion for some reminiscences in a letter to Lady Sunderland. Evelyn recalls how he took no felicity, as a young man, in the ordinary outdoor recreations 'because they did not contribute to any improvement of the mind', and so he took to the planting of trees and the writing of *Sylva*, which 'alone incited a world of planters to repaire their broken estates & woods, which the greedy rebells had wasted & made such havock of'.[2] Evelyn did not immediately accede to this demand, and in January 1696/7 was writing to Dr Richard Bentley about a new edition of *Sylva*, which still in his old age represented his happiest memories. 'I confess I am foolishly fond of these and other rustications, which had been my sweet diversions during the days of destruction and devastation both of woods and buildings, whilst the Rebellion lasted so long in this nation.'[3] William Wotton had now 'been so kind, as without my asking, to offer me his help in looking over, not overlooking, the typographical and other faults escaped in the last impression of the *Sylva*, which I am most earnestly called upon to reprint. The copy which I frankly gave about 30 years since to Allestry is now in the hands of Chiswell and your namesake Mr. Bentley (Booksellers), who have sold off three impressions, and are now impatient for the fourth: and it having been no unprofitable copy to them, I have promised some considerable improvements to it, upon condition of letting Benj. Took (for whom I have a particular kindness) into a share. This, though with reluctancy, they at last consented to do.' Evelyn then suggested that the book 'might have the honour to bear the character of Dr Bentley's new *Imprimerie*, which, I presume, the proprietors will be as proud of as myself'. Actually the fourth edition was not published until 1706, the year of Evelyn's death, with the imprint of Scott, Chiswell, Sawbridge, and Tooke. It was given the embellishment of an engraved portrait of the author by Nanteuil. This plate had been made many years before at Paris in 1650,[4] and so shows Evelyn as a man of 30.

Sylva, although it is at the present day superseded by more modern, perhaps more 'scientific', works, contains a wealth of interesting information and practical instruction in the growth and management of trees. Most kinds of tree found in the British Islands are systematically described, and the book shows

[1] Letter to Dr Beale, Wheatley, III, 191.
[2] Wheatley, III, 363–4.
[3] *Bentley Correspondence* (1842), I, 135–6.
[4] de Beer, III, 9–10.

throughout the fruits of the author's own experience. Its size renders it somewhat forbidding, but the value of its matter cannot be questioned.

The first edition of *Sylva* contained two appendixes entitled: *Pomona: or, an Appendix concerning Fruit-Trees in relation to Cider; The Making and several ways of Ordering it*, and *Kalendarium Hortense: or, Gard'ners Almanac: Directing what he is to do Monethly throughout the year.* The second of these was frequently reprinted separately and proved to be Evelyn's most popular work (see no. 57). To the second edition of *Sylva* Evelyn added a long chapter on 'An Historical account of the Sacredness and the use of standing Groves'. This is a tedious discourse in the manner, though unfortunately not in the spirit, of Sir Thomas Browne. The erudition is there, but the music and the artistry are lacking. The main additions to the third edition of 1679 were Abraham Cowley's poem entitled 'The Garden', addressed to Evelyn and first printed in Cowley's *Works*, 1668, a translation of the *Nemus* of Renatus Rapinus by John Evelyn junior,[1] and *Terra, a Philosophical Discourse of Earth*, which had been published separately three years before (see no. 93). To the fourth edition of 1706 he added *Acetaria, a Discourse of Sallets*, published separately in 1699. The fifth edition of 1729 was a reprint of the fourth. As will be seen from the bibliographical descriptions, the text in the four editions published up to 1706 also underwent considerable enlargement, every chapter being given additional matter each time the book was reprinted. Evelyn had advertised in the *Philosophical Transactions* of 1666 for additional matter to be inserted in the second edition (see no. 124), and a long and favourable notice of this edition appeared in the *Transactions* for 15 November 1669 (vol. IV, pp. 1071–4).

Evelyn gave a number of copies of *Sylva* to his friends. The edition of 1664 he gave to Dr Thomas Browne, whose letter of thanks is extant.[2] He had quoted a portion of an earlier letter from Browne on the Depeham lime tree in his book (p. 82). I have noted other copies of the first edition given to John Hopkins, perhaps the clergyman whose sermons he heard on 25 June 1654;[3] to Thomas Chiffing (Chiffinch), Keeper of the King's Closet, whose house and garden he visited in 1661;[4] and to Sir Edmund Bowyer, a friend mentioned several times in the Diary.[5] He gave the edition of 1670 to Sir John Narborow (or Narbrough),

[1] This is Book II from *Of Gardens, Four Books*, translated by the younger Evelyn from Rapinus, 1672 (see no. 181).

[2] See Browne's *Works*, ed. Keynes (1964), IV, 281.

[3] de Beer, III, 101. [4] *Ibid.* 305. [5] *Ibid.* 196.

Admiral and Commissioner of the Navy, to Elias Ashmole,[1] and to Sir Edward Bish (Bysshe), Garter King of Arms. Copies of the edition of 1679 went to Dr. Ralph Bathurst, President of Trinity College, Oxford, and later Dean of Wells;[2] to Sir Francis North, Lord Keeper; and to Charles Bertie Esq., probably the Mr. Bertie mentioned in the Diary, 3 June 1666.[3]

[1] This copy is now in the library of the Royal College of Physicians of London.
[2] de Beer, III, 401 etc. [3] *Ibid.* 438.

40 SYLVA [first edition W. E 3516] f° 1664

Title, in red and black: Sylva, Or A Discourse Of Forest-Trees, and the Propagation of Timber In His Majesties Dominions. [*rule*] By J. E. Esq; [*rule*] As it was Deliver'd in the Royal Society the xv^th^ of October, CIↃIↃCLXII. upon Occasion of certain Quæries Propounded to that Illustrious Assembly, by the Honorable the Principal Officers, and Commissioners of the Navy. [*rule*] To which is annexed Pomona; Or, An Appendix concerning Fruit-Trees in relation to Cider; The Making and several ways of Ordering it. Published by express Order of the Royal Society. Also Kalendarium Hortense; Or, Gard'ners Almanac; Directing what he is to do Monethly throughout the Year. [*rule*]

——Tibi res antiquae laudis & artis
Ingredior, tantos ausus recludere fonteis. Virg.

[*engraving of the arms of the Royal Society*, 10 × 9 cm., *between rules*]
London, Printed by Jo. Martyn, and Ja. Allestry, Printers to the Royal Society, and are to be sold at their Shop at the Bell in S. Paul's Church-yard. MDCLXIV.

Collation: A–R4 χ^2 A2 B–L4, one leaf inserted after C4, one leaf inserted between F2–F3, H1 cancelled, one leaf inserted after L4 (all in the second alphabet); 114 leaves.

Contents: A1*a* blank; A1*b Imprimatur* of the Royal Society, signed *Brouncker, P.R.S.*, Feb. 3, 1663/4; A2 title; A3*a–b The Epistle Dedicatory* to Charles II, signed *J. Evelyn, Says-Court, May* 29, 1663; A4*a*–B3*a To the Reader* signed *J. E.*; B3*b* blank; B4*a* Latin lines to Evelyn by *J. Beale, S.P.D.*; B4*b A Table of the Chapters*; C1*a*–R4*b* [C1 with sig. B] (pp. 1–120) *Sylva*; χ1*a*–G3*b Pomona* (see no. 52); G4*a*–L4*a Kalendarium Hortense* (see no. 57); L4*b* blank; one leaf inserted at the end with *errata*, 18 lines, to all three works on the recto.

Illustrations: (1) Woodcuts of various implements on p. 103 of *Sylva.*
(2) Woodcut of a cider vat on p. 49 of *Pomona.*

Note: C1 of *Sylva* has sig. B, and p. 111 is numbered 112. The signatures and pagination are otherwise correct. The three inserted leaves have no signatures. There is no indication of the contents of the cancelled leaf H1, pp. 53–4 of the second numbering. In one of my copies the engraving of the arms of the Royal Society has been omitted from the title-page and the *Imprimatur* is cut round and mounted, perhaps indicating a trial copy.

Copies: BLO (4, Douce.E.298, etc.), BM (2, 438.m.11; 447.i.9), CCE, K (2), ULC (Adams.4.66.3); CH, CLC, HCL (Arnold Arboretum).

SYLVA,

Or A DISCOURSE OF

FOREST-TREES,

AND THE

Propagation of Timber

In His MAJESTIES Dominions.

By *J. E.* Esq;

As it was Deliver'd in the *ROYAL SOCIETY* the xv[th] of *October*, CIↃIↃCLXII. upon Occasion of certain *Quæries* Propounded to that *Illustrious Assembly*, by the *Honorable* the Principal *Officers*, and *Commissioners* of the *Navy*.

To which is annexed

POMONA: Or, An *Appendix* concerning *Fruit-Trees* in relation to *CIDER*; The *Making* and several ways of *Ordering* it.

Published by express Order *of the* ROYAL SOCIETY.

ALSO,

KALENDARIUM HORTENSE; Or, *Gard'ners Almanac*; Directing *what* he is to do *Monethly* throughout the *Year*.

———*Tibi res antiquæ laudis & artis*
Ingredior, tantos ausus recludere fonteis. Virg.

LONDON, Printed by *Jo. Martyn*, and *Ja. Allestry*, Printers to the *Royal Society*, and are to be sold at their Shop at the *Bell* in S. *Paul's* Church-yard, MDCLXIV.

PLATE 13

Title-page of no. 40
(reduced)

41 SYLVA [second edition. W. E 3517] f° 1670

Title: Sylva, Or A Discourse Of Forest-Trees, and the Propagation of Timber in His Majesties Dominions. As it was Deliver'd in the Royal Society the xv[th] of October, CIϽIϽCLXII. upon occasion of certain Quæries propounded to that Illustrious Assembly, by the Honourable the Principal Officers, and Commissioners of the Navy. [*rule*] To which is annexed Pomona; Or, An Appendix concerning Fruit-Trees in relation to Cider; The Making, and severall wayes of Ordering it. Published by expresse Order of the Royal Society. Also Kalendarium Hortense; Or, the Gard'ners Almanae [*sic*]; Directing what he is to do Monthly throughout the Year. [*rule*] All which several Treatises are in this Second Edition much Inlarged and Improved by John Evelyn Esq; Fellow of the Royal Society. [*Latin quotation between rules, and engraving between rules as in no.* 40]

London, Printed for Jo. Martyn, and Ja. Allestry, Printers to the Royal Society MDCLXX.

Collation: $[A]^2$ $a–l^2$ C^2 $D–Z^2$ $Aa–Ii^4$ Kk^2 $[A]^2$ $B–I^4$ K^2 $Aa–Dd^4$ Ee^2, 1 leaf inserted after Z3 with sig. *Z; 199 leaves.

Contents: [A]1*a* blank; [A]1*b Imprimatur* of the Royal Society, undated; $[A]^2$ title; a1*a*–a2*a The Epistle Dedicatory* to the King; a2*b* blank; b1*a*–c2*b To the Reader*, list of seven *Books Publish'd by the Author of this Discourse* on c2*b*; d1*a* Latin lines by J. Beale, S.P.D.; d1*b*–d2*a* Latin lines by R. Bohun; d2*b* Greek lines by J. Evelyn jun.; e1*a*–*b Table of the Chapters*; e2*a*–l2*a The Table* of subjects; l2*b* blank; C1*a*–Kk2*a* (pp. 1–247 [should be 241; pp. 45–52 are omitted in the numbering and pp. 171–2 are repeated owing to the insertion of the leaf *Z]) text of *Sylva*; Kk2*b* blank; [A]1*a*–K2*a Pomona*, second edition (see no. 53); K2*b* blank; Aa1*a*–Ee1*a Kalendarium Hortense*, second edition in folio (see no. 60); Ee1*b* blank; Ee2*a Errata*, 20 lines, in all three works; Ee2*b* blank.

Illustrations: The woodcuts in the former edition are omitted. The following engravings have been added:

Sylva (1) p. 22. A winch for dragging out roots.
(2) p. 76. Method of drawing sap from a tree.
(3) p. 177 (full-page). Saw-mill and boring-engine.
(4) p. 195. Charcoal burning.

Pomona (5) p. 66. A cider press.

Note: The irregularities in the pagination of *Sylva* are noted above. This edition contains thirty-five chapters instead of thirty-two, the last being 'An historical Account of the Sacrednesse, and Use of standing Groves, &c.' The number of pages is increased by these and other additions from 120 to 241.

Copies: BLO (Douce.E.301), BM (1253.g.27), CCE, K, ULC (Fff.46); CLC, HCL (3, Arnold Arboretum, Gray Herbarium).

42 SYLVA [third edition. W. E 3518] f° 1679

Title, in red and black: Sylva, Or a Discourse of Forest-Trees, and the Propagation Of Timber In His Majesties Dominions. As it was Deliver'd in the Royal Society the xvth of October, MDCLXII. upon occasion of certain Quæries propounded to that Illustri-ous Assembly, by the Honourable the Principal Officers, and Commissioners of the Navy. Terra, A Philosophical Essay of Earth, being a Lecture in Course. To which is annexed Pomona: or, an Appendix concerning Fruit-Trees in relation to Cider; The Making, and several ways of Ordering it. Published by express Order of the Royal Society. Also Kalendarium Hortense; or, the Gard'ners Almanac; Directing what he is to do Monthly throughout the Year. [*rule*] All which several Treatises are in this Third Edition much Inlarged, and Improved. By John Evelyn Esq; Fellow of the Royal Society. [*Latin quotation between rules*]
London, Printed for John Martyn, Printer to the Royal Society, and are to be sold at the Bell in St Paul's Church-Yard. MDCLXXIX.

Collation: π^2 $*^4$ A^4 $a–n^2$ $B–Z^4$ $Aa–Zz^4$ $Aaa–Lll^4$ Mmm^2; 262 leaves.

Contents: π1 blank; π2 title; *1*a–b The Epistle Dedicatory* to the King; *2*a*–a1*b To the Reader*; a2*a–b Advertisement,* with glossary of unusual words, and list of nine *Books Publish'd by the Author of this Discourse*; b1*a*–b2*b* Latin and Greek lines as in second edition; c1*a*–d2*a The Garden,* signed *Abraham Cowley, Chertsea,* 16 *Aug.* 1666; d2*b* blank; e1*a–b A Table of the Chapters*; e2*a*–k1*b The Table to Sylva*; k2*a*–l1*b The Table to Rapinus's Nemus, and the Philosophical Discourse of Earth*; l2*a*–m1*b The Table to Pomona*; m2*a*–n2*a The Table to the Kalender*; n2*b* blank; B1*a*–Oo1*a* (pp. 1–281) *Sylva,* with Rapinus's *Nemus* printed at the end of the last chapter; Oo1*b* blank; Oo2–Uu3 *A Philosophical Discourse of Earth,* second edition (see no. 94); Uu4–Ggg2 *Pomona,* third edition (see no. 54); Ggg3–Mmm1 *Kalendarium Hortense,* third edition in folio (see no. 64); Mmm2*a Errata,* 23 lines; Mmm2*b* blank.

Illustrations: Five engravings as in the last edition, on pp. 24, 74, 196, 216, and 411. A woodcut of a cider vat is added on p. 399 of *Pomona.*

Note: This edition of *Sylva* is chiefly notable for the addition to it of Cowley's 'The Garden', a translation of Rapinus's *Nemus* by John Evelyn junior, and the author's *Discourse of Earth,* first published separately in 1676. The latter and *Pomona* are both dated 1678 on their sub-titles. *Sylva* is still divided into thirty-five chapters, though further additions have been made increasing the number of pages from 241 to 281. The arms of the Royal Society no longer appear on the title-page, and the *Imprimatur* is omitted.

Copies: BLO (C.8.3.Art.), BM (441.i.10), K, ULC (Fff.46); CH, CLC, HCL (2, Arnold Arboretum).

43 SILVA [fourth edition] f° 1706

Title, in red and black: Silva, Or a Discourse of Forest-Trees, and the Propagation of Timber In His Majesty's Dominions. As it was Deliver'd in the Royal Society the xv[th] of October, MDCLXII. upon occasion of certain Quæries propounded to that Illustrious Assembly, by the Honourable the Principal Officers and Commissioners of the Navy. In Two Books. Together with an Historical Account of the Sacredness and Use of Standing Groves Terra, A Philosophical Essay of Earth, being a Lecture in Course. To which is annexed Pomona: or, an Appendix concerning Fruit-Trees, in relation to Cyder; The Making, and several Ways of Ordering it. Published by Express Order of the Royal Society. Also Acetaria: Or, a Discourse of Sallets. With Kalendarium Hortense; or the Gard'ners Almanack; Directing what he is to do Monthly throughout the Year. [*rule*] All which several Treatises are in this Fourth Edition much Inlarg'd and Improv'd, By the Author John Evelyn, Esq; Fellow of the Royal Society [*quotation between rules*]
London: Printed for Robert Scott in Little-Britain; Richard Chiswell in St. Paul's Church-yard; George Sawbridge in Little-Britain; and Benj. Tooke in Fleetstreet. MDCCVI.

Collation: [A]^2 *–****^{4} B–Z^4 Aa–Zz^4 Aaa^4 Bbb–Ggg^2 Aaaa–Zzzz^4 Aaaaa–Mmmmm^4 Nnnnn^2; 356 leaves.

Contents: [A]1 title; [A]2*a–b* dedication; *1*a*–***1*b To the Reader*; ***2*a–b Advertisement*, etc. as in ed. 3; ***3*a*–4*b* Latin and Greek lines as in ed. 2; ****1*a*–4*a The Garden* by Abraham Cowley; ****4*b* blank; B1*a*–Bbb1*a* (pp. 1–361 [should be 369]) *Silva*, in four books with a translation of Rapinus's *Nemus* printed at the end of the fourth book; Bbb1*b*–Eee1*b* (pp. 362–374) *Appendix. A Table, shewing the several Sorts of Soil, or Places that are proper, or at least may serve, or that are unfit for certain Kinds of Trees*; Eee2*a*–Ggg2*b* (pp. 375–384) *A Table to Silva*; Aaaa1–Gggg4 *Terra, A Discourse of Earth*, third edition (see no. 95); Hhhh1–Rrrr3 *Pomona*, fourth edition (see no. 55); Rrrr4–Eeeee1 *Acetaria*, second edition (see no. 107); Eeeee2–Mmmmm4*a Kalendarium Hortense*, 'tenth edition' (see no. 72); Mmmmm4*b*–Nnnnn2*b A Table to Terra and the other Tracts*. (Pp. 337–44 occur twice over in the pagination.)

Frontispiece: Inserted facing the title-page is an engraved portrait of the author executed by Nanteuil. A bust of Evelyn, aged 30, is contained in an oval resting on a pediment, in front of which hangs a cloth inscribed: *Meliora Retinete.* / *Βούλου τὰς Εἰκόνας; τῆς ἀρετῆς ὑπόμνημα* / *μᾶλλον ἢ τοῦ σώματος, καταλιπεῖν* / ΙΣοκ. *πρὸς* Νικ. On each side of the cloth are two books; the cover of one on the left bears Evelyn's monogram, an open page of one on the right shows a geometrical figure (a variant of the pentacle). The plate is signed below: *R. Nanteüil delineabat, & Scul.* The plate-mark measures 24·3 × 17·2 cm. This print is found in five states as follows:

(1) Before all letters.

(2) With the motto and engraver's signature. Before the addition of the Greek quotation and the pentacle. The monogram is on the front volume on the left. The hindmost volume on the right bears the Evelyn coat of arms without any tints being indicated.

(3) The monogram added to the second volume on the left. The tints are indicated in the coat of arms. The Greek quotation and the pentacle added.

(4) The coat of arms erased. The monogram removed from the hindmost volume on the left.

(5) The whole plate retouched for later use (see p. 270).

State no. 4 is the one usually found in the fourth edition of *Silva*. An example of no. 1 is in the Print Room of the British Museum. No. 2 is in the Charrington collection, Fitzwilliam Museum, Cambridge. No. 3 is in the Hunterian Museum, Glasgow.

Illustrations: The five engravings which appeared in the last edition are on pp. 36, 96, 247, 271 of *Silva* and on p. 129 of *Pomona*. Five engravings have been added:

(1) p. 34. The arrangement of the roots of a tree.

(2) p. 306. The plan of a garden.

(3) p. 307. Plan of the walks in Mr Kirke's wood at Cookeridge in Yorkshire, and a table of the number of views.

(4) p. 309. Engraved plan showing how 'Forest-trees may be planted in Consort with Fruit-trees'.

(5) p. 269 of *Kalendarium*. The parts of a greenhouse.

Note: This edition of *Silva* (now so spelled for the first time) is the handsomest, as well as the most elaborate, of the original series. It is the first to contain *Acetaria* among the appended tracts, and its value is greatly enhanced by Nanteuil's portrait of the author. According to the Diary the drawing was made on 13 June 1650: 'I sate to the famous sculptor Nanteuil, who was afterwards made a Knight by the French King for his art. He engrav'd my picture in copper. At a future time he presented me with my own picture done all with his pen; an extraordinary curiosity.'[1] Nanteuil's drawing of Evelyn, together with those of his wife and Sir Richard and Lady Browne, is still in the Evelyn Collection, and is reproduced in Petitjean and Wickert's *Catalogue*.[2] It is signed and dated 1650. The engraved plate was now, 1706, first used in a book. It was copied by Worlidge for the second and later editions of *Sculptura* (see no. 34) and has served as the basis for other engravings.[3] The original plate was used again, though retouched, in the second edition of the *Memoirs and Correspondence* (1819), vol. 1, facing p. 245.

[1] de Beer, III, 9–10, 22.

[2] See Petitjean and Wickert, *Catalogue de l'Œuvre Gravé de Robert Nanteuil* (Paris, 1925), pp. 187–90. Six states are there recorded, but no. 5 was described in error. The accuracy of the above description was vouched for by the late John Charrington.

[3] See *Evelyn and Pepys on Engraving*, by Howard C. Levis (London, 1915), pp. 123–31.

The title-page states that *Silva* is in two books. Actually it is divided into four books, totalling thirty-five chapters as before. The number of pages is increased from 281 to 374, and there are four additional engravings in the text. The dedication to Charles II is omitted.

Copies: BM (1474.d.6), K, ULC (SSS.4.20); CH, CLC, HCL (3, Arnold Arboretum, Gray Herbarium).

44 SILVA [fifth edition] f° 1729

Title, in red and black: Silva: or, A Discourse of Forest-Trees, And the Propagation of Timber in His Majesty's Dominions: As it was delivered in the Royal Society the 15th of October, 1662, upon Occasion of certain Quæries propounded to that Illustrious Assembly, by the Honourable and Principal Officers and Commissioners of the Navy. [*rule*] In Two Books. [*rule*] Together with An Historical Account of the Sacredness and Use of Standing Groves. Terra, A Philosophical Essay of Earth; being a Lecture in Course. To which is annex'd, Pomona: Or an Appendix concerning Fruit-Trees, in relation to Cyder; the Making, and several Ways of Ordering it. Publish'd by express Order of the Royal Society. Also Kalendarium Hortense; Or, The Gardener's Almanack; Directing what is to do Monthly throughout the Year. [*rule*] By John Evelyn, Esq; Fellow of the Royal Society. [*rule*] The Fifth Edition. [*Latin quotation between rule and double rules*]
London: Printed for J. Walthoe, J. Knapton, D. Midwinter, A. Bettesworth, J. Tonson, W. Innys, R. Robinson, J. Wilford, J. Osborn and T. Longman, B. Motte, A. Ward; and sold also by F. Fayram. [*short rule*] M.DCC.XXIX.

Collation: π^2 a–g^2 A–Z^2 Aa–Zz^2 Aaa–Zzz^2 *Aaaa–*Bbbb^2 4A–4Z^2 5A–5Z^2 6A–6Z^2 7A–7G^2 [7F, 7G signed 6F, 6G]; 310 leaves.

Contents: π1 blank; π2 title; a1*a*–d2*a* (pp. i–xv) *To the Reader*; d2*b*–e1*a* (pp. xvj–xvij) *Advertisement*; e1*b* (p. xviij) *Books published by the Author of this Discourse*; e2*a*–f1*b* (pp. xix–xxij) Latin and Greek lines; f2*a*–g2*b* (pp. xxiij–xxviij) Cowley's *Garden*; A1*a*–4L1*b* (pp. 1–318 [should be 322, pp. 277–80 being repeated in the pagination]) *Silva*, as in ed. 4; 4L2*a*–4O1*a* (pp. 319–329) *Appendix*, as in ed. 4; 4O1*b* blank; 4O2*a*–4P2*b* (pp. j–vj) *A Table to Silva*; 4Q1*a*–5E1*b* *Terra. A Discourse of Earth*, fourth edition (see no. 96); 5E2*a*–5X1*b* *Pomona*, fifth edition (see no. 56); 5X2*a*–6Q1*a* *Acetaria*, third edition (see no. 108); 6Q1*b* blank; 6Q2*a*–7F2*a* *Kalendarium Hortense*, fifth edition in folio (see no. 73); 7F2*b*–7G2*b* *A Table to Terra and the other Tracts.*

Illustrations: The frontispiece is omitted. Also the first of the engravings added in the text of the last edition, though a space is left for it on p. 29. The other engravings are on pp. 32, 84, 214, 235, 267, 268, 270 of *Silva*, p. 110 of *Pomona*, and p. 230 of *Kalendarium.*

Note: Except that it does not have the frontispiece, this edition is a reprint of the fourth. The author had died in 1706, so that no further revision was possible.

Copies: BM (448.K.11), K, ULC (Hh.3.2); CLC, HCL (2, Arnold Arboretum, Gray Herbarium).

45 SILVA [abridged] 8° 1827

Title: Dendrologia; or, a Treatise of Forest Trees, with Evelyn's Silva revised, corrected and abridged; By a Professional Planter, and Collector of Practical Notes forty years. This Work will be found useful and entertaining to Noblemen, Gentlemen, Law-stewards, Land-stewards, Planters in general, and Landscape Gardeners: As it comprises the Seminary, Nursery, Transplanting, Training, Thinning, Pruning, Felling, Measuring, Valuing, Selling, Converting, and Final Decomposition by Age, Dry-rot, &c. By J. Mitchell, F.J.B.S. & M.N.A.

Keighley: Printed for the Author, by R. Aked, Low-Street, and sold by him, and all other booksellers. M,DCCC,XXVII.

Collation: 22 cm. pp. [ii], 280, [2]. Folding table inserted after p. 190.

Illustrations: Five engraved plates facing pp. 4, 94, 126 (2), 184, and some small woodcuts in the text.

Note: The author in a facetious dedication acknowledges his debt to Evelyn, Grew, and Hale. The work may be described as being based on Evelyn's *Silva* rather than as an abridgement. The copy collated came direct from an 'old library' at Keighley.

Copies: BM (442.b.17), K.

46 SYLVA [new edition] 2 vols. 8° [1908]

Title, in red and black: Sylva or a Discourse of Forest Trees: by John Evelyn F.R.S. with an Essay on the Life and Works of the Author by John Nisbet D.Œc. A Reprint of the Fourth Edition in Two Volumes Volume One [Two] London: Published by Arthur Doubleday & Company Limited at 8 York Buildings Adelphi

Collation: 25 cm. Vol. I, pp. cxv, [i], 335, [1]. Vol. II, pp. [iv], 287, [1].

Note: The text is printed, with typographical alterations, from the fourth edition of 1706, though the author's Introduction (pp. 1–7 of the fourth edition) is omitted without comment. The appended treatises are also omitted. The frontispiece in vol. I is a photogravure reproduction of the engraving by Nanteuil. Several of the engravings in the fourth edition are reproduced as line blocks. The two volumes were issued in green cloth, gilt.

HUNTER'S SILVA

1776

PREFACE

EVELYN'S *Silva* waned in popularity after its author's death, and after the edition of 1729 nearly fifty years elapsed before it was reprinted. The book was then given a fresh lease of life by the enthusiasm and industry of Dr Alexander Hunter of York, who published an extensively annotated edition in 1776. Dr Hunter, born in 1733, was a graduate of Edinburgh University, and studied medicine also in London, Rouen, and Paris. For the greater part of his life he practised in York, where he died in 1809. His mind was versatile like Evelyn's, and he varied his medical work by becoming an authority on agriculture and forestry. He also founded a lunatic asylum in York, and was a Fellow of the Royal Societies of London and Edinburgh. Hunter's edition of Evelyn's *Silva*, undertaken as a relaxation, proved to be a popular success, so that five editions of this ponderous work were called for up to 1825. His annotations are learned and extensive, and he claims that the text was collated with all five of the original editions, and corrected with the help of 'some Original Manuscripts'. The editions of 1706 and 1729 he states are exceedingly corrupt and there may, therefore, be some justification for his interference with the text. Further notes and plates were added to the editions of 1786 and 1801, and to the latter he also added an annotated edition of *Terra: A Philosophical Discourse of Earth*, which he had already published separately in 8° and 4° (see nos. 97, 98). After his death two more editions were published in 1812 and 1825. Some copies of the first two editions have the numerous engraved plates by J. Miller finely coloured by hand.

Proposals[1] for Hunter's new edition were issued in York about 1775. The *Advertisement* leaf thereof states that the few remaining copies of the fifth edition were being sold at three guineas; the price of the new edition could not be exactly ascertained, 'but the Editor engages that it shall not exceed one guinea and a half to subscribers'—though in the end they had to pay two guineas.

[1] The only copy seen (π^2 A–B^{4}C^2) appears to lack a title-page. It has an engraved plate of 'The Oak Tree' inserted.

47 HUNTER'S SILVA [first edition] 4° 1776

Title: Silva: or, A Discourse of Forest-Trees, and the Propagation of Timber in his Majesty's Dominions: As it was delivered in the Royal Society on the 15th Day of October, 1662, Upon Occasion of certain Quæries propounded to that illustrious Assembly, by the Honourable the Principal Officers and Commissioners of the Navy. Together with An Historical Account of the Sacredness and Use of Standing Groves. [*rule*] By John Evelyn, Esq; Fellow of the Royal Society. With Notes by A. Hunter, M.D. F.R.S. [*rule*] *Non caret Umbra Deo.—Statius.* [*double rule*]
York: Printed by A. Ward for J. Dodsley, Pall-Mall; T. Cadell, in the Strand; J. Robson, New-Bond-Street; and T. Durham, Charing-Cross, London. W. Creech and J. Balfour, Edinburgh. M.DCC.LXXVI.

Collation: [*a]–*d4 a–c4 A–Z4 Aa–Zz4 Aaa–Zzz4 4A–4N4 4O2; 358 leaves.

Contents: [*a]1 title; [*a]2*a* dedication to Sir Frederick Evelyn, Bart.; [*a]2*b* blank; [*a]3*a*–4*a* *Editor's Preface*; *a4*b* blank; *b1*a*–4*b* *Subscribers*; *c1 blank; *c2*a*–*d4*a* *The Life of Mr. John Evelyn*; *d4*b* blank; a1*a*–2*a* Evelyn's dedication to the King; a2*b* blank; a3*a*–c3*a* *To the Reader*; c3*b*–4*a* *Advertisement*; c4*b* Greek lines by J. Evelyn jun.; A1*a*–4N1*a* (pp. 1–649) *Silva*; 4N1*b* blank; 4N2*a*–4O2*a* Index; 4O2*b* blank. Folding table of the *Parts of Fructification* of trees inserted after 4N1.

Frontispiece: Engraved portrait in an oval, inscribed below *Joannes Evelyn Armr*, and signed *F. Bartolozzi del. et sculp.* 1776. Plate-mark 25 × 18·5 cm.

Illustrations: 39 engraved plates facing pp. 34, 69, 90 (not numbered), 119, 136, 143, 150, 159, 166, 170, 181, 182, 188, 190, 200, 201, 208, 218, 220, 224, 240, 244, 262, 263, 266, 267, 268, 299, 311, 349, 350, 362, 373, 378, 383 (misnumbered 283), 398, 500 (folding plate, not numbered), 502 (2, not numbered).

Note: Issued in boards with paper label on the spine. The volume was issued to over 700 subscribers at two guineas, and some copies contain the receipt for this amount signed by Dr Hunter. The portrait, drawn and engraved by Bartolozzi, was evidently made after the portrait by Kneller in the possession of the Royal Society. The hair and cloak have been altered to suit the artist's fancy, and the arm and hand holding a copy of *Silva* are not shown. Copies with the plates coloured by hand have been recorded; also printed on thick paper and bound in two volumes, with a specially printed title-page to the second part.

Copies: BLO (2, GG.38.Art.; Douce.E.297), BM (447.h.1) K; CLC, HCL (3, one with plates coloured, Arnold Arboretum, Gray Herbarium).

48 HUNTER'S SILVA [second edition] 2 vols. 4° 1786

Title: Silva:...[*rule*] By John Evelyn, Esq;...With Notes by A. Hunter, M.D. F.R.S. [*rule*] A New Edition. To which is added the Terra: A Philosophical Discourse of Earth. [*rule*] Volume I. [II.] [*double rule*]
York: Printed by A. Ward for J. Dodsley, Pall-Mall; T. Cadell, in the Strand; J. Robson, New Bond-Street; and R. Baldwin, Pater-noster-Row, London; J. Todd, York. M.DCC.LXXXVI.

Collation: Vol. I, pp. [xlvi], 311, [11]. Vol. II, pp. [ii], 343, [11], [viii], 74, [4]. A folding table of the parts of fructification of trees is inserted in both vols. at the end of the text of *Silva*. A folding table of clays and sands is inserted in *Terra*, facing p. 18.

Frontispiece: As in ed. I.

Illustrations: Vol. I, 28 plates. Vol. II, *Silva*, 13 plates. *Terra*, 1 plate.

Note: I have not seen a copy in original boards, though presumably it was issued thus. There have been no half-titles in the copies collated. Some copies were printed on thick paper and have the plates coloured by hand.

Copies: BLO (19182.c.16–17), BM (G.2467–68, coloured copy on thick paper), ULC (7400.b.12); CLC, HCL (3, one with plates coloured, Arnold Arboretum, Gray Herbarium).

49 HUNTER'S SILVA [third edition] 2 vols. 4° 1801

Title: Silva:...[*double rule*] By John Evelyn, Esq. F.R.S. With Notes, By A. Hunter, M.D. F.R.S.L. & E. [*double rule*] The Third Edition, revised, corrected, and considerably enlarged. To which is added The Terra: A Philosophical Discourse of Earth. [*short rule*] In Two Volumes.—Vol. I. [II.] [*short rule*]
York: Printed by T. Wilson and R. Spence, High-Ousegate. Sold by J. Mawman, (successor to Mr. Dilly,) Poultry; Cadell, jun. and Davies, Strand, London: Wilson and Spence, J. Todd, W. Tesseyman, and Sotheran and Son, York. Anno 1801.

Collation: Vol. I: pp. xii, 13–330, [4]. Vol. II: pp. [iv], 5–393, [1], [viii], 84, [4].

Frontispiece: As before.

Illustrations: Vol. I, 28 plates. Vol. II, *Silva*, 13 plates. *Terra*, 3 plates.

Note: Each volume has a half-title. Presumably issued in boards with labels, though I have not seen a copy in this state. At the end of vol. I or vol. II is a leaf with list of plates marked 'This leaf to be cancelled when the book is put into full binding'. Judicious binders have left it in position.

Copy: BM (7029.l.4); HCL.

50 HUNTER'S SILVA [fourth edition] 2 vols. 4° 1812

Title: Silva:...[*double rule*] By John Evelyn, Esq. F.R.S. With Notes, By A. Hunter, M.D. F.R.S.L. & E. [*double rule*] To which is added, The Terra: A Philosophical Discourse of Earth. The Fourth Edition, with the Editor's Last Corrections, and A Short Memoir of him. In Two Volumes.—Vol. I. [II.]
York: Printed by Thomas Wilson and Son, High-Ousegate; For Longman, Hurst, Rees, Orme and Browne, Pater-noster-row, London; and for Wilson and Son, York. 1812.

Collation: Vol. I, pp. xii, 13–330. Vol. II, pp. iv, 5–393, [1], [viii], 88, [2].

Frontispiece: As before.

Illustrations: Vol. I, *Silva*, 28 plates. Vol. II, *Silva*, 14 plates. *Terra*, 3 plates.

Note: Each volume has a half-title. Presumably issued in boards with labels, though I have not seen a copy in this state. At the end of vol. II is a leaf with sig. 3R marked, 'This leaf to be cancelled when the book is put into full binding'. The folding tables inserted in the previous editions are now printed on the leaves of the book. The brief memoir of Alexander Hunter, dated York, July 1812, is not signed. A folding plate has been added to vol. II, facing p. 155. It is referred to in the list as 'The Wheat-ear plate', though it seems to have been used before in another book as it is inscribed 'Page 372, Vol. III'.

Copy: BM (7073.e.13).

51 HUNTER'S SILVA [fifth edition] 2 vols. 4° 1825

Title: Silva:...To which is added The Terra: A Philosophical Discourse of Earth. By John Evelyn, Esq. F.R.S. With notes, by A. Hunter, M.D. F.E.S.L. & E. The Fifth Edition, with the Editor's last corrections. In Two Volumes. Vol. I. [II.]
London Henry Colburn, New Burlington Street. MDCCCXXV.

Collation: Vol. I, pp. 330. Vol. II, pp. 393, [1], [viii], 88, [2].

Frontispiece, illustrations: As in no. 50.

Note: Each volume has a half-title. Issued in boards, untrimmed, with green cloth backs, and paper labels on the spines: EVELYN'S | SILVA | AND | TERRA. | WITH NOTES | BY DR. HUNTER. | [*rule*] | FIFTH EDITION. | 46 Plates. | [*rule*] | IN TWO VOLUMES. | VOL. I. [II.]. The inscription on 'The Wheat-ear plate' has been corrected to 'Page 155, Vol. II'. The plates are together at the end of vol. II following the leaf with list of plates and instructions to the binder. These would be distributed in the two volumes when bound.

POMONA

1664

PREFACE

EVELYN'S *Pomona, or an Appendix concerning Fruit-Trees* appears to have been intended strictly as an appendix to *Sylva*, and was never printed by itself. The five editions of *Pomona* correspond, therefore, to the five of *Sylva* with which it was printed, and the work is given no separate mention in the Diary. It was always provided, however, with its own sub-title and for convenience it is here listed as a separate work. In his preface Evelyn is at pains to praise the virtues of cider as opposed to those of beer or wine. 'It is little more than an Age since Hops (rather a Medical, than Alimental Vegetable) transmuted our wholesome Ale into Beer', and as for wines, he wishes their admirers could but see 'the Cheat themselves; the Sophistications, Transformations, Transmutations, Adulterations, Bastardizings, Brewings, Trickings, not to say, even Arsenical Compassings of the Sophisticated God they adore'. He enlarges on the financial gain to be derived from planting fruit-trees, and gives reasons for preferring the Red-strake before other cider apples. *Pomona* was dedicated to the Earl of Southampton, Lord High Treasurer, on the ground that the author was designing to 'provide for the publick health, which is so necessary and precious to [the State] in your Excellent Person'. Robert Hooke, curator to the Royal Society, had invented a new cider-press, and Evelyn concludes the second and later editions of *Pomona* with an engraving and explanation of this engine. The treatise itself consists of eight short chapters on the cultivation of fruit-trees, and this is followed by a collection of six, afterwards increased to ten, contributions on the making of cider by other writers, of whom the principal is Dr Beale, of Yeovil in Somerset. These papers had been contributed at various dates to the proceedings of the Royal Society, though they had not been printed in the *Philosophical Transactions*. (See Birch's *History of the Royal Society*, 1756, vol I.)

52 POMONA [first edition W. E 3508] f° 1664

Sub-title: Pomona, or an Appendix concerning Fruit-Trees, In relation to Cider, The Making and Several ways of Ordering it. [*rule*] Virg. Eclog. ix.— *Carpent tua Poma nepotes.* [*device between rules*]

London, Printed by John Martyn and James Allestry, Printers to the Royal Society, and are to be sold at their Shop at the Bell in St Paul's Church-yard. MDCLXIV.

Collation: χ^2 A^2 B–C^4, 1 l. inserted, D–F, 1 l. inserted between F2–3, G^3; 29 leaves.

Contents: χ1 sub-title; χ2*a–b* *The Epistle Dedicatory* to the Earl of Southampton; A1*a*–C4*b* (pp. 1–20) *Pomona*; leaf inserted, *Animadversion*, verso blank; D1*a*–E1*a* (pp. 21–9) *Aphorisms concerning Cider, by Mr Beale*; E1*b*–F2*b* (pp. 30–40) *Sir Paul Neil's Discourse of Cider*; leaf inserted, *Sir Paul Neile's Second Paper*; F3*a*–G1*a* (pp. 41–5) *Observations Concerning the Making and Preserving of Cider, by John Newburgh Esq*; G1*b* (p. 46) *Concerning Cider, by Doctor Smith*; G2*a*–G3*b* (pp. 47–50) *Of Cider, By Capt. Taylor.*

Note: Appended to the first edition of *Sylva* (see no. 40). The work ends on G3, the sub-title to the succeeding work, *Kalendarium Hortense,* being printed on G4. The two inserted leaves have no pagination or signatures. The device on the sub-title to *Pomona* is a copy of one which belonged to J. Windet, 1592, and afterwards successively to W. Stansby and R. Bishop (McKerrow's *Printers' and Publishers' Devices,* no. 282). There is a woodcut illustration of a cider-vat on p. 49. *Errata* to all three works are given on a leaf inserted at the end of the volume.

53 POMONA [second edition. W. E 3509] f° 1670

Sub-title: Pomona, [etc. as in no. 52].

London, Printed by John Martyn and James Allestry, Printers to the Royal Society. MDCLXX.

Collation: $[A]^2$ B–I^4 K^2; 36 leaves.

Contents: [A]1 sub-title; [A]2*a–b* *The Epistle Dedicatory* to the Earl of Southampton; B1*a*–B3*a* (pp. 1–5) *The Preface*; B3*b* blank; B4*a*–E1*a* (pp. 7–25) text of *Pomona*; E1*b* blank; E2*a* (p. 27) *Animadversions*; E2*b* blank; E3*a*–F3*b* (pp. 29–38) *General Advertisements concerning Cider by Dr Beale*; F4*a*–H2*a* (pp. 39–51) *Sir Paul Neil's Discourse of Cider* and *Second Paper*; H2*b*–I1*a* (pp. 52–7) *Observations Concerning the Making and Preserving of Cider, by John Newburgh Esq*; I1*b* (p. 58) *Concerning Cider, by Doctor Smith*; I2*a*–I3*b* (pp. 59–62) *Of Cider, By Capt. Sylas Taylor*; I4*a–b* *An Account of Perry and Cider Out of Gloucester-shire, Imparted by Daniel Collwall Esq*; K1*a–b* *Another Account of Cider from a Person of great Experience*; K2*a* *Explication of the figures* (on K1*b*); K2*b* blank.

Note: Appended, with *Kalendarium Hortense*, to the second edition of *Sylva* (no. 41). A subject-index to *Pomona* is printed after the index to *Sylva* on k1*b*–l2*a*. The sub-title bears the same device as the first edition. The woodcut illustration used in the first edition has been omitted; an engraving of a cider-press 'brought into the *R. Society* by their *Curator*, the ingenious Mr. *Hooke*' is added on K1*b*, p. 66.

54 POMONA [third edition] f° 1678

Sub-title: Pomona, [etc. as in no. 52]. The Third Edition with Addition. [*quotation between rules, device, double rule*]

London, Printed for John Martyn, Printer to the Royal Society. MDCLXXVIII.

Collation: Uu4 Xx–Fff4 Ggg1–2; 39 leaves.

Contents: Uu4 sub-title; Xx1*a*–*b* dedication; Xx2*a*–Aaa2*a* (pp. 339–63) *Pomona*; Aaa2*b* blank; Aaa3*a* *Animadversion*; Aaa3*b* blank; Aaa4*a*–Bbb4*b* (pp. 367–76) *General Advertisements Concerning Cider: By Dr Beale*; Ccc1*a*–Ddd2*a* (pp. 377–87) *Sir Paul Neil's Discourse of Cider*; Ddd2*b*–3*a* (pp. 388–9) *Sir Paul Neile's second Paper*; Ddd3*b*–Eee2*a* (pp. 390–95) *Observations Concerning the Making, and Preserving of Cider by John Newburgh Esq*; Eee2*b* (p. 396) *Concerning Cider, by Doctor Smith*; Eee3*a*–4*b* (pp. 397–400) *Of Cider: By Capt. Silas Taylor*; Fff1*a*–*b* (pp. 401–2) *An Account of Perry and Cider Out of Gloucestershire, Imparted by Daniel Collwall Esq.*; Fff2*a*–*b* (pp. 403–4) *For Making of Cider out of Mr. Cook*, and *Another*; Fff3*a*–Ggg2*b* (pp. 405–412) *Another, sent me out of Wales by Sir Thomas Hanmer, Another Account of Cider from a Person of great Experience*, Explanation of the figures of Hooke's cider-press.

Note: Appended with other works to the third edition of *Sylva*, 1679 (no. 42). A *Table to Pomona* is printed on l2*a*–m1*b*. The device on the sub-title is the same as before. The woodcut of a cider-vat is on p. 399, and the engraving of Hooke's press on Ggg2*a*, p. 411.

55 POMONA [fourth edition] f° 1706

Sub-title: Pomona, [etc. as in no. 54, except that *Third* is altered to *Fourth Edition*].

London: Printed for Rob. Scot, Ric. Chiswell, George Sawbridge, and Benj. Tooke. MDCCVI.

Collation: Hhhh–Qqqq4 Rrrr3; 39 leaves.

Contents: Hhhh1 sub-title; Hhhh2*a*–*b* dedication; Hhhh3*a*–Rrrr3*b* (pp. 57–130) text.

Note: Appended with other works to the fourth edition of *Silva*, 1706 (see no. 43). There is a general index to all the appended works at the end of the volume. The woodcut is on p. 117 and the engraving on p. 129.

56 POMONA [fifth edition] f° [1729]

Sub-title: [*ornamental band*] Pomona: or, an Appendix Concerning Fruit-Trees, In relation to Cider, The Making, and several ways of Ordering it. [*Latin quotation between rules*] [*ornamental band*]

Collation: 5E2 5F–5U² 5X1; 32 leaves.

Contents: 5E2*a* sub-title; 5E2*b* dedication; 5F1*a*–5X1*b* (pp. 49–110) text.

Note: Appended with other works to the fifth edition of *Silva*, 1729 (see no. 44). The sub-title has no date or imprint. There is a general index to all the appended works at the end of the volume. The woodcut is on p. 100 and the engraving on p. 110.

KALENDARIUM HORTENSE

1664

PREFACE

'AS for the Kalendar your Ladyship mentions, what ever assistance it may be to some novice gardiner, sure I am his Lordship will find nothing in it worth his notice but an old inclination to an innocent diversion, & the acceptance it found with my deare (and while he liv'd) worthy friend Mr. Cowley, upon whose reputation only it has survived seaven impressions, & is now entering on the eighth with some considerable improvements, more agreeable to the present curiosity. 'Tis now, Madame, almost fourty yeares since first I writ it, when horticulture was not much advanc'd in England, and neere thirty since first 'twas publish'd, which consideration will I hope excuse its many defects. If in the meane time it deserve the name of no un-usefull trifle, 'tis all it is capable of.'[1] Thus Evelyn wrote to Lady Sunderland on 4 August 1690, and there is little to add to this account of its genesis and purpose. *Kalendarium Hortense, or, the Gard'ners Almanac* is a plain statement of how the garden is to be tended and planted month by month, and, being based on experience, can be used today as profitably as when it was first written. According to the letter quoted above, Evelyn compiled his *Almanac* about 1650, presumably for his own use. It was not until 1664, when *Sylva* was being printed for the Royal Society, that he thought of printing the *Kalendarium*, and it then appeared with Pomona as an appendix to the larger work. Its favourable reception encouraged him to reprint it before the folio was ready for a second edition, and it was accordingly published as an attractive small octavo in 1666. Evelyn now prefixed a graceful dedication to his friend, Abraham Cowley, who replied in his prose and verse essay entitled 'The Garden'. This was written as a letter addressed to Evelyn,[2] which was not printed until it was added to Cowley's *Works*, 1668. In this well-known poem Cowley apostrophized Evelyn most justly:

In Books and Gardens thou hast plac'd aright
    (Things which thou well dost understand;
And both dost make with thy laborious hand)
    Thy noble innocent delight.

[1] Wheatley, III, 463.

[2] Cowley's original MS, dated 26 August 1666, is now in the R. B. Adam collection. See *The R. B. Adam Library*, vol. III, p. 73, with facsimiles.

Evelyn's gratification may be imagined, though he did not immediately reprint Cowley's essay, as he might, in the next edition of the *Kalendarium*, which was published in 1669. Actually he did not use it until it was added to the preliminary matter in the third folio edition of *Sylva*, 1679. It was printed in the separate editions of the *Kalendarium* from 1691 onwards after the dedication or the introduction.

The *Kalendarium Hortense* proved to be one of Evelyn's most popular works, and was printed five times in folio and nine times in octavo. For twenty years it continued to be reprinted without much alteration. At length in 1691 it was furnished with a frontispiece (only copied, it is true, from that of *The French Gardiner*, see no. 5), perhaps in honour of Cowley's essay, and many additions were made to the text. The last separate edition appeared in 1706, the year of Evelyn's death, and since that date it has been printed only in the fifth edition of *Silva*, 1729, and the *Miscellaneous Writings*, 1825, pp. 425–98. Although the *Kalendarium* enjoyed a large circulation, most of the editions are now scarce. The book was made for use, and it was, indeed, used up. The first separate edition of 1666 is exceedingly uncommon, and only three copies are known to me.

There is a work entitled: *The Lady's Recreation: or The Third and Last Part Of the Art of Gardening Improv'd. By Charles Evelyn, Esq. London. J. Roberts.* 1717. This is stated on the title-page to contain 'Mr. John Evelyn's *Kalendarium Hortense*, methodically reduc'd: Interspers'd with many useful Additions'. This occupies pp. 152–94, and is referred to by the author as 'my *Kalendarium Hortense*', without any further acknowledgment of his debt to his namesake. It is in no sense a reprint of John Evelyn's work and the author has not been identified with any of his descendants. *The Lady's Recreation* is also found printed as Part IV of John Lawrence's *Gardening Improv'd*, Dublin: Reprinted for G. Grierson, 1719.

57 KALENDARIUM [first edition] f° 1664

Sub-title, in red and black: Kalendarium Hortense: or, the Gard'ners Almanac; Directing what He is to do Monethly, throughout the Year. [*rule*]

Columella *de cult. hort.* lib. 10
Invigilate viri, tacito nam tempora gressu
Diffugiunt, nullóque sono convertitur annus.

[*device between rules*]
London, Printed by J. Macock, for John Martin, and James Allestry, and are to be sold at their Shop, at the sign of the Bell in St Paul's Church-yard. MDCLXIV.

Collation: G4 H–L4 (H1 cancelled); 16 leaves.

Contents: G4 (pp. 51–2) sub-title; H2*a*–H3*a* (pp. 55–7) *Introduction*; H3*b*–L4*a* (pp. 58–83) *Kalendarium*; L4*b* blank. *Errata* to the whole volume on leaf inserted after L4.

Note: This, the first edition of *Kalendarium Hortense*, was printed at the end of the first edition of *Sylva*, 1664, and is paginated continuously with *Pomona* (see no. 40). There is no indication of what were the contents of the cancelled leaf H1.
The device on the sub-title is copied from one which belonged to J. Windet in 1592 and afterwards successively to W. Stansby and R. Bishop (McKerrow's *Printers' and Publishers' Devices*, no. 292).

58 KALENDARIUM [second edition. W. E 3491] 8° 1666

Title, in red and black: Kalendarium Hortense: or, the Gard'ners Almanac, Directing What he is to do Monethly through-out the Year. And What Fruits and Flowers are in Prime. [*rule*] The second Edition, with many useful Additions. [*rule*] By John Evelyn Esq; Fellow of the Royal Society. [*rule*]

Virg. Geo. 2.
—— *Labor actus in orbem.*

[*rule*] London, Printed by Jo. Martyn and Ja. Allestry, Printers to the Royal Society, and are to be sold at their Shops in St. Paul's Church-yard. MDCLXVI.

Collation: A4 B–H8 I2; 62 leaves.

Contents: A1 blank; A2 title; A3*a*–A4*b* *The Epistle Dedicatory to Abraham Cowley Esq.*; B1*a*–B5*b* (pp. 1–10) *Introduction to the Kalendar*; B6*a*–I2*a* (pp. 11–115) *Kalendarium*; I2*b* blank.

J Willughby A4:23

Kalendarium Hortense:

OR, THE

GARD'NERS ALMANAC,

DIRECTING

What he is to do *Monethly* throughout the *Year*.

AND

What *Fruits* and *Flowers* are in *Prime*.

The second Edition, *with many useful* Additions.

By *JOHN EVELYN* Esq;
Fellow of the *Royal Society*.

Virg. Geo. 2.
——*Labor actus in orbem*.

LONDON,
Printed by *Jo. Martyn* and *Ja. Allestry*, Printers to the *Royal Society*, and are to be sold at their Shops in St. *Paul's* Church-yard.
MDCLXVI.

Title-page of no. 58

Note: This is the first separate edition of the *Kalendarium,* though called the second on the title-page. The dedication to Cowley appears for the first time.

Copies: BLO (Antiq.f.E.1666/1), BM (G.2299),[1] K.[2]

59 KALENDARIUM [third edition. W. E 3492] 8° 1669

Title: Kalendarium Hortense: or, the Gard'ners Almanac, Directing What he is to do Monethly through-out the Year. And What Fruits and Flowers are in Prime. [*rule*] The third Edition, with many useful Additions. [*rule*] By John Evelyn Esq; Fellow of the Royal Society. [*rule*]

Virg. Geo. 2.
—— *Labor actus in orbem*

[*rule*] London, Printed by Jo. Martyn and Ja. Allestry, Printers to the Royal Society, MDCLXIX.

Collation: A–I⁸; 72 leaves.

Contents: A1 blank; A2 title; A3*a*–A4*b* *The Epistle Dedicatory to Abraham Cowley Esq.*; A5*a*–B1*b* (pp. 9–18) *Introduction to the Kalendar,* with advertisement of *The French Gard'ner,* ed. 2, and Rose's *Vineyard* on B1*b*; B2*a*–H8*a* (pp. 19–127) *Kalendarium Hortense*; H8*b* blank; I1*a*–I7*a* *The Table,* with prefatory note; I7*b* *Errata,* 4 ll., and advt. of *Sylva,* ed. 2; I8 (not seen; ? blank).

Note: Some copies seem to have been issued without section I containing the index and *errata.*

Copies: BLO (G.P.2311 (1)), CCE, K; CH.

60 KALENDARIUM [second edition in folio. W. E 3493] f° 1669

Sub-title: Kalendarium Hortense: or the Gard'ners Almanac; Directing what He is to do Monethly, throughout the Year. And What Fruits and Flowers are in Prime. [*rule*] The Third Edition, with many useful Additions. [*rule*] By John Evelyn, Esq; Fellow of the Royal Society. [*rule*] Virg. Geo. 2.---- *Labor actus in orbem.* [*device between rules*]

London, Printed by John Martin and James Allestry, Printers to the Royal Society, MDCLXIX.

Collation: Aa⁴ B⁴ Cc⁴ Dd⁴ Ee²; 18 leaves.

Contents: Aa1 sub-title; Aa2*a*–*b* *The Epistle Dedicatory*; Aa3*a*–Aa4*a* (pp. 5–7) *Introduction*; Aa4*b*–Ee1*a* (pp. 8–33) text; Ee1*b* blank; Ee2*a* *Errata*; Ee2*b* blank.

1 On the fly-leaf is a signed presentation inscription from Evelyn to Lord Arlington.

2 From the Wollaton House library, with signature of Thomas Willughby, first Lord Middleton.

Note: Printed at the end of the second edition of *Sylva*, 1670, but paginated separately. It is called on the sub-title *The Third Edition*. Actually it is the second edition in folio, but was published in the same year as an octavo edition which is also called the third.
The device on the sub-title was used for S. Waterson in 1605 (McKerrow's *Printers' and Publishers' Devices*, no. 317).

61 KALENDARIUM [fourth edition. W. E. 3494] 8° 1671

Title: Kalendarium Hortense: or the Gard'ner's Almanac, Directing What he is to do Monethly through-out the Year. And What Fruits and Flowers are in Prime. [*rule*] The fourth Edition, with many useful Additions. [*rule*] By John Evelyn Esq; Fellow of the Royal Society [*rule*]

Virg. Geo. 2.
—— *Labor actus in orbem*

[*rule*] London, Printed by John Martyn, Printer to the Royal Society. MDCLXXI.

Collation: A–I^8; 72 leaves.

Contents: A1 [? blank]; A2 title; A3*a*–A4*b* *The Epistle Dedicatory*; A5*a*–B1*b* (pp. 9–18) *Introduction*, with advt. on B1*b*; B2*a*–H8*a* (pp. 19–127) text; H8*b* blank; I1*a*–I7*a* *The Table*, with prefatory note; I7*b* advt. of *Sylva*, ed. 2; I8 blank.

Note: An exact reprint of the octavo edition of 1669, except for the correction of the *errata*.

Copy: BM (7032.b.22).

62 KALENDARIUM [fifth edition. W. E 3495] 8° 1673

Title: Kalendarium Hortense: or, the Gard'ners Almanac, Directing What he is to do Monthly through-out the Year. And What Fruits and Flowers are in Prime. [*rule*] The Fifth Edition, with many useful Additions. [*rule*] By John Evelyn Esq; Fellow of the Royal Society. [*rule*]

Virg. Geor. 2
——*Labor actus in orbem*

[*rule*] London, Printed by John Martyn, Printer to the Royal Society. MDCLXXIII.

Collation: A–H^8 I^4; 68 leaves.

Contents: A1 blank; A2 title; A3*a*–A4*b* *The Epistle Dedicatory*; A5*a*–B1*b* (pp. 9–18) *Introduction*; B2*a*–H8*a* (pp. 19–127) text; H8*b* blank; I1*a*–I4*b* *The Table.*

Note: A reprint of the preceding edition, with the index on four leaves instead of seven.

Copies: BLO (Th.8°.B.298), K; CLC, HCL.

63 KALENDARIUM [sixth edition] & DISCOURSE OF EARTH [W. E 3496] 8° 1676

Title: Kalendarium Hortense: or, the Gardner's Almanac, Directing What he is to do Monthly through-out the Year. And What Fruits and Flowers are in Prime. To which is Added, a Discourse of Earth, Relating to the Culture and Improvement of it for Vegetation, and the Pro-pagation of Plants, &c. [*rule*] The Sixth Edition, with many useful Additions. [*rule*] By John Evelyn Esq; Fellow of the Royal Society. [*rule*]
London. Printed by John Martyn, Printer to the Royal Society. MDCLXXVI.

Collation, contents: As in no. 62, with *A Discourse of Earth,* as in no. 93, appended.

Note: This is the only octavo edition containing *A Philosophical Discourse of Earth,* which consists of the same sheets as were also issued separately in 1676.

Copies: BLO (Wood. 573), K, ULC (M. 18. 61), VAF; CLC, HCL (Arnold Arboretum).

64 KALENDARIUM [third edition in folio] f° 1679

Sub-title, in red and black: Kalendarium Hortense: or the Gard'ners Almanac;... [etc. as in no. 60]. The Fifth Edition, with many useful Additions...[etc. as in no. 60].
London, Printed for John Martyn, Printer to the Royal Society. 1679.

Collation: Ggg3–4 Hhh–Lll4 Mmm2; 20 leaves.

Contents: Ggg3 sub-title; Ggg4*a–b* *The Epistle Dedicatory*; Hhh1*a*–Hhh2*a* (pp. 5–7) *Introduction*; Hhh2*b*–Mmm1*b* (pp. 8–38) text; Mmm2*a* *Errata*; Mmm2*b* blank.

Note: Printed at the end of the third edition of *Sylva,* 1679, but paginated separately. It is called on the sub-title *The Fifth Edition.* Actually it is the third edition in folio, and octavo editions called the fifth and the sixth had already been published in 1673 and 1676.

The text concludes with a list 'For those who affect to have their Fruit out of France', and a 'Catalogue of Fruit-trees to be had out of the Nurseries near the City of London'. Neither of these lists is printed in any other edition. Cowley's poem 'The Garden', included in the octavo editions of *Kalendarium* from 1691, was first reprinted from Cowley's *Works,* 1668, in this, the third, edition of *Sylva* among the preliminary matter (see no. 42).

65 KALENDARIUM [seventh edition. W. E 3497] 8° 1683

Title: Kalendarium Hortense: or, the Gard'ners Almanac, Directing What he is to do Monthly through-out the Year. And What Fruits and Flowers are in Prime. [*rule*] The Seventh Edition, with many useful Additions. [*rule*] By John Evelyn Esq; Fellow of the Royal Society. [*rule*]

Virg. Geor. 2.
——*Labor actus in Orbem.*

[*rule*] London, Printed for T. Sawbridge in Little-Britain, G. Wells in St. Paul's Church-yard, and R. Bently in Russel-street in Covent-Garden, MDCLXXXIII.

Collation, contents: As in no. 62.

Note: A Philosophical Discourse of Earth, which was bound with the preceding edition, is not included.

Copies: BLO (191.k.57), BM (967·c·7), K (2);[1] CH, CLC, HCL, PL.[2]

66 KALENDARIUM [eighth edition, first issue. W. E 3498] 8° 1691

Title, in red and black: Kalendarium Hortense: or, the Gard'ners Almanac, Directing what he is to do Monthly throughout the Year. And What Fruits and Flowers are in Prime. [*rule*] The Eighth Edition, with many useful Additions. [*rule*] By John Evelyn Esq; Fellow of the Royal Society. [*rule*]

Virg. Geor. 2
——*Labor actus in orbem.*

Columell. lib. ix. cap. 1.

Satis admirari nequeo, quod primo scriptorum meorum exordio jure conquestus sum: Cæterarum Artium minus Vitæ neces-sariarum repertos Antistites, Agriculturæ neque Discipu-los, neque Præceptores inventos.

[*rule*] London, Printed for R. Chiswell in St. Paul's Church-yard, T. Sawbridge in Little-Britain, and R. Bently in Russel-Street in Covent-garden. MDCXCI.

Collation: A^4 B–N^8 O^4 P^2; 106 leaves.

Contents: A1 frontispiece; 2 title; A3*a*–A4*b* *The Epistle Dedicatory*; B1*a*–B7*b* *The Garden* [by Abraham Cowley] *To J. Evelyn Esq*; B8*a*–C4*b* (pp. 1–10) *Introduction*; C5*a*–N7*a* (pp. 11–175). text, with headings to each month in red; N7*b*–P2*a* *The Table*; P2*b* *Errata*, 26 lines.

Illustrations: i. A1*b*. Frontispiece. A copy, reversed, of the frontispiece to *The French Gardiner*, 1658 (see no. 5). Plate-mark 12·5 × 7·5 cm. Signed *P. P. Bouche Scul:*.
ii. M6*a* (p. 157). Engraving representing the constituent parts of the greenhouse described in the text. Plate-mark 13 × 8 cm.

[1] From the libraries of White Kennett and Francis Wrangham.

[2] With a long inscription from Evelyn to an unnamed 'noble Ld.'.

Note: To this edition Evelyn added a description of *A New Conservatory, or Green-house* (pp. 150–62), and a *Catalogue of Fruit Trees* (pp. 163–75), as well as the illustrations described above. These additions were not at first mentioned on the title-page, and when this was afterwards cancelled and reprinted for another publisher the omission was made good (see next entry). Cowley's poem, 'The Garden', written in 1666, is here printed in the preliminary matter of the *Kalendarium* for the first time, though without his name. It had already appeared in Cowley's *Works*, London, 1668, fo., pp. 115–20, and in *Sylva*, third edition, 1679 (see no. 42).

Copies: BM (988.b.15), K; CLC, HCL.[1]

67 KALENDARIUM [eighth edition, second issue. W. E 3499] 8° 1691

Title, in red and black: Kalendarium Hortense: or the Gard'ners Almanac,... [etc. as in no. 66]. To which is now added in this Eighth Edition, A New Conservatory, or Green-House. With many other useful Additions. [*rule*]... [etc. as in no. 66].

London, Printed for Matthew Gillyflower, at the Spread-Eagle in Westminster-Hall, and James Partridge, at the Post-House at Charing-Cross. 1691.

Collation, contents, illustrations: As in no. 66.

Note: A re-issue of the sheets of the preceding entry with a new title-page.

Copy: K.

68 KALENDARIUM [ninth edition, first issue. W. E 3500] 8° 1699

Title, in red and black: Kalendarium Hortense; or, the Gard'ner's Almanac,... [etc. as in no. 66]. The Ninth Edition, with many useful Additions...[etc. as in no. 66].

London, Printed for Rob. Scott, Ri. Chiswell, Geo. Sawbridge, and Benj. Tooke. 1699

Collation: A^4 B–N^8 n^2 O^8; 110 leaves.

Contents: A1 frontispiece; A2 title; A3*a*–A4*b* *The Epistle Dedicatory*; B1*a*–B7*b* *The Garden* by *A. Cowley*, dated *Chertsea*, 1666; B8*a*–C4*b* (pp. 1–10) *Introduction*; C5*a*–N8*b* (pp. 11–178) text, with headings to each month in red; n1*a*–n2*a* (pp. 179–81) *A Letter from Sir Dudley Cullum*; n2*b* blank; O1*a*–O7*b* *The Table*; O8*a* *Errata*, 8 lines; O8*b* blank.

Illustrations: Engravings as before on A1*b* and M7*b* (p. 160).

Note: The contents are the same as in the preceding edition with the addition of a letter from Sir Dudley Cullum about the greenhouse stove. This was first printed in *Philosophical*

[1] With presentation inscription to Dr Ashe.

Transactions, vol. XVIII, no. 212, p. 191, and was now reprinted as an afterthought and inserted as a gathering of two leaves before the index. The title-page in this issue does not appear to be a cancel, and presumably, therefore, preceded the other two issues described below.

Copy: K; CLC.

69 KALENDARIUM [ninth edition, second issue. W. E 3501] 8° 1699

Title, in red and black: Kalendarium Hortense; or, the Gard'ner's Almanac,... [etc. as in no. 66]. The Ninth Edition, with many useful Additions...[etc. as in no. 66].

London, Printed for George Huddleston at the Black-Moor's Head near Exeter Exchange in the Strand. 1699.

Collation, contents, illustrations: As in no. 68.

Note: The sheets of no. 68 with cancel title.

Copies: BM (966.a.11); CLC, HCL.

70 KALENDARIUM [ninth edition, third issue. W. E 3502] 8° 1699

Title, in red and black: Kalendarium Hortense; or, the Gard'ner's Almanac,... [etc. as in no. 66]. The Ninth Edition, with many useful Additions...[etc. as in no. 66].

London, Printed for Francis Fawcet, at the King's Head and Crown near Durham-Yard, in the Strand, 1699.

Collation, contents, illustrations: As in no. 68.

Note: The sheets of no. 68 with a second cancel title.

Copies: BLO (Douce.E.58), K, ULC (Hhh.223).

71 KALENDARIUM [tenth edition] 8° 1706

Title, in red and black: Kalendarium Hortense: or, the Gard'ner's Almanac,... [etc. as in no. 66]. The Tenth Edition, with many useful Additions...[etc. as in no. 66].

London: Printed for Rob. Scot, Ric. Chiswell, George Sawbridge, and Benj. Tooke, 1706.

Collation: A–N^8 O^4; 108 leaves.

Contents: A1 frontispiece; A2 title; A3*a*–A4*b* *The Epistle Dedicatory*; A5*a*–B1*b* (pp. i–x) *Introduction*; B2*a*–B8*b* *The Garden*, by *A. Cowley*, dated *Chertsea*, 1666; C1*a*–N4*a* (pp. 1–167) text, with headings to each month in red; N4*b*–N5*b* (pp. 168–70) *A Letter from Sir Dudley Cullum*; N6*a*–O4*b* *The Table.*

Illustrations: Engravings as before on A1*b* and M3*a* (p. 149).

Note: Similar to the preceding edition except that the *Introduction* and Cowley's poem have been transposed. The publishers are the same as those of the first issue of the preceding edition. The book is sometimes found bound up with the second issue of *Acetaria* published by Tooke in the same year.

Copies: BLO (19185.f.18), BM (988.b.16), CCE, K, VAF; CLC, HCL (Arnold Arboretum).

72 KALENDARIUM [fourth edition in folio] f° 1706

Sub-title: Kalendarium Hortense: or, the Gard'ner's Almanac,...[etc. as in no. 66]. The Tenth Edition with many useful Additions...[etc. as in no. 66]. London: Printed for Rob. Scot, Ric. Chiswell, George Sawbridge, and Benj. Tooke. MDCCVI.

Collation: Eeeee2–4Fffff–Mmmmm^4; 31 leaves.

Contents: Eeeee2 sub-title; Eeeee3*a*–*b* (pp. 217–18) *Dedication*; Eeeee4*a*–Fffff1*a* (pp. 219–21) *Introduction*; Fffff1*b*–Mmmmm4*a* (pp. 222–75) text.

Note: Printed at the end of the fourth edition of *Silva*, 1706, with which it is paginated continuously. It is called on the sub-title *The Tenth Edition*. Actually it is the fourth edition in folio, but it was published in the same year as the octavo edition which is called the tenth. The text has the additions which had been made to the octavo editions in 1691 and 1699 (see nos. 66 and 68), and therefore has the engraving of the parts of a greenhouse on Mmmmm1*a* (p. 269). Cowley's poem, 'The Garden', is printed, as in the folio of 1679, among the preliminary matter to *Silva* (see no. 42). Page 217 is numbered 216.

73 KALENDARIUM [fifth edition in folio] f° 1729

Sub-title: Kalendarium Hortense: or, the Gardiner's Almanack,...Prime. [*rule*] By John Evelyn, Esq;...[*rule*] [*quotations*] [*line of ornaments*]

Collation: 6Q2 6R–6Z 7A–7F^2; 27 leaves.

Contents: 6Q2 sub-title; 6R1*a* (p. 185) *To Abraham Cowley, Esq*; 6R1*b*–6R2*b* (pp. 186–88) *Introduction*; 6S1*a*–7F2*a* (pp. 189–235) text.

Note: Printed at the end of the fifth edition of *Silva*, 1729, with which it is paginated continuously. It is not numbered on the sub-title, which has no date or imprint. It is the fifth edition in folio, and is the last edition of *Kalendarium Hortense* except for the reprint in *Miscellaneous Writings*, 1825. The text is the same as that of 1706. The engraving is on 7E1*b* (p. 230).

PARALLEL OF ARCHITECTURE

1664

PREFACE

ROLAND FRÉART, Sieur de Chambray, published his *Parallele de l'Architecture Antique et de la Moderne*[1] at Paris in 1650. It was a sumptuous work, embellished with an engraved title-page by Tournier, containing a portrait of the author, and 49 other engravings, mostly of full-page size. A copy of the book was in Evelyn's library according to the catalogue of 1687. He would have been attracted both by the matter and by the manner of its production, and soon after reading it began, about 1652, to 'interpret' it 'to gratify a Friend in the Countrey'. It was, however, laid aside, until, some ten years later, he was encouraged to complete it by his friend Mr Hugh May, architect at Windsor and elsewhere, who had somehow procured 'a most accurate Edition of the Plates'. The result was the publication in 1664 of Evelyn's most splendid book, *A Parallel of Architecture*, containing excellent copies of all the engravings in the original edition and extended by an *Account of Architects and Architecture* from his own pen. Further padding was added in the shape of a translation of Leon Baptista Alberti's treatise *Of Statues* illustrated with two more engravings.

Evelyn records in his Diary that he dined at the Lord Chancellor's on 15 October 1664, and gave him his 'booke on Architecture, as before I had don to his Mat^y and the Queene Mother'.[2] The King's copy, in a royal binding of red morocco, is now in the British Museum. It was natural that he should wish Dr Christopher Wren to have the book, and so he wrote on 4 April 1665, 'There has layne at Dr Needham's a copy of the Parallel bound up for you, & long since design'd you, which I shall entreate you to accept.'[3] This copy,[4] too, is extant and contains an inscription in Evelyn's hand. Another, now in the Evelyn Collection, was given to John Beale, the King's Chaplain and author of the Latin lines to Evelyn printed at the beginning of the *Parallel*.

Evelyn was already associated with Mr Hugh May and Sir John Denham as

[1] Parallele de l'Architecture Antique et de la Moderne. A Paris, De l'Imprimerie d'Edme Martin, ruë S. Iacques, au Soleil d'or. M.DC.L. a^6 A–O⁴ (BM: 560*.e.1).

[2] de Beer, III, 380.

[3] Wheatley, III, 305–6.

[4] Sold at Sotheby's, 31 October 1928, lot 818 (T. Thorp). It has been rebound in half-calf and lacks a leaf of preliminary matter. Inscribed 'For my most honor'd Friend Dr. Wren, from his most humble ser^t J. Evelyn'.

commissioners of high-ways and sewers (see no. 177), and in his dedication to Denham, the poet and surveyor-general of works, Evelyn wrote, 'It is from the *Asymmetry* of our *Buildings*, want of *decorum* and proportion in our *Houses*, that the irregularity of our *humours* and *affections* may be shrewdly discerned', an observation which might perhaps apply with even more force in our present age. He undoubtedly felt a deep enthusiasm for the art of architecture, and genuinely believed that a grand reformation of buildings in London was to begin under the auspices of Charles II. He even saw evidences of this in 1663 in the new paving stones which Denham had caused to be laid down in Holborn, and an extension of this was to bring 'incredible advantage to the Publick', even to 'the *preserving* of both the *Mother* and the *Babe*, so many of the *Fair-Sex* and their *Offspring* having *perished* by *mischance* (as I am credibly inform'd) from the ruggedness of the unequal *Streets*'. To Evelyn, therefore, the Great Fire of London came almost as an inspiration. On 27 August 1666 he had surveyed with Wren and several others the fabric of old St Paul's, and had come to the conclusion that it was in so sad a state that it needed rebuilding from the foundations. He and Wren 'had a mind to build it with a noble cupola, a forme of church-building not as yet known in England, but of wonderfull grace'.[1] On the night of 2 September the fire began in Pudding Lane and on the 5th Evelyn was sadly examining the smoking ruins of what had been St Paul's. But he was an architectural enthusiast and forthwith set to work, so that on the 13th he was able to present the King 'with a survey of the ruines, and a plot for a new City'.[2] Evelyn was first in the field and the King was greatly interested in his plans, though neither these nor Wren's, as far as concerned a deliberate replanning of the City, were to be realized. Evelyn's plans remained in manuscript and lay until his death among those pieces that he had a mind to revise and complete but never did.[3]

The first edition of the *Parallel of Architecture* had been printed by Thomas Roycroft, one of the foremost craftsmen of the seventeenth century, and sold by the bookseller, John Place. The book was an elaborate production and no doubt

[1] de Beer, III, 448–9. [2] de Beer, III, 462–3.

[3] Three plans for the rebuilding of London, including Evelyn's, were engraved by Vertue for the Society of Antiquaries in 1748. An abridgment of a text belonging to Evelyn's plan was printed in W. Maitland's *History of London*, second edition (1756), pp. 447–50, and the whole text in the *Journal of the Royal Institute of British Architects*, 3rd ser., vol. XXVII (1919–20), pp. 467–70. This was edited by Dr de Beer in 1938 (see no. 121*a*).

expensive to produce. It seems not to have sold well, and in 1680 the unsold copies were provided with a new title-page on which Place added after his own initials the names of five other booksellers. In August 1696 Evelyn wrote a letter to Place[1] proposing a revision and reprinting of the work, but the expense and probability of small returns evidently discouraged the publisher, who is spoken of by Evelyn in a letter to Dr Richard Bentley dated 20 January 1696/7 as having 'made so many difficulties about my book of architecture'.[2] Evelyn even suggested to Place that the new edition should be one of the first books to be printed at Dr Bentley's new press at Cambridge. The revision actually was done, for he greatly enlarged his *Account of Architects and Architecture* and provided it with a dedication to Sir Christopher Wren dated 21 February 1696/7. He had been encouraged thereto by a visit to the new St Paul's, where he was informed by some of Wren's chief workmen of the assistance they had obtained from his book. There seem, however, still to have been difficulties, for the second edition was not published until after his death, being dated 1707, and was printed for a syndicate of booksellers of whom Place was not one.

Two further editions were published in 1723 and 1733. To these was prefixed Sir Henry Wotton's *Elements of Architecture*, first printed in 1624.

Evelyn's dedications and his enlarged *Account of Architects and Architecture* were reprinted in *Miscellaneous Writings*, 1825, pp. 337–424.

[1] Wheatley, IV, 8–11.

[2] Wheatley, IV, 14.

74 PARALLEL OF ARCHITECTURE [W. C 1923] f° 1664

Title: A Parallel of the Antient Architecture with the Modern, In a Collection of Ten Principal Authors who have written upon the Five Orders,

viz. {Palladio and Scamozzi, Serlio and Vignola} {D. Barbaro and Catanoe, L. B. Alberti and Viola} {Bullant and De Lorme, Compared with one another.

The three Greek Orders, Dorique, Ionique, and Corinthian, comprise the First Part of this Treatise. And the two Latine, Tuscan and Composita the Latter. [*rule*] Written in French by Roland Freart, Sieur de Chambray; Made English for the Benefit of Builders. [*rule*] To which is added an Account of Architects and Architecture, in an Historical, and Etymological Explanation of certain Tearms particularly affected by Architects. With Leon Baptista Alberti's Treatise of Statues. [*rule*] By John Evelyn Esq; Fellow of the Royal Society. [*rule*] [*engraved vignette*]
London, Printed by Tho. Roycroft, for John Place, and are to be sold at his Shop at Furnivals-Inn Gate in Holborn. M DC LXIV.

Collation: π^2 a^4 $*b^2$ $A^4BC^2D–Y^4$; 88 leaves.

Contents: π1*a* blank; π1*b Imprimatur* dated *Nov.* 21, 1663; π2 engraved title with portrait of Fréart; a1 title; a2*a*–a4*b* dedication to *Charles II* dated *Says-Court* 20. *Aug.* 1664; *b1*a*–*b2*b* dedication to *Sr John Denham, Superintendent of His Majesties Buildings and Works*; A1*a* lines in Latin to Evelyn by *Jo. Beale, S.P.D.*; A1*b* blank; A2*a*–A4*b* Fréart's dedication *To my most Dear Brothers*, dated *Paris the* 22. *of May* 1650; B1*a*–Q4*a* (pp. 1–111) *A Parallel*; Q4*b* blank; R1*a–b* (pp. 113–14) *The Interpreter to the Reader*, signed *J. Evelyn*; R2*a*–V3*b* (pp. 115–42) *An Account of Architects & Architecture*, signed *J. E.*; V4*a To the Reader*, signed *Evelyn*; V4*b Cosimo Bartoli to Bartolomeo Ammanti*; X1*a*–Y4*a* (pp. 145–59) *L. B. Alberti of Statues, Errata*, 5 lines, on Y4*a*; Y4*b Books Printed for John Place.*

Engravings: 1. Engraved title.
2. Vignette on printed title.
3–10. Vignettes on A2, B1, D4, K4, N4, P1(2), P3.
11–50. Large engravings on E1, E2, E3, F1, F2, F3, F4, G1, G2, G4, H1, H2, H3, H4, I1, I2, I3, I4, K1, K2, K3, L1, L2, L3, L4, M1, M2, M3, M4, N1, N2, N3, O3, O4, P1, P4, Q1, Q2, Q3, Q4.
51, 52. Smaller engravings on X4, Y1.

Copies: BLO (2, Arch. Antiqu. A.II.1;[1] Savile.E.7), BM (60.h.6[2]), CCE,[3] K,[4] ULC (M.8.14); CH, HCL.

75 PARALLEL OF ARCHITECTURE [first edition, second issue. W. E 1924] f° 1680

Title: The Whole Body Of Antient and Modern Architecture: comprehending What has been said of it by these Ten Principal Authors who have written upon the Five Orders,... [etc., as in no. 74].
Also an Account of Architects and Architecture, in an Historical, and Etymological Explanation of certain Terms particularly used by Architects. With Leon Baptista Alberti's Treatise of Statues. The three Greek Orders, Dorique, Ionique, and Corinthian, comprise the First Part of this Treatise. And the two Latine, Tuscan and Composita the Latter. [*rule*] Published for the Benefit of Builders, Limners, and Painters. [*rule*] By John Evelyn Esq; Fellow of the Royal Society. [*rule*] Adorned with Fifty one Copper Plates. [*rule*]
London, Printed for J. P. Sold by C. Wilkinson, T. Dring, C. Harpur, R. Tonson, and J. Tonson. MDCLXXX.

Collation, contents: As in no. 74.

Note: The sheets of no. 74, with a new title-page from which the engraved vignette is omitted. It appears that the original printed title-page has been cancelled and a new one inserted, together with a2–4, between the *Imprimatur* leaf and the engraved title.

Copies: BM (7820.i.13; no frontispiece or *Imprimatur* leaf), TCC; CLC, HCL.

76 PARALLEL OF ARCHITECTURE [second edition] f° 1707

Title: A Parallel of the Antient Architecture with the Modern,... [etc. as in no. 75]. The Second Edition With Large Additions. [*rule, and vignette as before*]
London, Printed for D. Brown at the Black Swan without Temple Bar, J. Walthoe in the Middle-Temple-Cloysters, B. Took at the Middle-Temple-Gate in Fleet-street, and D. Midwinter at the Rose and Crown in St. Paul's-Church-Yard. 1707.

1 Inscribed: *For the pub: Library at Oxon: J. Evelyn.*
2 Bound in red morocco for King Charles II.
3 Inscribed by Evelyn for *Mr Beale.*
4 Large-paper copy from the library of the Earl of Essex.

Collation: a–e² B–Z² Aa–Gg² A–X²; 110 leaves.

Contents: a1 title; a2*a*–b2*a* first dedication; b2*b* blank; c1*a*–c2*b* second dedication; d1*a*–e1*b* author's dedication; e2*a* lines to Evelyn by J. Beale; e2*b* blank; B1*a*–Gg2*a* (pp. 1–115) *A Parallel*; Gg2*b* blank; A1 sub-title to *An Account of Architects and Architecture*, 1706; A2*a*–*b* dedication to *Sir Christopher Wren, Kt.*, dated *Wotton*, 21 *Feb.* 1696/7; B1*a*–*b* *To the Reader*; B2*a*–Q2*a* (pp. 1–57) *An Account*, etc.; Q2*b* blank; R1*a* *To the Reader*, signed *J. Evelyn*; R1*b* *Bartoli to Amanti*; R2*a*–X1*a* (pp. 61–75) *Alberti of Statues*; X1*b* *Books printed for Dan. Brown*, etc.; X2 blank.

Engravings: Engraved title-page inserted, vignette on the title-page, and 50 engravings in the text as in no. 74. One of the HCL copies has a variant imprint: *Printed by E. Midwinter for D. Brown*...

Note: In this edition Evelyn has considerably extended his *Account of Architects and Architecture*, and has dignified it with a separate title-page and a dedication to Sir Christopher Wren.

Copies: BLO (Radcliffe.c.26), ULC (A.16.7); CLC, HCL (2, one variant).

77 PARALLEL OF ARCHITECTURE [third edition] f° 1723

Title, in red and black: A Parallel of the Antient Architecture with the Modern,... [etc. as in no. 74]. The Third Edition, with the Addition of The Elements of Architecture; Collected by Sir Henry Wotton Knt. from the best Authors and Examples; and also other large Additions. [*rule and woodcut*]
London: Printed by T. W. for D. Browne, J. Walthoe, B. and S. Tooke, D. Midwinter, W. Mears, and F. Clay. MDCCXXIII.

Collation: (a)–(e)² a–i² k¹ B–Z² Aa–Gg² A–U²; 127 leaves.

Contents: (a)1 title; (a)2*a*–(b)2*a* first dedication; (b)2*b* blank; (c)1*a*–(c)2*b* second dedication; (d)1*a*–(e)2*a* author's dedication; (e)2*b* lines to Evelyn by J. Beale; a1 sub-title to *The Elements of Architecture by Sir Henry Wotton*; a2*a*–*b* *The Preface*; b2*a*–k1*b* (pp. i–xxxviii [should be xxxiv]) *The Elements of Architecture*; B1*a*–Gg2*a* (pp. 1–115) *A Parallel*; Gg2*b* blank; A1 sub-title to *An Account of Architects and Architecture*, 1723; A2*a*–*b* dedication to Wren; B1*a*–*b* *To the Reader*; B2*a*–Q2*a* (pp. 1–57) *An Account*, etc.; Q2*b* blank; R1*a* *To the Reader*; R1*b* *Bartoli to Amanti*; R2*a*–U2*b* (pp. 61–75) *Alberti of Statues*.

Engravings: Engraved title-page inserted and 50 engravings in the text as in no. 74. A woodcut is substituted for the engraving on the title-pages of the previous editions. Pp. xxi–xxiv are omitted in the pagination.

Note: To this edition the publishers have added Wotton's *Elements of Architecture*. It is otherwise the same as the second.

Copies: ULC (A.16.8); CLC.

78 PARALLEL OF ARCHITECTURE [fourth edition] f° 1733

Title, in red and black: A Parallel of the Antient Architecture with the Modern, ...[etc. as in no. 74]. The Fourth Edition...[etc. as in no. 77].
London: Printed by T. W. for J. Walthoe, D. Midwinter, and A. Ward; W. Mears, F. Clay, B. Motte, and D. Browne. [*short rule*] MDCCXXXIII.

Collation: a–e² a–i² k¹ A–Z² Aa–Gg² A–P² R–U²; 127 leaves.

Contents: a1–Gg2 as in no. 77; A1 sub-title to *An Account*, no date; A2*a–b* dedication to Wren; B1*a–b To the Reader*; B2*a*–P2*a* (pp. 1–53) *An Account*, etc.; P2*b* blank; [sign. Q omitted]; R1*a Bartoli to Amanti*; R1*b To the Reader*; R2*a*–U2*b* (pp. 61–75) *Alberti of Statues*.

Engravings: Engraved title-page inserted and 50 engravings in the text as in no. 74.

Note: A close reprint of the preceding edition, except that Evelyn's *Account of Architects and Architecture* is made to occupy four pages less. As a result signature Q has been omitted, though the pagination beyond this point does not allow for the omission.

Copies: BM (1264.g.25).; CLC, HCL (Architecture Library).

THE PERNICIOUS CONSEQUENCES OF THE NEW HERESIE

1666

PREFACE

IN January 1664/5 Evelyn had published his translation of Jansenist papers by Arnauld and Nicole under the title Μυστήριον τῆς Ἀνομίας. *That is, Another Part Of The Mystery of Jesuitism* (see no. 39). This had been undertaken at the instance of Lord Cornbury, son of Lord Chancellor Clarendon, and was published anonymously. It attracted the attention of the King, so that Evelyn had some satisfaction for the pains he had taken in translating it. Perhaps because of this success he was not left long in peace, and on 9 February of the same year he was writing to Lord Cornbury:

'My Lord, Being late come home, imagine me turning over your close printed memoires, and shrinking up my shoulders; yet with a resolution of surmounting the difficulty, animated with my Lᵈ Chancellors & your Loᵖˢ com'ands, whom I am perfectly dispos'd to serve, even in the greatest of drudgeries, the translation of bookes. But why call I this a drudgery? Who would not be proud of the service? By the slight tast of it, I find God & King concerned, and I will in due tyme endeavour to p'sent your Lordᵖ & the world with the fruites of my obedience, cherefully, & with all due regards.'[1]

Evelyn added a note to his copy of the letter that this refers to: 'Mysterie of Jesuitisme, & its pernicious consequences as it relates to Kings & States, w'h I published this yeare.' This note has usually been taken to mean the book already mentioned, partly owing to Evelyn's inaccuracies in title and date. It is now plain, however, that he meant to name another publication first identified and described in 1937 under the title *The Pernicious Consequences of the New Heresie of the Jesuites against The King and the State*, London, 1666. It was again printed by James Fisher for Richard Royston, who had produced the former book, and was a translation of a treatise by Pierre Nicole, *Les Pernicieuses Conséquences De la nouvelle Heresie des Jesuites contre le Roy & contre l'Estat. Par un Advocat en Parlement.* This was written in 1662 and, according to the catalogue of the Bibliothèque Nationale, was published in 1664.[2] Evelyn's zeal for Church and State and his hatred of popery overcame his dislike for the drudgery of translating, and on 1 March 1665/6 he recorded in his Diary, 'To London,

[1] Wheatley, III, 299.

[2] The only edition to be found in the British Museum is a quarto pamphlet without date or title-page (4091.g.16).

and presented his Ma^ty^ my book intituled The pernicious Consequences of the New Heresy of the Jesuits against Kings and States'.[1] Hitherto this has again been erroneously taken by Evelyn's editors to mean the former book, in spite of his having given on this occasion the correct title and date. Evelyn also sent a copy to Dr Wilkins, Dean of Ripon, with a letter in which he wrote, 'S^r^, that I presume to send you the consequence of what I formerly publish'd in English, in the Controversy 'twixt the Jesuits and Jansenists, speakes rather my obedience to a com'and from that greate person (My Lord Chancellor) than my abilities to have undertaken, or acquitted myself of it as I ought: I have annexed an Epistolary Preface, not to instruct such as you are in anything which you do not know: but for their sakes, who reading the booke, might possibly conceive the French Kings to have ben the onely persons in danger; & because I hope it may receive your suffrage as to the pertinence of it *pro hic et nunc.*'[2]

Evelyn's *Dedicatory Preface* extends to thirty pages and is a learned account, written with much feeling, of the iniquities of the Roman Church and the danger it held for other kingdoms besides that of France. It was addressed to Lord Clarendon, though the elaborate cipher which Evelyn caused to be engraved for the heading of the dedication (see next page) effectively conceals his patron's identity. Dr Barlow, however, noted in his copy of the book 'that Mr John Evelyn of Depthford translated this booke, and made the Preface to my Ld Chancellor Hide'. Evelyn also wrote to Lord Cornbury on 9 September 1665 mentioning 'that piece your Lo^p^ enjoyn'd me to publish in consequence of the former, and which I have made bold to inscribe to my Ld Chancellor, under somewhat an ænigmatical character, because of the invidiousenesse of the argument'.[3]

The existence of Evelyn's book was suspected by Miss Ruth Clark,[4] though she had failed to locate a copy. It is to be found, however, at Oxford, where there are two copies in the Bodleian Library (ascribed in the catalogue to Arnauld) and one at Queen's College with a note by the Provost, Dr Thomas Barlow, and there is another in the Cambridge University Library, from which the accompanying facsimiles have been made. Others will no doubt be found now that its authorship is established. Evelyn's interest in the Jansenist controversies was clearly very great, though there is no evidence connecting him directly with any of the other books to which they gave rise (see also p. 124).

No part of this work has yet been reprinted.

[1] de Beer, III, 431. [2] Wheatley, III, 342. [3] Wheatley, III, 319.

[4] See her *Strangers and Sojourners at Port Royal* (Cambridge, 1932), p. 111.

THE

Pernicious Consequences

OF THE

New Heresie of the *Jesuites*

AGAINST

The KING and the STATE.

By an *Advocate* of *Parliament*.

LONDON,
Printed by *J. Flesher*, for *Richard Royston*,
Bookseller to His most Sacred MAJESTY. 1666.

THE

Dedicatory Preface.

My LORD,

THE *title your* Honour *has to these ensuing* Papers, *and to the* Person *who makes them* English, *defends him from being thought* presumptuous, *that now they are* publish'd *and come abroad in the* World: *They wear this* Cypher *in front*, *as a* Periapta *or* Amulet *to pro-*

A 2 *tect*

Title-page and second leaf of no. 79

79 PERNICIOUS CONSEQUENCES OF THE NEW HERESIE

[W. N 1138] 8° 1666

Title within double lines: The Pernicious Consequences of the New Heresie of the Jesuites against The King and the State. [*rule*] By an Advocate of Parliament. [*type ornament between rules*]
London, Printed by J. Flesher, for Richard Royston, Bookseller to His most Sacred Majesty. 1666.

Collation: A^8 a^8 B–K^8; 88 leaves.

Contents: A1 title; A2*a*–a8*b* *The Dedicatory Preface*, unsigned, with engraved device on A2*a*; B1*a*–I6*b* (pp. 1–124) *The Pernicious Consequences*; I7*a* (p. 125) *An Advertisement upon the following Discourse*; I7*b*–K8*b* (pp. 126–44) *A Refutation of Certain Cavils.*

Note: The *Dedicatory Preface* is by Evelyn, who has translated the text from Pierre Nicole's *Les Pernicieuses Conséquences*, 1664. The cipher in the device on A2*a* will be seen to contain all the letters of the name CLARENDON, the Lord Chancellor to whom the *Preface* is addressed.

Copies: BLO (2, Bliss.a.79; 8° N.44.Th), K, QCO, ULC (F.12.46);[1] HCL.

[1] With note by Dr Thomas Barlow.

THE ENGLISH VINEYARD
1666

PREFACE

THE *ENGLISH VINEYARD VINDICATED* appears to have been really written by Evelyn, although the matter was derived from the lips of the King's Gard'ner, John Rose. In the *Preface* Evelyn explains thus: 'Being one day refreshing my self in the Garden at Essex-house, and amongst other things falling into discourse with Mr. Rose, (then Gard'ner to her Grace the Dutchess of Somerset) about Vines, and particularly the Cause of the neglect of Vineyards of late in England; he reason'd so pertinently upon the Subject (as indeed he does upon all things, which concern his hortulan Profession) that... I was easily perswaded to gratifie his modest and charitable inclinations, to have them communicated to the world. The Matter therefore of the ensuing Discourse being totally his, receives from me onely its forme, and the putting of his conceptions together; which I have dress'd up in as rural a garbe as I thought might best become, and recommend them for Practice.' He adds that he has consulted many larger books, but none appeared more rational than 'these short observations of Mr. Rose, and which I so much the more value, as I consider them the native production of his own Experience, without obtruding anything upon the reputation of others, which is now become the most pernitious Imposture that flatters us into so many mistakes and errours; whilst men follow such Directions as they meet withall in Print, or from some Monsieurs new come over, who thinke we are as much oblig'd to follow their mode of Gard'ning, as we do that of their Garments, 'till we become in both ridiculous.' Yet John Rose's plea that neglect of the culture of the vine in England was 'not altogether from the defect of Climate' does not seem to have been successful in promoting the industry or in commending English wines to the King's table.

Although Evelyn signed his *Preface* under the pseudonym of *Philocepos*[1] he did not preserve his anonymity, as he referred at the end to his *Sylva*, published under his name two years earlier.

The first edition of *The English Vineyard* seems to be an exceedingly scarce book. It was not reprinted separately, but, in spite of Evelyn's contempt for the 'Monsieurs', was appended to the second and subsequent editions of *The French Gardiner*, 1669, etc. (see nos. 8–11). Evelyn then, at Rose's request,

[1] From κῆπος, a *garden* or *plantation*.

added 'some Directions concerning Making and Ordering of Wines'. This contribution is headed *The Vintage* and occupies ten pages. Upcott does not appear to have noticed Evelyn's authorship of the whole book, and only reprinted the *Preface* in *Miscellaneous Writings*, 1825 (p. 101).

A review of *The English Vineyard* of nearly a page, 4°, appeared in *Philosophical Transactions* for 18 July 1666 (vol. 1, p. 262). It describes the work as 'a very thin Pocket-book', and is favourable to the author's pretensions.

THE *ENGLISH*

VINEYARD

VINDICATED

BY

JOHN ROSE

Gard'ner to His *MAJESTY*,
at his Royal *GARDEN*
in St. *James's*.

Formerly *Gard'ner* to her *Grace*
the *Dutchess* of *Somerset*.

With an Addrefs,

Where the beſt Plants *may be had at*
eafie *Rates*.

LONDON,
Printed by *J. Grifmond* for *John Crook*,
at the *Ship* in *St. Pauls Church-yard*,
1666.

Title-page of no. 80

80 THE ENGLISH VINEYARD [first edition. W. R 1935] 8° 1666

Title: The English Vineyard Vindicated by John Rose Gard'ner to His Majesty, at his Royal Garden in St James's. Formerly Gard'ner to her Grace the Dutchess of Somerset. With an Address, Where the best Plants may be had at easie Rates. [*rule*]
London, Printed by J. Grismond for John Crook, at the Ship in St. Pauls Church-yard, 1666.

Collation: A–D^8; 32 leaves.

Contents: A1 blank; A2 title; A3*a*–A5*b* *Epistle Dedicatorie to the King*, signed *John Rose*; A6*a*–B1*b* *The Preface or Occasion of this Discourse*, signed *Philocepos*; B2*a*–D6*a* (pp. 1–41) *The English Vineyard Vindicated*; D6*b*–D7*a* *To the Reader*; D7*b* –D8*b* blank.

Illustration: Folding plate facing p. 1. The cultivation of vines. Plate-mark 13 × 14 cm.

Note: In one of my copies, bound in contemporary mottled calf, gilt, gilt edges, there is a correction in the author's hand, *strong* in line 3, p. 5, being altered to *stony*.

Copies: BM (448.a.17), K (2); HCL, PL.

81 THE ENGLISH VINEYARD [second edition. W. R 1936] 8° 1669

Appended to *The French Gardiner*, 1669 (see no. 8), with an addition by Evelyn entitled *The Vintage*.

82 THE ENGLISH VINEYARD [third edition. W. R 1937] 8° 1672

Appended to *The French Gardiner*, 1672 (see no. 9).

83 THE ENGLISH VINEYARD [fourth edition. W. R 1938] 8° 1675

Appended to *The French Gardiner*, 1675 (see no. 10).

84 THE ENGLISH VINEYARD [fifth edition. W. R 1939] 12° 1691

Appended to *The French Gardiner*, 1691 (see no. 11).

PUBLICK EMPLOYMENT

1667

A

MORAL ESSAY,

PREFERRING

SOLITUDE

TO PUBLICK

EMPLOYMENT,

And all it's Appanages; ſuch as Fame, Command, Riches, Pleaſures, Converſation, *&c,*

---

2 King. 4. 13.

—*Wouldeſt thou be ſpoken for to the King, or to the Captain of the hoſt? And ſhe anſwered, I dwell among mine own people.*

EDINBURH,
Printed for *Robert Brown*, and are to be ſold at his Shop, at the Sign of the *Sun*, on the North-ſide of the Street, over againſt the Croſs, 1665.

Title-page of Mackenzie's *Essay*

PREFACE

IN 1665 Mr George Mackenzie, a distinguished Scottish advocate, published at Edinburgh *A Moral Essay, preferring Solitude to Publick Employment, And all it's Appanages; such as Fame, Command, Riches, Pleasures, Conversation, &c.*[1] Mackenzie was afterwards knighted, and, as Lord Advocate, became known as 'Bloody Mackenzie' for his harsh treatment of the Covenanters. He was addicted to the composition of 'Moral Essays',[2] and these writings betray the character of a bigot. Perhaps it was his sense of this that incited Evelyn to compose in 1667 his reply, in which *Publick Employment and an Active Life with all its Appanages, Such as Fame, Command, Riches, Conversation, &c.* are *Prefer'd to Solitude.* He dedicated this exercise in casuistry to his father-in-law, Sir Richard Browne, who had held several public offices, and it was published, according to the Diary, on 15 February 1666/7.[3] Evelyn's advocacy of an active life might seem at variance with his known delight in country solitude and pursuits, and in truth his attack upon Mackenzie is but a half-hearted affair. He can only counter a plea for books by exclaiming, 'Not to *read men*, converse with *living Libraries*, is to deprive our selves of the most useful and profitable of studies,'[4] and by recounting the names of the authors of famous books who had themselves been men of action. A reference by Mackenzie to 'seraphick Mr Boyle', as an example of virtue shaded by a private life, goads him to claim for Boyle that 'there lives not a *Person* in the *World* whose *moments* are more *employ'd*...and that more confirms his *contemplations* by his *actions* and *experience*: And if it be objected, that his employments [that is, chemistry and physics] are not *publick*, I can assure him, there is nothing more *publick*, than the *good* he's always *doing*.' In the end Evelyn is forced to descend to caricature, for after painting a picture on the one side of King and subjects working for the common good, he represents on the reverse 'the *goodliest* piece of the *Creation*, sitting on a Cushion *picking* his *teeth*; His Country-Gentleman taking *Tobacco*, and *sleeping*

[1] *A Moral Essay, preferring Solitude to Publick Employment...Edinburh, Printed for Robert Brown*, 1665. A⁴ B–H⁸; pp. 6 + 2 + 112. Re-issued with a new title-page dated 1666. Reprinted London, 1685 and 1693. K (3, 1665, 1666, and 1685).

[2] *Religio Stoici*, 1663; *Moral Gallantry*, 1669; *A Moral Paradox*, 1669; *The Moral History of Frugality*, 1691; *Reason, an Essay*, 1695.

[3] de Beer, III, 475.

[4] *Publick Employment*, p. 77.

after a *gorgeous meal*: There *walks* a *Contemplator* like a *Ghost* in a *Church-yard*, or sits *poring* on a *book* whiles his *family starves*: Here lies a *Gallant* at the *foot* of his *pretty female*, *sighing* and looking *babies* in her *eyes*, whilst *she* is *reading* the last new *Romance* and *laughs* at his folly: On yonder *rock* an *Anchorite* at his *beads*: *There* one *picking daisies*, another *playing* at *push pin*, and abroad the *young Potcher* with his *dog* and *kite* breaking his neighbours *hedges*, or *trampling* o're his *corn* for a *Bird* not worth *six-pence*: *This*, sitts *lowsing* himself in the *Sun*, that, *quivering* in the *cold: Here* one *drinks poyson*, another *hangs himself*; for *all* these, and a *thousand* more seem to prefer *solitude* and an *inactive life* as the most *happy* and *eligible* state of it: And thus have you *Land-skip* for your *Land-skip*.'[1]

The truth was, of course, that Evelyn's inclinations lay on both sides, so that he could honestly attack Mackenzie's thesis, and at the same time write to Abraham Cowley: 'You had reason to be astonish'd at the presumption, not to name it affront, that I who have so highly celebrated recesse, and envied it in others, should become an advocate for the enemie, which of all others it abhorrs and flies from. I conjure you to believe that I am still of the same mind, & that there is no person alive who dos more honor and breathe after the life and repose you so happily cultivate and adorne by your example: But as those who prays'd dirt, a flea, and the gowte, so have I *Publiq Employment* in that trifling Essay, and that in so weake a style compar'd to my antagonists, as by that alone it will appeare I neither was nor could be serious; and I hope you believe I speake my very soule to you.'[2]

The mild 'attack' on Mackenzie produced, therefore, no rancour. Writing in his Diary on 9 March 1690, he says: 'I din'd at the Bp. of St Asaph's...with the famous lawyer Sr Geo. Mackenzie...against whom both the Bp. and myselfe had written and publish'd books, but now most friendly reconcil'd.'[3] But the 'reconciliation' had taken place at the moment of the attack. Exceedingly polite letters passed between the antagonists in March 1667, immediately after the publication of Evelyn's book, in which Mackenzie says it was 'rarely weel writ', and Evelyn assures Mackenzie that he is a person 'infinitely obliging' to him.[4]

Samuel Pepys did not read the book until 26 May 1667 when, after amusing himself with Mistress Martin: 'I away to my boat, and up with it as far as Barne Elmes, reading of Mr. Evelyn's late new book against Solitude, in which I do

[1] *Publick Employment*, pp. 117–18.
[2] Wheatley, III, 349.
[3] de Beer, V, 12.
[4] *Miscellaneous Writings*, 1825, pp. 503–4.

not find much excess of good matter, though it be pretty for a bye discourse. I walked the length of the Elmes, and with great pleasure saw some gallant ladies and people come with their bottles, and basket, and chairs, and form, to sup under the trees by the waterside, which was mighty pleasant. I to boat again and to my book, and having done that I took another book, Mr. Boyle's of Colours, and there read, where I laughed, finding many things worthy of observation.'[1] Boyle on *The Experimental History of Colours* was more amusing than Evelyn on *Solitude*.

Evelyn's little volume is attractive in a plain way, and is not uncommon, though the copies in circulation belong to three different issues with the same date, which were first distinguished in 1937. Two of these belong to the first edition; the third is a line-for-line reprint and constitutes a second edition. The only later reprint of the text is that in the *Miscellaneous Writings*, 1825, pp. 505–52.[2]

[1] Wheatley's *Pepys*, vol. VI, pp. 318–19.

[2] The late Gilbert R. Redgrave wrote to me in 1938 that he believed there was an eighteenth-century reprint of Mackenzie's book printed with Evelyn's reply in one volume, but I have been unable to find any trace of it.

85 PUBLICK EMPLOYMENT [first edition, first issue. W. E 3510]
8° 1667

Title: Publick Employment and an Active Life Prefer'd to Solitude, and all its Appanages, Such as Fame, Command, Riches, Conversation, &c. In Reply to a late Ingenious Essay of a contrary Title. [*rule*] By J. E. Esq; S.R.S. [*rule*]

Arist. I. Polit.

Ἄνθρωπος ζῶον πολιτικόν·

Sen. Ep. XXII.

Excute istos qui, quæ cupiere, deplorant, & de earum rerum loquuntur fuga, quibus carere non possunt: videbis voluntariam esse illis in eo moram, quod æque ferre & misere loquuntur.

[*rule*] London, Printed by J. M. for H. Herringman at the Sign of the Blew Anchor in the Lower Walk of the New-Exchange. 1667.

Collation: A–H⁸ I⁴; 68 leaves.

Contents: A1*a* blank; A1*b* *Imprimatur, Roger L'estrange. Dec.* 13 1666; A2 title; A3*a*–A6*b* *The Epistle Dedicatory* to Richard Browne, dated *Says-Court, Feb.* 5. 166$\frac{6}{7}$; A7*a*–A8*b* *To the Reader*, signed *J. E.*; B1*a*–I4*b* (pp. 1–120) text.

Copies: BM (527.f.14), K, VAF; CLC, HCL.

86 PUBLICK EMPLOYMENT [first edition, second issue. W. E 3511]
8° 1667

Title: Publick Employment and an Active Life with all its Appanages, Such as Fame, Command, Riches, Conversation, &c. Prefer'd to Solitude. [*rule*] By J. E. Esq; S.R.S. . . . [etc. as in no. 85]. 1667.

Collation, contents: As in no. 85, with the addition of a small *errata* slip pasted on A1*b* below the *Imprimatur*.

Note: The sheets of no. 85 with cancel title.

Copies: BLO (2, Wood.730 (5), lacking A7 and *errata* slip; Mason.A.A230), CCE, K; CLC, HCL (2).

PUBLICK EMPLOYMENT
AND AN
ACTIVE LIFE
PREFER'D TO
SOLITUDE,
AND ALL ITS
APPANAGES,
Such as Fame, Command, Riches, Conversation, &c.
In Reply *to a late Ingenious* Essay *of a* contrary Title.

By J. E. *Esq*; S. R. S.

Arist. 1. Polit.
Ἄνθρωπος ζῷον πολιτικόν.
Sen. Ep. XXII.
Excute istos qui, quæ cupiere, deplorant, & de earum rerum loquuntur fuga, quibus carere non possunt: videbis voluntariam esse illis in eo moram, quod æque ferre & misere loquuntur.

LONDON,
Printed by *J. M.* for *H. Herringman* at the Sign of the *Blew Anchor* in the Lower Walk of the *New-Exchange.* 1667.

Title-page of no. 85

PUBLICK EMPLOYMENT
AND AN
ACTIVE LIFE
WITH ALL ITS
APPANAGES,
Such as Fame, Command, Riches, Conversation, &c.
PREFER'D TO
SOLITUDE.

By J. E. *Esq*; S. R. S.

Arist. 1. Polit.
Ἄνθρωπος ζῷον πολιτικόν.
Sen. Ep. XXII.
Excute istos qui, quæ cupiere, deplorant, & de earum rerum loquuntur fuga, quibus carere non possunt: videbis voluntariam esse illis in eo moram, quod æque ferre & misere loquuntur.

LONDON,
Printed by *J. M.* for *H. Herringman* at the Sign of the *Blew Anchor* in the Lower Walk of the *New-Exchange.* 1667.

Title-page of no. 86

87 PUBLICK EMPLOYMENT [second edition. W. E 3512] 8° 1667

Title: Publick Employment and an Active Life, with its Appanages, Such as Fame, Command, Riches, Conversation, &c. Preferr'd to Solitude: In Reply to a late Ingenious Essay of a contrary Title. [*rule*] By J. E. Esq; S.R.S.[*rule*] [quotations as in no. 85]

London, Printed by J. M. for H. Herringman at the Sign of the Blew Anchor in the Lower Walk of the New-Exchange, 1667.

Collation: A–H8 I4; leaves.

Contents: A1*a* blank; A1*b Imprimatur*; A2 title; A3*a*–A5*b To the Reader*; A6*a*–A8*b The Epistle Dedicatory*; B1*a*–I4*b* (pp. 1–120) text.

Note: This is a line-for-line reprint of no. 85, except that the positions of *The Epistle Dedicatory* and *To the Reader* have been reversed. There are also some small alterations on the title-page. It is clearly the second edition of the book, for the *errata* noted on the slip added to no. 86 have been corrected. It is more roughly printed than the first edition and on inferior paper. Collated from a copy offered by Messrs Pickering and Chatto in May 1926.

Copies: CLC, Y.

PERFECTION OF PAINTING

1668

PREFACE

EVELYN'S *Idea of the Perfection of Painting* was published, according to his Diary, on 28 August 1668.[1] It was a translation of Roland Fréart's *Idée de la Perfection de la Peinture*, Le Mans, 1662, 4°. He had already translated the same author's work on architecture (see no. 74), and had published his own work on engraving (*Sculptura*, 1662). He protests in his preface to the present volume that he believed he had done with the drudgery of translating books, but felt constrained to add this one in order to round off his contribution to the arts. He also wished to add his testimony to the versatility of the great painters, who were so well equipped in other arts, and he instances Dr Christopher Wren, 'that *Miracle* and *Ornament* of our *Age* and *Countrey*', as another who was able to perform in all the arts if he were so disposed.

Evelyn dedicated his book to Henry Howard, heir apparent to the Duke of Norfolk, who had given to the Royal Society the library at Arundel House and had provided it with meeting-rooms from 1667 to 1673. Evelyn had also suggested to him the noble gift of the Arundel marbles to the University of Oxford, so that he fully deserved the tribute of this dedication. The translation includes the author's *Preface* and *Advertisement to the Reader*, but omits his dedication to the Duc d'Orléans and the *Table des Articles*.

The book is not rare, and was no doubt given by Evelyn to a number of his friends. Only one such gift-copy has so far come to my notice. This has an inscription on the fly-leaf addressed to Mr (Sir Peter) Lely as follows: 'For my honour'd Friend Mr Lilly, from his humble ser^t^ J. Evelyn.'[2] In this copy a word in the Preface that was left blank by the printer has been filled in by Evelyn.

The dedication and preface were reprinted in the *Miscellaneous Writings*, 1825, pp. 553–62; the rest of the work has not been reprinted. A very favourable notice of the book was printed in the *Philosophical Transactions*, no. 39, 21 Sept 1668, pp. 784–5.

[1] de Beer, III, 514.

[2] Sold at Sotheby's, 29 Nov. 1927, lot 352.

AN

IDEA

Of the *Perfection*

OF

PAINTING:

DEMONSTRATED

From the *Principles* of Art, and by *Examples* conformable to the *Observations*, which *Pliny* and *Quintilian* have made upon the most celebrated *Pieces* of the *Antient* PAINTERS, Parallel'd with some *Works* of the most famous *Modern Painters*, LEONARDO *da* VINCI, RAPHAEL, JULIO ROMANO, and N. POUSSIN.

Written in *French*

By *Roland Freart*, *Sieur de Cambray*,

And rendred *English*

By *J. E.* Esquire,

Fellow of the ROYAL SOCIETY.

In the *SAVOY*:

Printed for *Henry Herringman* at the Sign of the *Anchor* in the Lower-walk of the *New-Exchange*. 1668.

Title-page of no. 88

88 PERFECTION OF PAINTING [W. C 1922] 8° 1668

Title, within double lines: An Idea Of the Perfection of Painting: Demonstrated From the Principles of Art, and by Examples conformable to the Observations, which Pliny and Quintilian have made upon the most celebrated Pieces of the Antient Painters, Parallel'd with some Works of the most famous Modern Painters, Leonardo da Vinci, Raphael, Julio Romano, and N. Poussin. [*rule*] Written in French By Roland Freart, Sieur de Cambray, And rendred English By J. E. Esquire, Fellow of the Royal Society. [*rule*]
In the Savoy: Printed for Henry Herringman at the Sign of the Anchor in the Lower-walk of the New-Exchange. 1668.

Collation: A^8 a^4 b^8 B–I^8 K^4; 88 leaves.

Contents: A1 title; A2*a*–A8*b The Preface*; a1*a*–a4*b An Advertisement to the Reader* (explanation of terms); b1*a*–b3*b* dedication *To Henry Howard*, dated *Says-Court, June* 24, 1668; b4*a*–b8*a To the Reader*, signed *J. Evelyn*; b8*b Errata*, 19 lines; B1*a*–K4*b* (pp. 1–136) text.

Note: A word in the *Preface* on A8*a*, left blank by the printer, is supplied in the *errata*.

Copies: BLO (2, Douce. F. 304; Lister. A. 240), BM (1043.e.10), CCE, K, ULC (M.11.66); CLC, HCL.[1]

[1] With presentation inscription to Sir Peter Lely.

HISTORY OF THE IMPOSTORS

1669

PREFACE

HENRY BENNET, first Earl of Arlington, was a great figure at the Court of Charles II, and was Secretary of State from 1662 to 1674. He came much into contact with Evelyn and is mentioned very frequently in the Diary during these years; it was to him that Evelyn dedicated his *History Of the Three late famous Impostors*. This was printed early in 1669, and under the date 13 February 1668/9 Evelyn wrote: 'I presented his Ma^ty^ with my Historie of the Foure Imposters; he told me of other like cheates. I gave my booke to Lord Arlington to whom I dedicated it.'[1] *Foure* is here an error for *Three*, the characters described being Padre Ottomano, Mahomed Bei, and Sabbatei Sevi, the first two being pretenders in the Turkish Imperial Family, the third a Jewish pseudo-Messiah, Shabbethai Zebi. In his *Epistle Dedicatory* to Lord Arlington Evelyn explains that his stories are of 'undoubted *Verity*', having been obtained from eye-witnesses, whose names are suppressed lest they should be exposed thereby to inconvenience. The narrator of the first two impostures, 'a Persian stranger', is, however, easily identified. At the beginning of the first story a beautiful slave is obtained for Kefler Aga, the Sultan's Eunuch, by a merchant, Jacobo Cesii. It can hardly be a mere coincidence that the following entry occurs in the Diary under the date 29 September 1668: 'I had much discourse with Sign^r^. Pietro Cesij, a Persian gent., about the affaires of Turkey to my infinite satisfaction.'[2] The narrator (or, perhaps, author) of the third imposture, Sir Paul Rycaut, remained anonymous, though he had 'already gratified the *Publique* with the *Fruit* of many rare and excellent *Observations*', presumably in his book on the Turkish Empire, *The Capitulations and Articles of Peace*, Constantinople, 1663. He reprinted his contribution to Evelyn's book in his *History of the Turkish Empire from 1623 to 1677*, London, 1680, pp. 200–19, a continuation of Richard Knolles's *General History of the Turks*, 1602, &c. The editor of the *Miscellaneous Writings*, 1825, noted that Evelyn's first narrative is also reprinted by Rycaut almost verbatim, pp. 55 ff. Evelyn's book is concluded by a brief account of 'The History Of the Late Final Extirpation And Exilement of the Jewes Out of the Empire of Persia'. This, together with the third narrative, is to be found in Henry Timberlake's *Two Journeys to Jerusalem*, London, 1683, &c.

[1] de Beer, III, 522–3.

[2] *Ibid.* 516.

The whole work has only been reprinted in *Miscellaneous Writings*, 1825, pp. 563–620. The book was translated into German, 1669, and was reprinted with a preface in 1739 (see nos. 90, 91).

According to Brunet[1] it was also translated into French and published by Robinet at Paris in 1673, 12°. This statement has not been verified. On the other hand a translation of Evelyn's narratives did appear in a somewhat altered form in *Les Imposteurs Insignes. Par Jean Baptiste de Rocoles. A Amsterdam Chez Abraham Wolfgang*. 1683. 12° (BM: 10604.a.19).

[1] See *Le Traité des Trois Imposteurs...par Philomneste junior. Paris*, 1867, p. xxxiii. This has a new French translation and a bibliography.

THE

HISTORY

Of the THREE late famous

IMPOSTORS,

viz. { *Padre Ottomano,*
Mahomed Bei, and
Sabatai Sevi. }

The *One*, pretended *Son* and *Heir*
to the late *Grand Signior*;
The *Other*, a *Prince* of the *Ottoman* Family,
but in *truth*, a *Valachian Counterfeit.*
And the Last,
The Suppos'd *MESSIAH* of the *Jews*,
in the *Year* of the true *Messiah*, 1666.

With a brief *Account* of the *Ground*, and *Occasion*
of the present *War* between the
TURK and the *VENETIAN.*
Together with the *Cause* of the final
Extirpation, Destruction, and *Exile*
of the *JEWS* out of the
EMPIRE of PERSIA.

In the *SAVOY*,
Printed for *Henry Herringman* at the Sign
of the *Anchor* in the Lower-Walk of
the *New-Exchange.* 1669.

Title-page of no. 89

89 HISTORY OF IMPOSTORS [W. E 3490] 8° 1669

Title, within double lines: The History Of the Three late famous Impostors, viz. Padre Ottomano, Mahomed Bei, and Sabatai Sevi. The One, pretended Son and Heir to the late Grand Signior; The Other, a Prince of the Ottoman Family, but in truth, a Valachian Counterfeit. And the Last, The Suppos'd Messiah of the Jews, in the Year of the true Messiah, 1666. With a brief Account of the Ground, and Occasion of the present War between the Turk and the Venetian. Together with the Cause of the final Extirpation, Destruction, and Exile of the Jews out of the Empire of Persia. [*rule*]
In the Savoy, Printed for Henry Herringman at the Sign of the Anchor in the Lower-Walk of the New-Exchange. 1669.

Collation: A–I^8; 72 leaves.

Contents: A1 title; A2*a*–A4*b* *The Epistle Dedicatory* to Lord Arlington; A5*a*–A8*a* *To the Reader*, with *Errata* on A8*a*; A8*b* blank; B1*a*–I7*b* (pp. 1–126) *The History* etc.; I8 blank.

Copies: BLO (Art.8°.D.87), BM (278.b.3), CCE, K, ULC (T.5.44), VAF; CH, CLC, HCL.

90 HISTORY OF IMPOSTORS [German translation] 8° 1669

Title, in red and black: Historia De tribus hujus seculi famosis Impostoribus, Dass ist Beschreibung der dreyen unlängst beruffenen Betriegere / Nehmlich des Padre Ottomano Mahomed Bei oder Johann Michael Cigala, und Sabatai Sevi . . . Aus dem Englischen in Teutsche übersetzet [*double rule*]
Gedruckt im Jahr 1669.

Collation:)(^{4} A–F^8 G^4; 56 leaves.

Contents:)(1*a* title;)(1*b*–)(3*a* dedication;)(3*b*–)(4*b* *An dem Leser*; A1*a*–G2*b* (pp. 1–100) text; G3*a*–G4*a* *Relation von Johann Michael Cigala*; *Errata* at bottom of G4*a*; G4*b* blank.

Note: I have a note of another issue or edition of this translation dated 1676 (Hertzberger's catalogue, Amsterdam, Dec. 1963).

Copies: BM (701.b.59); HCL.

91 HISTORY OF IMPOSTORS [German translation] 8° 1739

Title, in red and black: Historia de Tribus Seculo XVII. famosis Impostoribus, Oder Historische Nachricht von dreyen im XVII. Jahrhundert beruffenen Ertz-Betrügern, als nemlich dem Padre Ottomanno, dem Mahomed Bei, oder Iohan. Mich. Cigala, und dem Sabbatei Sevi. Aus dem Englischen ins Deutsche übersetzet, nebst ihren Bildnissen, und einer Vorrede, Darinnen noch mehrere, und zur Continuation dienliche Nachrichten und Umstände ertheilet werden. [*rule*]
Gedruckt im Jahr 1739.

Collation:)(^{8} 𝔄–𝔉^8; 56 leaves.

Contents:)(1 title;)(2*a*–)(8*b* *Vorrede*; 𝔄1*a*–𝔉6*b* (pp. 1–92) text; 𝔉7*a*–𝔉8*a* *Relation von Johann Michaël Cigala*; 𝔉8*b* blank.

Illustrations: Engraved portraits of Ottomanus, Cigala, and Sabbatei Sevi facing pp. 1, 16 and 32.

Note: The text is the same as that of no. 90. The preface is by Martin Schmizel.

Copy: K.

NAVIGATION AND COMMERCE

1674

PREFACE

IN the year 1664 Evelyn became heavily involved in his country's affairs. War had been declared against 'the Hollanders', and on 27 October he was appointed one of the Commissioners for the care of the sick and wounded and of the prisoners. He performed his duties with characteristic care and thoroughness, so that in 1665 and 1666 he was greatly occupied by this public service, carried through in spite of the danger of the plague, to which he was often exposed. In this connexion Evelyn was constantly brought to the notice of the King, who not unnaturally came to regard him, with his literary reputation, as the ideal historian of this conflict. On 13 February 1668/9 Evelyn presented the King with his *History of the Three Impostors*, and it was on this occasion, according to the Diary, 'that he began to tempt me about writing the Dutch War'.[1] Evelyn at first declined the task, but he records that in June 1670, finding that his refusal had displeased the King, and being given many promises of assistance, he was persuaded to undertake it.[2] In fact, however, as his extant letters to Lord Treasurer Clifford show, he was already at work on his History in January 1670, and in August 1671 was calculating that the main part of the work would amount to 800 or 1000 pages in folio.[3] He found the bulk of the available material exceedingly irksome, and only after valiant struggles did he lay aside his uncongenial task long before it had been completed.

Some years later, in 1681, he handed the History, so far as it was written, to Samuel Pepys, writing on 6 December: 'I send you the sheets I have long since blotted with the Dutch War. . . . As to the compiler's part, 'tis not easy to imagine the infinite fardles of papers, treaties, declarations, relations, journals, original letters, and other volumes of print and writings, &c. which I was obliged to reade & peruse.'[4] Evelyn's sheets were accompanied by a number of miscellaneous papers of great interest, evidently intended to gratify Pepys's insatiable appetite for collecting, and so the results of Evelyn's labours came to rest in appreciative hands.[5]

[1] de Beer, III, 523.
[2] *Ibid.* 550.
[3] Wheatley, III, 375–81.
[4] *Ibid.* 407.
[5] Pepys kept these papers for ten years, and in March, 1692, wrote a letter to Evelyn expressing his intention of returning them. Presumably he did so, for they are not now in the Pepys Library; neither, however, are they to be found elsewhere (see *Private Correspondence of Pepys*, ed. Tanner, 1926, vol. I, p. x) except for 'Progresse of the Dutch War, The Third Booke', now at Christ Church (MS 134).

The History had not, however, proved to be an entirely abortive task, for in 1674 Evelyn published the introduction to his work under the title *Navigation and Commerce, their Original and Progress*. This gave great offence to the Dutch, as was intended, and the Ambassador demanded its suppression. An account of the affair is given by Evelyn in his Diary under the date 19 August 1674 as follows:

'His Ma^{ty} told me how exceedingly the Dutch were displeas'd at my treatise of the Historie of Commerce; that the Holland Ambass^{r} had complain'd to him of what I had touch'd of the Flags and Fishery, &c. and desired the booke might be call'd in; whilst on the other side he assur'd me he was exceedingly pleas'd with what I had done, and gave me many thanks. However, it being just upon conclusion of the treaty at Breda[1] (indeed it was design'd to have been publish'd some moneths before and when we were at defiance), his Ma^{ty} told me he must recall it formally, but gave order that what copies should be publiqly seiz'd to pacifie the Ambass^{r}, should immediately be restor'd to the printer, and that neither he nor the vendor should be molested. The truth is, that which touch'd the Hollander was much lesse than what the King himself furnish'd me with, and oblig'd me to publish, having caus'd it to be read to him before it went to the presse; but the error was, it should have ben publish'd before the peace was proclaim'd. The noise of this book's suppression made it presently be bought up, and turn'd much to the stationer's advantage. It was no other than the Preface prepar'd to be prefix'd to my History of the whole Warr; which I now pursued no further.'[2]

Another similar account was written by Evelyn on the fly-leaf of a copy of the book[3] given by him to Sir Henry Capel, afterwards Lord Capel of Tewkesbury. In this he added: 'The passages for which this Treatise...was call'd in at the Instance of the Dutch Ambass^{r} you will find in severall pages when I perstringe them for the insolence of the Hollanders, especially pp. 62, &c...where I speake of the Dominion of the Sea, duty of the Flags & Fishery.'

Evelyn continued to think about the questions raised in his book, and some years later, in 1682, he wrote Samuel Pepys a long letter[4] concerning the claim

[1] Evelyn was here in error. The treaty of Breda was concluded in 1667; the treaty of 1674, here mentioned, was signed on 19 February and has no distinctive name.

[2] de Beer, IV, 41.

[3] Offered for sale by Messrs Maggs Bros. in June 1921.

[4] Wheatley, III, 414–19.

of England to 'Dominion on the seas'. He confessed that he did not find the claim to be altogether valid in spite of the arguments advance in *Navigation and Commerce*, and he begged Pepys to 'Let this ingenuous Confession com'ute for my faults in that Treatise, & put amongst the Retractations of S^r your &c.'.

Some capital is being made out of 'the noise of this book's suppression' even at the present day, for the booksellers invariably advertise the work as having been 'suppressed' and as therefore being scarce, but suppress the fact that the suppression never took effect. *Navigation and Commerce* is an interesting compilation of facts concerning the economic history of Great Britain and Holland, but it cannot command a high price on the score of rarity, being in reality one of the commoner of Evelyn's books.

The treatise was reprinted in *Miscellaneous Writings*, 1825, pp. 625–86, and in Lord Overstone's *Select Collection of Tracts on Commerce*, London, 1859, pp. 29–103.

A notice of it appeared in *Philosophical Transactions*, vol. IX (June 1674), no. 104, p. 88.

NAVIGATION
AND
Commerce,
THEIR
ORIGINAL
AND
PROGRESS.

Containing

A succinct Account of Traffick *in General*; *its* Benefits *and* Improvements: *Of* Discoveries, Wars *and* Conflicts *at* Sea, *from the Original of* Navigation *to this Day; with special Regard to the* ENGLISH Nation; *Their several* Voyages *and* Expeditions, *to the Beginning of our late Differences with* HOLLAND; *In which His* Majesties Title *to the DOMINION of the SEA is Asserted, against the* Novel, *and* later Pretenders.

By *J. EVELYN* Esq; *S.R.S.*

Cicero ad *Attic.* L. 10. Ep. 7.
Qui MARE *tenet, eum necesse est* RERUM *Potiri.*

LONDON,
Printed by *T.R.* for *Benj. Tooke*, at the Sign of the *Ship* in St. *Pauls Churchyard*, 1674.

Title-page of no. 92

92 NAVIGATION AND COMMERCE [W. E 3504] 8° 1674

Title: Navigation and Commerce, their Original and Progress. Containing A succinct Account of Traffick in General; its Benefits and Improvements: Of Discoveries, Wars and Conflicts at Sea, from the Original of Navigation to this Day; with special Regard to the English Nation; Their several Voyages and Expeditions, to the Beginning of our late Differences with Holland; In which His Majesties Title to the Dominion of the Sea is Asserted, against the Novel, and later Pretenders. [*rule*] By J. Evelyn Esq; S.R.S. [*rule*]

Cicero ad *Attic.* L. 10. Ep. 7.
Qui MARE *tenet, eum necesse est* RERUM *Potiri.*

[*rule*] London, Printed by T. R. for Benj. Tooke, at the Sign of the Ship in St. Pauls Churchyard, 1674.

Collation: $[A]^4$ $B–I^8$ K^4; 72 leaves.

Contents: [A]1 blank; [A]2 title; [A]3*a*–[A]4*a* *To the King* signed *J. Evelyn*; [A]4*b* blank; B1*a*–I4*b* (pp. 1–120) text; I5*a*–K2*b* *The Table*; K3*a* *Errata*, 11 lines; K3*b* blank; K4*a*–*b* *Books sold by Benj. Tooke*.

Note: In October 1950 Messrs McLeish and Sons showed me a copy of the book printed on thicker paper than usual and carrying on the fly-leaf an inscription by Evelyn: *For the Rg^t: hon^le my L^d: Gorges*, i.e. Richard Gorges, 1620–1712, second Baron Gorges of Dundalk, mentioned several times in the *Diary*. This may be evidence of a special issue for presentation.

Copies: BLO (Art.8°.I.54), BM (2, 288.a.4.; 713.b.3[1]), CCE, K, ULC (4, O.4.72; R·11·72; Bb*.14.11; Dd*.4.11[1].E), VAF; CH, CLC, HCL.

[1] Inscribed on the fly-leaf in Evelyn's hand *For Mr. Slingsby*, and on the title-page is the signature *H. Slingesby*, probably Henry Slingsby, Master of the Mint (BM, second copy).

DISCOURSE OF EARTH

1676

PREFACE

ON 28 December 1674 the Council of the Royal Society addressed to Evelyn an invitation to present the Society 'at one of their Publick Meetings with a Discourse (grounded upon, or leading to Philosophical Experiments)'[1] on a subject of his own choice. This was to be given on any Thursday after 14 January 1675 that he cared to name. Thus it came about that on 29 April following Evelyn read, according to the Diary, his 'first discourse of Earth and Vegetation before the Royall Society as a lecture in course after Sir Rob. Southwell had read his the weeke before on Water'.[2] The second discourse was delivered on 13 May and the book containing both was printed soon afterwards by an order of the Council of the Royal Society made at a meeting held on 24 June. This small octavo volume was well printed by John Martyn, printer to the Royal Society, and it bears the title *A Philosophical Discourse of Earth*. In his dedication to Lord Brouncker, the then President of the Royal Society, Evelyn protests that the Society might have found a thousand things among the matters enriching their collections more worth producing, and in his preamble to the *Discourse* observes that he himself had 'once indeed pitch'd upon a Subject of somewhat a more brisk and lively nature; for what is there in Nature so sluggish and dull as Earth? What more spiritual and active than Vegetation, and what the Earth Produces?' But perhaps there was no harm in bringing the noses of the members of the Royal Society down to earth, so given as they were 'to converse among the brighter Orbs and Heavenly Bodies'. Evelyn certainly did bring them down to earth and rubbed them in it. His 'dull Discourse of *Earth*, *Mould* and *Soil*', as he called it,[3] may not appeal to our literary or aesthetic senses, for it deals strictly with earthy matters—kinds of soil, the characters of different kinds of dung, the science of stercoration, how to treat soil for every kind of cultivation, and so on; but it must have had a real value in its time, for it is an honest, practical treatise on matters of great importance to countrymen, and was based on the author's own observations and experience. Within the limitations of its period it merits the term 'scientific', and was worthy of the Society that sponsored it.

[1] The letter to Evelyn is printed with the third edition of the *Discourse of Earth* (see no. 95).

[2] de Beer, IV, 62.

[3] *Discourse of Earth*, 1676, p. 181.

The book is usually dated 1676 on the title-page, though it was entered in the Term Catalogue of 24 November 1675, and a long notice of it was printed in no. 119 of the *Philosophical Transactions*[1] for 22 November 1675. Part of the edition was bound up in one volume with the sixth edition of *Kalendarium Hortense*, 1676 (see no. 63), both works being mentioned on the first title-page. *A Discourse of Earth* was, however, not reprinted in its original form, the second and later editions being part of the third and subsequent folio editions of *Sylva*. In the edition of 1706 the title *Terra* was prefixed to the longer title used before in order that it might range with its companion works *Silva* and *Pomona*. It was reprinted separately with notes by Hunter in 8° in 1778, and again in 4° in 1787. It was added to his second and later editions of *Silva*, 1786, &c. (see no. 48). For this reason it was not included in the *Miscellaneous Writings* of 1825.

[1] Vol. x, pp. 454–6.

At a Meeting of the Council of the *Royal Society*, *June* 24. 1675.

Ordered,

THAT *a Discourse, made before the* Royal Society *the* 29th *of* April, *and* 13th *of* May 1675. *by* John Evelyn *Esquire, concerning Agriculture, be printed by the Printer of the said Society.*

BROUNCKER P.R.S.

A

Philosophical Discourse

OF

EARTH,

Relating to the

Culture and *Improvement* of it for *Vegetation*, and the *Propagation* of *Plants*, *&c.* as it was presented to the *Royal Society*, *April* 29. 1675.

By *J. Evelyn* Esq; *Fellow* of the said *SOCIETY.*

Πόλλακι τοὶ κηπωρὸς ἀνὴρ κατακαίριον εἶπε.

LONDON,

Printed for *John Martyn*, Printer to the *Royal Society*. 1676.

Imprimatur and title-page of no. 93

93 DISCOURSE OF EARTH [first edition W. E 3507] 8° 1676

Title, within lines: A Philosophical Discourse of Earth, Relating to the Culture and Improvement of it for Vegetation, and the Propagation of Plants, &c. as it was presented to the Royal Society, April 29. 1675. [*rule*] By J. Evelyn Esq; Fellow of the said Society. [*rule*]

Πόλλακι τὸι κηπωρὸς ἀνὴρ κατακαίριον εἶπε.

[*rule*] London, Printed for John Martyn, Printer to the Royal Society. 1676.

Collation: A–L4 M4; 92 leaves.

Contents: A1*a* blank; A1*b* order for printing by the Royal Society, signed *Brouncker P.R.S.*; A2 title; A3*a–b* *Dedication* to Lord Brouncker; A4*a*–M3*b* (pp. 7–182) text; *erratum* on M3*b*; M4 blank.

Note: Except that p. 108 is numbered 118, the pagination is correct. The copy in my library, which was formerly in that of the Duke of Leeds, contains three corrections in the hand of the author, of which only the first was recorded in the *erratum* on M3*b*. The binding suggests that it was a presentation copy, though it contains no inscription.

Copies: BLO (3, Lister.A.252; Wood.573; Art.8°.M.25), BM (967.c.5), K, ULC (Dd*.4.60[1].E); CH, CLC, HCL (2, one Arnold Arboretum).

94 DISCOURSE OF EARTH [second edition] f° 1678

Sub-title: A Philosophical Discourse of Earth, . . . [etc., as in no. 93]. The Second Edition Improv'd [*rule*] [*device*] [*double rule*]

London, Printed for John Martyn, Printer to the Royal Society. MDCLXXVIII.

Collation: Oo2–4 Pp–Tt4 Uu1–3; 26 leaves.

Contents: Oo2 sub-title; Oo3*a* dedication; Oo3*b* blank; Oo4*a*–Uu3*b* (pp. 287–334) text.

Note: This forms part of the third edition of *Sylva*, 1679 (see no. 42). The archaic word *redevable* in the last line but one of the dedication in the first edition is here altered to *accountable*, and there are various additions to the text. The device on the sub-title was used by J. Windet in 1592, and probably passed to W. Stansby in 1611 and to R. Bishop in 1634–8 (McKerrow, *Printers' and Publishers' Devices*, 1913, no. 292).

95 DISCOURSE OF EARTH [third edition] f° 1706

Sub-title: Terra. [*rule*] A Philosophical Discourse of Earth, . . . [etc. as in no. 93]. The third Edition Improv'd [*double rule*]

London: Printed for Rob. Scot, Ric. Chiswell, George Sawbridge, and Benj. Tooke. MDCCVI.

Collation: Aaaa–Gggg[4] 28 leaves.

Contents: Aaaa1*a* sub-title; Aaaa1*b* *For John Evelyn, Esq*; *&c.* signed *Brouncker, P.R.S. Lond. Dec.* 28, 1674; Aaaa2 dedication; Aaaa3*a*–Gggg4*a* (pp. 1–51) text; Gggg4*b* blank.

Note: This forms part of the fourth edition of *Silva*, 1706 (see no. 43). The address from the Council of the Royal Society, dated 28 Dec. 1674, requesting Evelyn to contribute a discourse at one of their meetings, is printed here for the first time, and the name *Terra* is prefixed on the title-page.

96 DISCOURSE OF EARTH [fourth edition] f° 1729

Sub-title: [*ornamental band*] Terra. [*rule*] A Phililosophical Discourse of Earth, . . . [etc. as in no. 93] [*Greek quotation*] [*rule*] [*ornamental band*] [*Sign.* 4Q, *catchword* FOR]

Collation: 4Q–4Z[2] 5A–5D[2] 5E1; 25 leaves.

Contents: 4Q1 sub-title; 4Q2*a* *For John Evelyn Esq*; 4Q2*b* dedication; 4R1*a*–5E1*b* (pp. 1–46) text.

Note: This forms part of the fifth edition of *Silva*, 1729 (see no. 44). The sub-title has no date or imprint. There is a general index to *Terra* and the other appended works at the end of the volume.

97 DISCOURSE OF EARTH [fifth edition] 8° 1778

Title: Terra: A Philosophical Discourse of Earth. Relating To the Culture and Improvement of it for Vegetation, and the Propagation of Plants, as it was presented to the Royal Society, By J. Evelyn, Esq; F.R.S. [*short rule*] A New Edition. With Notes By A. Hunter, M.D. F.R.S. [*double rule*]
York: Printed by A. Ward, for J. Dodsley, Pall-Mall; T. Cadell, in the Strand; J. Robson, New Bond-Street; T. Durham, Charing-Cross, London; and W. Creech, Edinburgh. MDCCLXXVIII.

Collation: a[4] A–Z[4] Aa[4], 1 leaf inserted after Z4; 101 leaves. Folding leaf inserted.

Contents: a1 title; a2*a*–*b* *Editor's Preface*, dated *York, March* 1, 1778; a3*a*–*b* *To John Evelyn. Esq.*; a4*a*–*b* dedication; A1*a*–Z*b*4 and leaf inserted (pp. 1–185) text; Aa1*a*–Aa4*b* (pp. 187–194) *Index*. Folding leaf, *A Table of sands*, inserted to face p. 42.

Note: The editor states in his preface that he had intended to add *Terra* to his edition of *Silva* (1776), but this was not done as it was not ready. It was added to the second edition, 1786 (see no. 48).

Copies: BM (2, 452.c.29; 42.c.28), K; CLC.

98 DISCOURSE OF EARTH [sixth edition] 4° 1787

Title: Terra: A Philosophical Discourse of Earth. Relating to the Culture and Improvement of it for Vegetation, and the Propagation of Plants, as it was presented to the Royal Society. By J. Evelyn, Esq; F.R.S. With Notes By A. Hunter, M.D. F.R.S. [*double rule*]
York: Printed by A. Ward, for J. Dodsley, Pall-Mall; T. Cadell, in the Strand; J. Robson, New Bond-Street; and R. Baldwin, Pater-noster-Row, London: J. Todd, York. [*short rule*] M.DCC.LXXXVII.

Collation: a^4 A–L^4; 48 leaves. Folding leaf inserted.

Contents: a1 title; a2 *Editor's Preface*, dated *January* 1, 1787; a3 *To John Evelyn Esq.*; a4 dedication; A1*a*–K1*b* (pp. 1–74) text; K2*a*–K3*b* *Index*; K4*a*–L4*a* advt. of *A New* [second] *Edition of Mr Evelyn's Silva: With Notes by A. Hunter, M.D. F.R.S. To which is added the Terra*; L4*b* blank. Folding leaf inserted to face p. 18.

Illustration: Facing p. 48. Aquatint of *The Tartarian Lamb*, signed *J. Halfpenny fecit.* Plate-mark 23·5 × 19·5 cm.

Note: This was published simultaneously with Hunter's second edition of *Silva*, 1786, and was evidently intended to be for the satisfaction of the purchasers of the first edition, which did not contain it. The 'only Notes of consequence' added to the second edition of *Silva* are therefore added on K4–L4 after the advertisement.

Copies: BLO (B.S. 4° 557), BM (7028.ee.36), K (in original wrappers, untrimmed); HCL (Gray Herbarium).

MUNDUS MULIEBRIS

1690

PREFACE

EVELYN'S eldest daughter, Mary, was born at Wotton in 1665, and to his great grief died of the smallpox when still under nineteen and a half. According to her epitaph in the Church of St Nicholas, Deptford, she died on 17 March 1685, though Evelyn states in his Diary that she died on 14 March. There, in the entry under the date 10 March, he gives a beautiful and moving account of her virtues, her piety, comeliness, and cheerfulness, her intelligence and learning. 'I have been assisted by her', he writes, 'in reading and praying by me; comprehensive of uncommon notions, curious of knowing every thing to some excesse, had I not sometimes repressed it. Nothing was so delightfull to her as to go into my study, where she would willingly have spent whole dayes, for as I sayd she had read aboundance of history, and all the best poets, even Terence, Plautus, Homer, Virgil, Horace, Ovid; all the best romances and modern poemes; she could compose happily, and put in pretty symbols, as in the Mundus Muliebris, wherein is an enumeration of the immense variety of the modes and ornaments belonging to the sex; but all these are vaine trifles to the interior virtues which adorn'd her soule.'[1]

Evelyn does not refer again to *Mundus Muliebris* in his Diary, but the memory of Mary and her poem remained in his mind, until in 1690, five years after her death, it was issued as a thin quarto pamphlet. It was produced by Richard Bentley, the well-known publisher of plays, novels and romances, as well as of more solid works such as Evelyn's *Sylva*.[2] Mary's poem is preceded by a preface, apparently from her father's pen, and is followed by a *Fop-Dictionary*, which is provided with a separate title-page. The whole pamphlet is intended to burlesque the manners of the time. The frenchified jargon of the world of foppery is amusingly recorded, and the *Fop-Dictionary* defines in detail many of Mary's 'pretty symbols', which might otherwise puzzle a later age, such as:

Plumpers. Certain very thin, round and light Balls, to plump out, and fill up the Cavities of the Cheeks, much us'd by old Court-Countesses.

Sprunking. A *Dutch* term for Pruning, Tiffing, Trimming, and setting out, by the Glass or Pocket *Miroir*.

Mundus Muliebris is now an uncommon trifle though comparison of the examples in my collection shows that it was printed three times in 1690. There were two

[1] de Beer, IV, 420–2.

[2] See p. 131.

distinct issues of the first edition, and it was printed a third time for the second edition, to which a burlesque receipt for making 'Pig, or Puppidog water for the Face' was added at the end. The second edition was re-issued with a new title-page in 1700. In 1691 an answer to *Mundus Muliebris* was published under the

Mundus Foppensis:

OR, THE

Fop Difplay'd.

BEING

The Ladies VINDICATION,

In Anfwer to a late Pamphlet, Entituled,

Mundus Muliebris: Or, The Ladies Dreffing-Room Unlock'd, *&c.*

In Burlefque.

Together with a fhort SUPPLEMENT to the *Fop-Dictionary*: Compos'd for the ufe of the Town-*Beaus*.

Prifca juvent alios; Ego me nunc denique natum,
Gratulor hac ætas moribus apta meis.
Non quia nunc terra lentum fubducitur aurum
Lectaque diverfo littore Concha venit.
Sed quia cultus adeft; nec noftros manfit in Annos,
Rufticitas Prifcis illa fuperftes avis.
Ovid de Arte Amandi. *Lib.* 3.

London, Printed for John Harris at the Harrow in the *Poultry*, 1691.

title *Mundus Foppensis*, with 'a short Supplement to the Fop-Dictionary: Compos'd for the use of the Town-*Beaus*'. The above reduced facsimile of the title-page has been made from a copy in the Evelyn Collection.

The first edition of *Mundus Muliebris* was reprinted in *Miscellaneous Writings*, 1825, pp. 697–713.

99 MUNDUS MULIEBRIS [first edition, first issue. W. E 3521]

4° 1690

Title: Mundus Muliebris: or, the Ladies Dressing-Room unlock'd, And her Toilette spread. [*rule*] In Burlesque. [*rule*] Together With the Fop-Dictionary, Compiled for the Use of the Fair Sex. [*rule*]

> ——*Tanquam famæ discrimen agatur,*
> *Aut Animæ: tanta est quærendi cura decoris.*
> Juvenal. Sat. 6.
> Such care for a becoming Dress they take,
> As if their Life and Honour were at Stake.

[*rule*] London: Printed for R. Bentley in Russel-Street in Covent Garden. 1690.

Collation: A–D4; 16 leaves.

Contents: A1 title; A2*a*–A4*b* *Preface* [by John Evelyn]; B1*a*–C2*b* (pp. 1–12) *A Voyage to Maryland: or the Ladies Dressing-room*; C3 sub-title to *The Fop-Dictionary*; C4*a*–D3*b* (pp. 15–22) *The Fop-Dictionary*; D4 blank.

Copies: BLO (Douce.E.238), BM (11626.bb.42), CCE, K, VAF; CH.

100 MUNDUS MULIEBRIS [first edition, second issue. W. E 3522]

4° 1690

Title: Mundus Muliebris: or, the Ladies Dressing-Room unlock'd, . . . [etc. as in no. 99].

[*rule*] London: Printed for R. Bentley in Russel-Street in Covent-Garden. 1690.

Collation: A–D4; 16 leaves.

Contents: As in no. 99.

Note: Another issue of no. 99. Sections A and B have been reset, and a few minor corrections have been made, notably the addition of a hyphen after *Covent-* in the last line but one of the title-page, and the alteration of *Maryland* to *Marryland* in the heading to the text on B1*a*. Sections C and D appear to be unchanged and to have been printed from the same setting as before. This second issue is printed on rather better paper than the first.

Copies: K; CLC, HCL.

Mundus Muliebris:

OR, THE

LADIES Dreſſing-Room

UNLOCK'D,

And her TOILETTE

SPREAD.

In Burleſque.

Together
With the FOP-DICTIONARY, Compiled
for the Uſe of the FAIR SEX.

——*Tanquam famæ diſcrimen agatur,*
Aut Animæ: tanta eſt quærendi cura decoris.
Juvenal. Sat. *6.*
Such care for a becoming Dreſs they take,
As if their Life and Honour were at Stake.

LONDON:
Printed for *R. Bentley* in *Ruſſel-Street* in *Covent Garden.* 1690.

Title-page of no. 99

101 MUNDUS MULIEBRIS [second edition, first issue. W. E 3523]

4° 1690

Title: Mundus Muliebris: or, the Ladies Dressing-Room unlock'd, . . . [etc. as in no. 99]. The Second Edition. To which is added a most rare and incomparable Receipt, to make Pig, or Puppidog-Water for the Face. [quotation between rules as in no. 99]

London: Printed for R. Bentley, in Russel-Street in Covent-Garden. 1690.

Collation: A–D4; 16 leaves.

Contents: As in no. 99, except that the text here extends onto D4*a*.

Note: A reprint of no. 100 with the addition of thirteen lines on 'Pig, or Puppidog, water'. The whole type has been reset, an occasional correction being made, such as the alteration of the word 'bequirtle' to 'bespertle' on C1*a*. The copy in my collection is untrimmed and stitched in its original blue paper wrapper as issued. It measures 20·5 × 15·5 cm.

Copies: BLO (2, Linc.C.2.4; Malone.289), BM (G.18918), K, VAF; CLC, HCL.

102 MUNDUS MULIEBRIS [second edition, second issue. W. E 3520]

4° 1700

Title: The Ladies Dressing-Room unlock'd, And her Toilette Spread. Together, With a Fop-Dictionary, and a Rare and Incomparable Receipt to make Pig, or Puppidog-Water for the Face. [*rule*]

——Tanquam famæ discrimen agatur,
Aut Animæ: Tanta est quærendi cura decoris.
Juvenal. Sat. 6.

[*rule*] Such care for a becoming Dress they take,
As if their Life and Honour were at Stake.

[*rule*] London: Printed for Joseph Wild, at the Elephant at Charing-Cross, 1700.

Where Gentlemen and Ladies may pick Novels at 6s. per Doz. And be furnish'd with most Sorts of Plays.

Collation: A–D4; 16 leaves.

Cancels: A1 has been cancelled, and a new leaf substituted; C3, the sub-title to the *Fop-Dictionary*, has been removed.

Contents: As in no. 101, except for the cancels noted above.

Copy: BM (11631.bb.47).

THE LADIES DRESSING-ROOM UNLOCK'D,

And her TOILETTE Spread.

TOGETHER,

With a *Fop-Dictionary*, and a Rare and Incomparable Receipt to make *Pig*, or *Puppidog-Water* for the Face.

——Tanquam famæ discrimen agatur,
Aut Animæ: Tanta est quærendi cura decoris.
Juvenal. Sat. 6.

Such care for a becoming Dress they take,
As if their Life and Honour were at Stake.

LONDON:

Printed for *Joseph Wild*, at the *Elephant* at *Charing-Cross*, 1700.

Where Gentlemen and Ladies may pick Novels at 6 *s.* *per* Doz. And be furnish'd with most Sorts of Plays.

Title-page of no. 102

THE COMPLEAT GARD'NER

1693

PREFACE

IT was about the year 1670 that Monsieur de la Quintinye, Chief Director of all the gardens of the French King, visited Evelyn at Sayes Court and inspected his gardens.[1] The event is not recorded in the Diary, though it must have had much significance for Evelyn. The English King even tried, by the offer of a pension, to induce de la Quintinye to stay in England as superintendent of the Royal Gardens.[2] He preferred, however, to remain in the service of his own King, and after his return to Paris gratified Evelyn by sending him 'some directions concerning the ordering of melons', which he translated into English and distributed to his friends. De la Quintinye wrote his great work on gardening some years later,[3] but did not live to put the finishing touches to his book, and this, Evelyn conjectured,[4] was the reason for the omission of his remarks on melons and for some repetitions and long-windedness which obtruded themselves on the translator's notice. In spite of this the qualities of the book induced Evelyn to undertake the immense task of translating it so that it could be published in 1693 under the title *The Compleat Gard'ner*, and he made good the omissions by including translations of de la Quintinye's 'Treatise of Orange Trees' and the notes on melons which had been sent. Evelyn sent a copy of the book to his brother George and wrote in a letter[5] accompanying it: 'I do not attribute the whole to my selfe; the toile of meere translating would have been very ungrateful to one who had not so much time to spend thrashing: but as a considerable part of it has, and the rest under my care, the publishers & printers will have it go under my name, altogether against my intentions.' He also wrote to his brother's gardener on the same day saying that the book which he had 'interpreted' was worth his perusal. It is evident, therefore, that the responsibility for the translation was mainly Evelyn's, and the style is his, though he had no doubt employed a professional translator as assistant, perhaps George London. The result was a large folio, almost the last of Evelyn's major publications. A fine engraved portrait of the author was prefixed, and the text was embellished with a charming series of small copper-plates illustrating various garden activities of the

[1] Evelyn's note, *Compleat Gard'ner*, 'Concerning Melons', p. 1.

[2] *Miscellaneous Writings*, 1825, p. 718 n.

[3] *Instruction pour les Jardins Fruitiers et Potagers. Avec un Traité des Orangers, suivy de Réflexions sur L'Agriculture. Paris. Barbin.* 1690. Second edition, 1692.

[4] 'Concerning Melons', p. 4.

[5] Now in the Evelyn Collection at Christ Church.

period.[1] The dedication to Lord Capel was signed by the publishers, Gillyflower and Partridge, Evelyn's name being attached to an *Advertisement*, following the author's preface. It is a little surprising to find that this is nothing more than an elaborate 'puff' of the nursery gardens at Brompton Park near Kensington, a business under the direction of two very capable men, George London and Henry Wise.[2] London had been apprenticed to John Rose, the King's gardener and nominal author of one of Evelyn's books (see no. 80). He was sent to France to study at Versailles, and afterwards became successively head gardener to the Bishop of London and superintendent of the Royal Gardens. With several partners he established the Brompton Nurseries, and later, with Henry Wise, developed them into a very large business, combining it with tours of inspection to the gardens of the noblemen of England.[3] Evelyn refers in his Diary to only one visit to Brompton Park, with Richard Waller on 24 April 1964,[4] though it is clear from his *Advertisement* that he had been familiar with London's establishment for many years before 1693. In addition to the *Advertisement*, Evelyn wrote for *The Compleat Gard'ner* a note on his translation of de la Quintinye's 'Directions concerning Melons', and *An Advertisement to the Curious* regarding his translation in general. These three pieces were all reprinted in the *Miscellaneous Writings*, 1825, pp. 714–20. A copy of the book containing some marginal notes in Evelyn's hand was inscribed by him for Lord Godolphin.[5] No other presentation copies have come to my notice.

The Compleat Gard'ner was never reprinted as a whole. London and Wise, however, saw that it might be turned to good account if it were pruned and condensed, and accordingly an abridged version was published under their names in 1699 with the following title: *The Compleat Gard'ner: or, Directions for Cultivating and Right Ordering of Fruit-Gardens, and Kitchen-Gardens. By Mounsieur De la Quintinye. Now Compendiously Abridg'd, and made of more Use, with very Considerable Improvements. By George London, and Henry Wise. London, Printed for M. Gillyflower, at the Spread Eagle in Westminster-Hall*, MDCXCIX. (8°, pp. [iv], xxxv, [i], 309, [7]). The book has an attractive frontispiece in the same style as the small engravings which decorated the folio, and some of the large plates were used again on folding leaves. This volume, though it was based

[1] Both the portrait and the small plates are reversed copies of those in the French edition.

[2] See David Green's *Gardener to Queen Anne*, Oxford University Press, 1956.

[3] *Miscellaneous Writings*, 1825, p. 715 n.

[4] de Beer, v, 176.

[5] Sold at Hodgson's, 30 Oct. 1930, lot 587 (Lee £20).

on Evelyn's work, contained at first nothing that was specifically his, and his name did not appear in it nor any acknowledgment. The abridgers presently awoke, however, to the fact that Evelyn's *Advertisement* in the folio was indeed an advertisement of some value to their business, and they therefore had it printed on two leaves which were inserted between pp. xiv and xv of the unsold copies. Soon afterwards the title-page was cancelled, and a new one was printed on which the book is called 'The Second Edition, Corrected'. There were five subsequent editions dated 1701–1719.[1]

[1] The editions of the abridgment are as follows: First edition, *M. Gillyflower*, 1699; 'second' edition, *M. Gillyflower & Andrew Bell*, 1699; third edition, *Andrew Bell*, 1701; fourth edition, *Andrew Bell*, 1704; fifth edition, *Andrew Bell*, 1710; sixth edition, *A. and W. Bell*, 1717; seventh edition, *A. and W. Bell*, 1719. My collection formerly contained copies of all of these, including two copies of the first edition, one with Evelyn's *Advertisement* and one without it.

103 THE COMPLEAT GARD'NER [W. L 431] f° 1693

Title in red and black, within double lines: The Compleat Gard'ner; or Directions for Cultivating and Right Ordering of Fruit-Gardens and Kitchen-Gardens; With Divers Reflections On several Parts of Husbandry. [*rule*] In Six Books. [*rule*] By the Famous Mon^sr.^ De La Quintinye, Chief director of all the Gardens of the French-King. [*rule*] To which is added His Treatise of Orange-Trees, with the Raising of Melons, omitted in the French Editions. [*rule*] Made English by John Evelyn Esquire, Illustrated with Copper Plates. [*rule*] London, Printed for Matthew Gillyflower, at the Spread Eagle in Westminster-Hall, and James Partridge, at the Post-house at Charing-Cross, MDCXCIII.

Collation: Collation: π^2 a**^{4} b^4 b***^{1} c*^{4} [a]^4 [b]^3 B–O^4 P–Q^6 R–Z^4 Aa^4 Bb^2 B–P^4 Q^2 T–Z^4 Aa–Dd^4 [a]^2 A–K^4; 248 leaves.

Contents: π1 title; π2*a* dedication to Henry Lord Capel, signed *Matthew Gillyflower, James Partridge*; π2*b* blank; a*1*a*–b4*a* *The Preface*; b4*b*–b**1*b* *Advertisement*, signed *J. Evelyn*, with advts. of books at end; c*1*a*–2*b* Latin verses to the author signed *Santolius Victorinus*; c*3*a*–4*b* the same translated;[1] [a]1*a*–[b]3*b* *The Dictionary* of gardening terms, with advt. of where to buy gardening tools[2] at end; B1*a*–Aa3*a* (pp. 1–183 [should be 191]) text of Vol. I, parts i–iii; Aa3*b*–Bb2*b* (p. 184 with four pp. unnumbered) *The Table*; B1*a*–Dd2*b* (pp. 1–204 [should be 184]) text of Vol. II, parts iv–vi; Dd3*a*–4*a* *The Table*; Dd4*b* blank; [a]1*a*–2*a* (pp. 1–3) *Directions Concerning Melons*, with prefatory paragraph signed *J. Evelyn*; [a]2*b* (p. 4) *An Advertisement to the Curious*, signed *J. Evelyn*; A1*a*–E1*a* (pp. 1–33) *A Treatise of Orange Trees*; E1*b* (p. 34) *A Table*; E2*a*–K4*a* (pp. 35–79) *Reflections Upon some parts of Agriculture*; K4*b* (p. 80) *A Table*.

Frontispiece: Engraved portrait of de la Quintinye in an oval, inscribed *F. de la Mare Richart pinx: acad: W. Elder sculpsit.* On the pediment below the oval are engraved four Latin lines by Santolius Victorinus.

Illustrations: (1) Eleven full-page or folding plates as follows: Vol. I, facing p. 1. Vol. II, facing pp. 2, 10, 11, 20, 22, 24, 32, 68 (two), 177 (the last is wrongly marked *Pag: 17 in the Orange Tree*).

(2) Eleven small engravings in the text as follows: Vol. I, pp. 1, 16, 34, 40, 62. Vol. II, pp. 1, 78, 137, *Melons*, p. 1, *Orange Trees*, pp. 1, 35.

(3) Four woodcuts in the text as follows: Vol. I, p. 41. Vol. II, pp. 62, 108, 110.

[1] According to Wood's *Athenæ Oxonienses* the translator was Thomas Creech, Fellow of All Souls College, Oxford.

[2] 'The best Pruning-Knives, and other Instruments for *Gard'ning*, made according to the Directions of *Mons*^r^. *de la Quintinye* when last in *London*, are Sold at Mrs. *Gillyflowers* a *Toy-Shop*, next to the *Kings-Bench* in *Westminster-Hall* the Corner-Shop.'

Note: Both the collation and the pagination are irregular. In the preliminary matter it seems probable that the single leaf with sig. b** was imposed as the fourth leaf of the gathering with sig. [b], since this has only three leaves. In the division of the book called Vol. I, sigs. P and Q contain six leaves each. In these signatures P2–5 and Q2–5 are paginated on the recto only, so that eight pages are dropped in the numbering. Furthermore, sigs. Q2 and Q3 are printed as Q3 and Q5 and the page number 118 is printed as 116. In Vol. II, pp. 117–36 are omitted altogether in the numbering.

Copies: BLO (2, Douce.Q.subtus 1; Mason.G.G.234), BM (448.K.10), K, ULC (L.2.17); CH, CLC, HCL (2).

NUMISMATA

1697

PREFACE

EVELYN'S curiosity was unquenchable, and he was already an old man when he began in 1692 to collect notes for a work on medals. He had found that little had been written on the subject in English and, animated by a commendable regard for portraits and portraiture, sought in his *Numismata, A Discourse of Medals* to remedy this defect. After he had begun his book Obadiah Walker, Master of University College, Oxford (until evicted in 1689 as a Roman Catholic), published a work on Greek and Roman history illustrated by coins and medals, and Evelyn was for a time discouraged.[1] But he soon determined to make the scope of his work wider than Walker's, and by June 1694 he was arranging with the printer and publisher Benjamin Tooke for setting up the book in type and for engraving the illustrations. He intended that his book should be worthy of its subject, and his letter[2] to Tooke illustrates well his solicitude for every aspect of its make-up:

Mr. Tooke,

Tarde, sed tandem. At last I send you the copy you have so long expected; never the worse, I hope, for coming no sooner. I wish it may answer the paines I have taken in compiling: for it would amount to the value of many Medals. I was indeede unwilling it should scape from me without some thing more than an ordinary treatise. It will therefore require a more than ordinary supervisor. You tell me, such a one you have; if not, pray make use of the poore man I directed to you, who is also acquainted with my hand, & will be ready to assist you. There being aboundance of writers on this subject in all other polite European languages, & but one very short & partial one in ours, will I hope render this the more acceptable, & give ferment to the curious. I expect attaques from some peevish quarter, in this angry age, but so it make for your interest, & satisfy equitable judges, I shall not be much concern'd.

The Medals which are here sent you, pray take care of, & deliver but one by one to your graver, nor supply him with any other till he returnes you that he is graving with the plate. You'l find I have mark'd the paper, wherein you must keepe the plates, and apply to the pages as directed, by which you'l avoid mistakes, easily fallen into without some such method. Such as you are to have from the Earle of Clarendon, Dr. Plot, &c. I will take care to procure you by the time these are dispatch'd. As for the graving, so the contours and outlines be well design'd, I am not solicitous for the hatching (as they call it), since we have laudable examples of the other in Gruter, Spanheim, & other excellent authors. Mr White, if he have leisure, will be your best man; & for the volume, I should think a thin moderat folio, with a faire

[1] *Numismata*, To the Reader.

[2] Wheatley, III, 478–9.

letter, most desireable. As for the title, epistle, & preface, I shall provide you in good time, & as I see cause; onely I pray take special care of the insertions & paragraphs which I have marked [: when all this is finish'd, I purpose a very accurate index. This being all at present, I wish you good successe, and am

Y^r &c.

Wotton, 2 *June*, 1694.

On 16 June 1696 he wrote[1] to his friend Sidney Godolphin, one of the Commissioners of the Treasury, a letter concerning the monetary system and trade of the country, and sent him the seventh chapter of *Numismata*, dealing with mints and coinage. The long delay in completing the work he attributed to the time taken in engraving the numerous plates of medals which were to decorate and illustrate the text. Some of his difficulties were illustrated by a letter written by Charles Hatton to Viscount Hatton on 7 August 1697:

Mr. Evelyn is putting forth a book in folio of English medallions, in immitation of the Historie Metallique of Holland. But he can heare of soe few that, instead of medailles with the inscriptions and reverses, he is forced to make up his booke with severall discourses relating to that subject. His book hath been long in the press and is not yet ready to come out, the medailles being not yet all engraven. If your Lo^ppe hath any or cou'd procure any relating to any eminent English person or any actions done in England, if your Lo^ppe would please either to send a design of the meddaille or lend the meddail to be here designed, it shou'd carefully be restored with thankes. Mr. Evvelyn desired me and all his acquaintances here in London to try what medailes they can procure to illustrate his worke.[2]

At last, at the end of the year 1697, *Numismata* was published. But it brought no satisfaction to its author, for he was deeply mortified to find that, in spite of all the trouble he had taken, it was full of errors amd misprints. He was so angry that he wished to complain of this even in his preface, but was dissuaded therefrom by Dr Bentley[3] and by Tooke, who pointed out truly enough that to draw attention to the book's defects in the preface would scarcely help to sell it. He therefore contented himself with inserting an immense list of *Emendanda* after the contents list. His own copy of the book, in his cipher binding, is extant,[4] and

1 See the letter in Wheatley, IV, 3.

2 *Correspondence of the Family of Hatton 1601–1704*, ed. E. Maunde Thompson (Camden Society 1878, n.s. XXIII, p. 228).

3 *Correspondence of Richard Bentley, D.D.*, 1842, vol. I, p. 153. Bentley had, in fact, undertaken to 'reform' the proofs, but, it seems, attended to no more than the first two sheets (Hiscock, pp. 177–8). Evelyn also sent a copy to William Wotton with an apologetic letter (Hiscock, p. 198).

4 Britwell Court library, Sotheby's, 31 March 1925, lot 278 (£80).

contains three pages of his MS corrections and additions at the end. He also vented some of his feelings in an outspoken letter[1] written on the fly-leaf of a copy[2] sent to Sir Hans Sloane, expressing himself as follows:

Worthy S^r^,

I no sooner send you this Book, with the *Errata* (of which I im̄ediately gave an Account in the *philos. Transactions*)[3] but finding it too late to Recall what had ben dispers'd; you will easily guesse how sensibly I was Afflicted; not onely to see how the *printer* had Abus'd me (by leaving out many the most material *Corrections*) but how ill I was dealt with by those who in my Absence all the Sum̄er (in *Surry*, many Miles from London) undertook to supervise and repaire my failings: I do not by this go about to Extenuate my Mistakes & Follys, (which are in̄umerable) But deplore my Rashnesse and presumption, in not Consulting Mr Charleton, and such other Learned Friends, as out of Tenderness to my Reputation, would either have dehorted me from publishing it at all; or Incourag'd me with their kind Assistance. But, as I sayd, tis now too late; the Wounds so deepe, & so many; that the Crazy Vessel must never hope to make a more fortunate Adventur, unless Repair'd by such Masterly hands as yours: You would therefore Infinitely Oblige me with your free Animadversions: I should (I assure you) most thankfully Receive & Acknowledge them, as becomes

S^r^,

Your most humble &
most obliged servant
J. Evelyn

I have endeavor'd to reforme some of the grosser *errata*; but the paper is so bad, that I should but have multiply'd faults instead of mending them. I have (in the mean time also) provided some considerable Materials for my owne satisfaction and to leave it with some Improvements but without any intention of publishing them, after this miscarriage.

To Sir Hans Sloane Bar^t^. [in another hand]

In at least one copy[4] of the book formerly in the Evelyn library vignette no. lxxix was printed twice, appearing correctly on p. 145 and again in place of no. lxxxi on p. 146; the correct print has been pasted over the duplicate.

Numismata is a handsome folio, and the engravings of medals are excellently done. But a pleasant appearance cannot compensate in a work of this kind for faulty scholarship and typography. It has, in consequence, never been held in

[1] First printed in Beloe's *Anecdotes of Literature*, 1807, vol. II, pp. 430–1.

[2] Now in the British Museum.

[3] This account does not seem to have been published; there is, however, a long notice of the book in *Phil. Trans.* vol. XX (1699), pp. 57–61, which does not mention the *errata*.

[4] In a catalogue of Wm. Dawson & Sons some years ago.

esteem, and Horace Walpole even criticized the index, complaining that in the twenty-six entries under the letter N he found the following, 'which I believe would puzzle any man to guess how they found their way into a discourse on medals':

Nails of the Cross	Negros
Narcotics	Neocoros
Nations, whence of such various dispositions	Nightingale
	Noah
Natural and artificial curiosities	Noses
Navigation	Nurses, of what importance their temper and dispositions
Neapolitans, their character	

It is true enough that the book is garrulous and digressive. One thing leads to another, and it would not be easy to reconstruct the passages by which Evelyn arrived at reminiscences of what Queen Henrietta Maria said to him about her spaniels and why, in Evelyn's opinion, the creatures had unsavoury breath.[1]

Ch. viii, in which Evelyn gives a list of all those persons who he thinks should be honoured by a portrait medal, is of some interest.

Evelyn dedicated his book to Francis, the only son of Lord Godolphin, in a Latin address dated from Wotton 7 November 1697. Francis was still under twenty but, if his attainments were all that Evelyn fondly supposed (he had superintended the boy's education at Eton and King's), it is to be feared that he cannot have been blind to his aged tutor's failure.

No part of *Numismata* has ever been reprinted.

[1] *Numismata*, p. 295.

104 NUMISMATA [W. E 3505] f° 1697

Title in red and black, within double lines: Numismata. [*rule*] A Discourse of Medals, Antient and Modern. Together with some Account of Heads and Effigies of Illustrious, and Famous Persons, in Sculps, and Taille-douce, of Whom we have no Medals extant; and Of the Use to be derived from them. To which is added A Digression concerning Physiognomy. [*rule*] By J. Evelyn, Esq; S.R.S. [*rule*]

Effigies hominum non solebant exprimi, nisi aliquâ illustri causâ perpetuitatem merentium.
Plin. Nat. Hist. Lib. XXXIV. Cap. 4.

[*rule*] London, Printed for Benj. Tooke at the Middle-Temple-Gate, in Fleetstreet. MDCXCVII.

Collation: A–Z⁴ Aa–Xx⁴ Yy² Zz² Aaa²; 182 leaves.

Contents: A1 title; A2*a–b* *Dedicatio Francisco Godolphin*; A3a–*b* *To the Reader*; A4*a* *Table of the Chapters*; A4*b* *Emendanda*, 44 lines; B1*a*–Xx3*b* (pp. 1–342) text; Xx4*a*–Aaa2*b* *Index.*

Illustrations: 97 engraved vignettes of medals in the text. These are numbered up to XCIX in the margins, but the numerals do not correspond to the actual numbers owing to various omissions and insertions.

Copies: BLO (3, Lister.E.16; Douce.E.subtus 1; Arch. Numm. xl.23), BM (602.i.1),[1] CCE,[2] K, ULC (R.8.43); CH, CLC, HCL.

[1] Presentation copy to Sir Hans Sloane.
[2] Presentation copy to the Earl of Clarendon.

ACETARIA

1699

PREFACE

IN 1699 Evelyn had been for forty years amassing notes for a real *magnum opus* beside which any of his published works would have faded into insignificance. This was his *Elysium Britannicum*, a book intended to describe and show 'the *Amplitude* and *Extent* of that Part of *Georgicks*, which belongs to *Horticulture*'.[1] Already in November 1669 it had been announced in the *Philosophical Transactions* as preparing for the press,[2] but thirty years later the immense folios containing a thousand pages of notes[3] had not been reduced to any sort of order, and their author, then in his eightieth year, had abandoned all hope of completing his task. He had compiled, however, at some date, perhaps about 1659, a brief synopsis of his work, which he divided into three Books and forty-two Chapters and entitled 'The Plan of a Royal Garden'. This was printed on a single folio leaf and headed *Elysium Britannicum*. A copy was found by Upcott among the Evelyn papers, and is now in the BM (Add. MS. 15950, f. 143). Book II, chapter 3, of this *opus* is headed 'Of Sallets', and this chapter he decided with many misgivings to print separately, thus giving to the world his last book, called *Acetaria, A Discourse of Sallets*. The project had been in his mind for twenty years, and had been discussed in a letter to Dr Beale dated 11 July 1679, but the possibility of completing his whole scheme had deterred him.[4] He prided himself on his knowledge of the subject, as Charles Hatton wrote to Viscount Hatton on 28 September 1699: 'Mr. Evelyn hath been with me and tells me he hath a new book of sallating just finish'd at the press, and will be publish'd next week. He setts up for a great virtuoso in sallating. In his booke he takes notice that juice of oranges in salets is preferable to vinegar. But the oranges must be cut with a silver knife, for a steele blade will give a tincture of steel to the juice.'[5]

The dedication to John Lord Somers of Evesham, Lord High Chancellor of

[1] *Acetaria*, a8*a*.

[2] *Phil. Trans.* vol. IV, no. 53, 15 Nov. 1669, p. 1073.

[3] *Acetaria*, a5*a*. In the Evelyn library at Christ Church is a MS volume representing this work, but it now contains only about 300 leaves with many slips added. Portions were probably removed by Upcott. One specimen 2½ pp. 4°, headed 'A catalogue for Tryals', was sold at Sotheby's, 3 May 1967, lot 76, inserted in a copy of the *Memoirs*, 1819, with a statement by Upcott that it had belonged to the *Elysium Britannicum*.

[4] Wheatley, III, 190.

[5] *Correspondence of the Family of Hatton 1601–1704*, ed. E. Maunde Thompson (Camden Society, 1878, n.s. XXIII, p. 242).

England and President of the Royal Society, is written with even more than his usual long-winded solemnity, so that he feels constrained to explain what his meaning is, 'to usher in a *Trifle*, with so much Magnificence, and end at last in a fine Receipt for the *Dressing* of a *Sallet*, with an Handful of *Pot-Herbs*'.[1] He has to clear himself of the suspicion of being unable to mind 'anything serious besides the gratifying a sensual Appetite with a Voluptuary *Apician* Art', and asserts that when 'a well drest and excellent *Sallet*' is before him, he is yet a very moderate Eater of it; so that, as to this *Book-luxury*, he can affirm with the Poet, *Lasciva pagina, vita proba*.[2] It is evident, in fact, that in writing the dedication for *Acetaria* he imagined himself composing it for his complete *Elysium*, and so was shaken somewhat off his balance. The author records in his Diary under the date 22 October 1699, 'I presented my *Acetaria* dedicated to my Lord Chancellor, who return'd me thanks by a most extraordinary civil letter.'[3]

Acetaria is a small octavo containing, after the Dedication and Preface, 'The Plan of a Royal Garden'. The text describes 73 sorts of pot-herbs, and then enters on a discussion of the philosophy of salads, including an account of their medicinal properties. Directions how to gather, prepare and dress them are followed by a seasonal table of salad-plants, compiled in response to an anonymous enquiry made many years before by the great Robert Boyle in the *Philosophical Transactions*.[4] There follows a discourse of salads and their eaters worthy almost of Sir Thomas Browne in its eloquence and learning. Numerous recipes for preparing, mixing, and dressing salads are given in an appendix, and there is an unusually full index.

Acetaria is by no means the least attractive or interesting of Evelyn's books, and it is surprising that, except in the *Miscellaneous Writings*, 1825, pp. 721–812, it has been reprinted only once since the eighteenth century. In 1706 the unsold sheets were provided with a new title-page which describes them as 'The Second Edition', but this was only for purposes of sale. Evelyn himself was clearly pleased with his book, for there is evidence that he thought it worth giving to a number of his friends among the nobility. Ordinary copies are printed, except for sheets B and C, on thin paper of very poor quality which has turned brown all through the book in every copy I have seen. There was, however, a special edition printed entirely on good paper, which has remained white. These copies are in pretty gold-tooled bindings of calf or morocco, and the pages are rubricated

[1] *Acetaria*, A4*b*. [2] *Acetaria*, a1*a*. [3] de Beer, v, 361.
[4] *Phil. Trans.* vol. III, no. 40, 19 Oct. 1668, pp. 799–801.

throughout. Their uniformity shows that they were bound to Evelyn's order in the same shop at the same time. Two of these special copies now in my library belonged to Hugh Earl of Loudoun and Charles Lord Halifax. A third, now in the Morgan Library, New York, belonged later to Philip Lord Hardwicke, and a fourth was formerly in the library at Badminton. None of these has a presentation inscription, though the Badminton copy still contains a letter from Evelyn addressed to the Duchess of Beaufort, in which the expression of polite nothings is brought to a fine point of meaninglessness:

For HER GRACE THE DUTCHESSE OF BEAUFORT

Madame

Receiving from a Young Oxford Scholar (my Grandson) an Account of his Late Excursion, to see what might be most worthy his Observation in those parts of the Country where he has ben this Sũmer; He is Return'd with such a Description of *Badminton*, as can agree with none save to those whose noble Seate it is: But it is (after all the Magnificence, becoming the Dignity of so Illustrious a Family, of which your Grace's personal Vertues, & rare Oeconomy (which sets the Lustre on all that's shining there) he superadds, that, of making the Garden no meane part of your Graces Care, as well as of your Diversion:

This is that Madame, which has perswaded me, your grace will not reject this meane Oblation, tho' but of an hand full of Herbs; Since tho' they are not the Birth of the more glorious partners (sweets onely to be gather'd by your Graces faire hands) They are yet the products of the same greate Author, and have their peculiar Vertues and Uses too; which has made them to be cherish't, & Cultivated by the greatest Princes, and now come to Offer what they have of Estimable, to Madame,

Your Graces
Most Obedient, most
humble most devoted Servant

J. EVELYN

I have a note of another copy with a presentation inscription to the Earl of Chesterfield (1633–1713).[1]

An ordinary copy was given by the author to Sir Christopher Wren, being inscribed on the fly-leaf *Sr Chr: Wren: J. E.* and having at the end 13 lines of additional recipes in the author's hand in reference to the cooking of cucumbers and carrots.[2] Another copy has a presentation inscription with the date 21 October 1699; there is no recipient's name, however, though Evelyn's pentacle sign is found at the top of the last leaf.[3]

[1] Bookseller's catalogue, Levinson, California, April 1956.

[2] Dowden sale, Hodgson's, 16 Dec. 1913, lot 114.

[3] Sotheby's, Paulin Martin library, 7 April 1930, lot 34.

Acetaria was first reprinted in folio with the fourth edition of *Silva*, 1706, and this, containing some alterations and additions by the author, is to be regarded as the final text. It was again printed with the fifth edition of *Silva*, 1729.

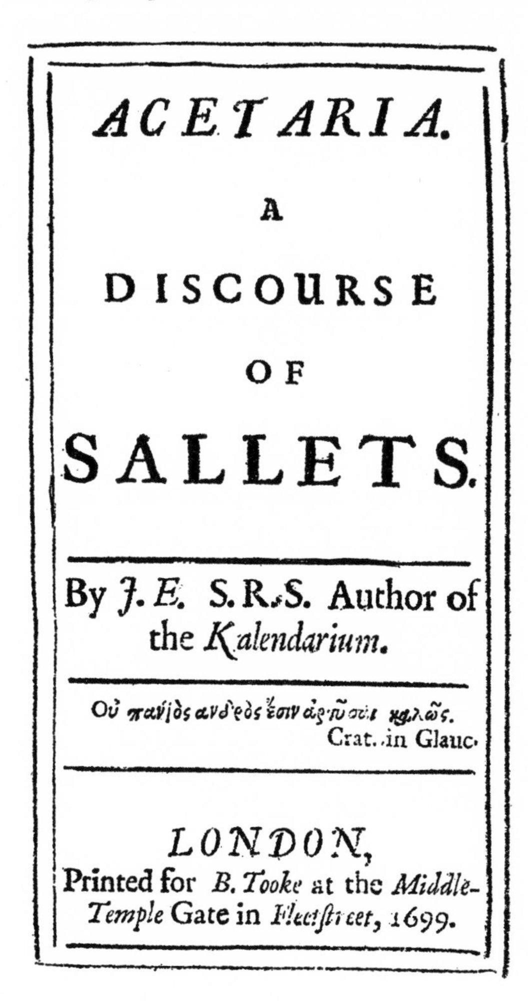

ACETARIA.

A

DISCOURSE

OF

SALLETS.

By *J. E.* S.R.S. Author of the *Kalendarium.*

Οὐ παντὸς ἀνδρὸς ἐστιν ἀρτῦσαι καλῶς.
Crat. in Glauc.

LONDON,
Printed for *B. Tooke* at the *Middle-Temple* Gate in *Fleetstreet*, 1699.

Title-page of no. 105

105 ACETARIA [first edition. W. E 3480] 8° 1699

Title within double lines: Acetaria. A Discourse of Sallets. [*rule*] By J. E. S.R.S. Author of the *Kalendarium*. [*rule*]

Οὐ παντὸς ανδρὸς ἔστιν ἀρτῦσαι καλῶς.
Crat. in Glauc. [*rule*]

London, Printed for B. Tooke at the Middle-Temple Gate in Fleetstreet, 1699.

Collation: π² A⁸ a⁸ b⁴ B–R⁸; 150 leaves, 1 folding leaf inserted.

Contents: π1 blank; π2 title; A1*a*–a2*b* *The Dedication* to Lord Somers of Evesham; a3*a*–a7*b* *The Preface*; a8*a*–b3*b* *The Plan of a Royal Garden*; b4*a* *Errata*, 36 lines; b4*b* blank; B1*a*–N8*b* (pp. 1–192) text; O1*a*–R2*a* *Appendix*; R2*b*–R8*b* *The Table*. Folding leaf, with classification of vegetables by months, inserted between H6 and H7 to face p. 108.

Note: In the ordinary issue sheets B and C are printed on a thicker and better paper than the rest of the book. In the special issue the whole book is on the better paper. In many copies the *errata* leaf has been transferred to the end of the book.

Copies: (*a*) Special issue: K (2); CLC, HCL.[1] (*b*) Ordinary issue: BLO (Douce.E.58), BM (1038.b.11), K, ULC (Syn.8.69.26), VAF; CH, CLC, HCL.

106 ACETARIA [second issue] 8° 1706

Title, within double lines: Acetaria. A Discourse of Sallets. [*rule*] The Second Edition. [*rule*]...[etc. as in no. 105].
London: Printed for B. Tooke at the Middle-Temple Gate in Fleetstreet, 1706.

Collation, contents: As in no. 105.

Note: The sheets of no. 105 with cancel title-page.

Copies: K, VAF; CLC.

107 ACETARIA [second edition] f° 1706

Sub-title: Acetaria. [*rule*] A Discourse of Sallets. [*rule*] By J. E. S.R.S. Author of the Kalendarium. [*rule*] The Second Edition much Enlarged. [*Greek quotation between rules*] [*type ornaments*].
London: Printed for Rob. Scot, Ric. Chiswell, George Sawbridge, and Benj. Tooke. MDCCVI.

[1] From the Badminton library with a letter to the Duchess of Beaufort. Sold at Sotheby's, 25 July 1932, lot 48.

Collation: Rrrr4 Ssss–Zzzz^4 Aaaaa–Ddddd^4 Eeeee1; 42 leaves.

Contents: Rrrr4 sub-title; Ssss1*a*–3*b* (pp. 133–8) dedication; Ssss4*a*–*b* (pp. 139–40) *The Preface*; Tttt1*a*–2*a* (pp. 141–3) *The Plan of a Royal Garden*; Tttt2*b*–Eeeee1*a* (pp. 144–213) text; Eeeee1*b* blank.

Note: Appended with other works to the fourth edition of *Silva*, 1706 (see no. 43). There is a general index to all the appended works at the end of the volume. This, the first reprint of *Acetaria*, contains some alterations and additions as advertised on the title-page.

108 ACETARIA [third edition] f° [1729]

Sub-title: [*ornamental band*] Acetaria. [*rule*] A Discourse of Sallets. [*rule*] By J.E. S.R.S. Author of the Kalendarium. [*Greek quotation between rules*] [*ornamental band*]

Collation: 5X2 5Y–5Z^2 6Z–6P^2 6Q1; 36 leaves.

Contents: 5X2 sub-title; 5Y1*a*–5Y2*b* (pp. 113–16) dedication; 5Z1*a*–*b* (pp. 117–18) *The Preface*; 5Z2*a*–*b* (pp. 119–20) *The Plan of a Royal Garden*; 6A1*a*–6Q1*a* (pp. 121–81) text; 6Q1*b* blank.

Note: Appended with other works to the fifth edition of *Silva*, 1729 (see no. 44). The sub-title has no date or imprint. There is a general index to all the appended works at the end of the volume.

108a ACETARIA 8° 1937

Acetaria: A Discourse of Sallets, by John Evelyn, Esq.... Brooklyn [N.Y.] published by the Women's auxiliary, Brooklyn Botanic Garden, 1937. 22 cm. pp. 21,1,148.

Note: This is a reprint of the first edition with correction of some obvious typographical errors and of those noted in the *errata*. One thousand copies were issued in cloth binding with facsimile of the original title-page and a portrait.

WORKS PUBLISHED POSTHUMOUSLY

THE LIFE OF

MRS. GODOLPHIN

BY JOHN EVELYN

OF WOOTTON ESQ.

Now firſt publiſhed and

Edited by SAMUEL Lord Biſhop of OXFORD

Chancellor of the Moſt Noble

Order of the Garter

LONDON

WILLIAM PICKERING

1847

Title-page of no. 109

PREFACE

EVELYN'S liking for making everything into a book has already been described, and the titles of a number of his bound MSS have been mentioned (see p. 21). During the eighteenth century no one appears to have taken any serious interest in those of his literary remains that were preserved at Wotton House or elsewhere. Even after the publication of the Diary in 1818 almost another thirty years passed before it was thought worth while to print one of his most charming and characteristic productions, *The Life of Mrs. Godolphin*, published by William Pickering in 1847. This was followed soon afterwards in 1850 by a treatise of less attraction, *The History of Religion*. Nothing more of Evelyn's was printed until 1926, when I was allowed to transcribe and edit *Memoires for my Grandson*, and this was followed in 1932 by the *Directions for the Gardiner at Says-Court*. Finally in 1936 Dr Frere performed the same office for the book of devotions which Evelyn composed for his private use during the Commonwealth. A number of other MSS remain unpublished, and it may be doubted whether any of them will ever be considered worthy of being printed.

109 The Life of Mrs. Godolphin By John Evelyn of Wootton Esq. Now first published and Edited by Samuel Lord Bishop of Oxford Chancellor of the Most Noble Order of the Garter [*Pickering's device*] London William Pickering 1847

17 cm, pp. [ii], xviii, 265, [1]. Frontispiece, portrait of Mrs Godolphin engraved by W. Humphreys from a painting at Wotton. Issued in brown cloth, with paper label on the spine.

110 The Life of Mrs. Godolphin...[second edition] London William Pickering 1848

17 cm, pp. [ii], xviii, 291, [1]. Frontispiece and binding as before.

111 The Life of Mrs. Godolphin...[Third edition] London William Pickering 1848

17 cm, collation etc. as before.

112 The Life of Mrs. Godolphin...[Third edition] London Longman, Green, Longman, Roberts, & Green 1864

The sheets of no. 111 with cancel title. Issued in blue cloth.

113 The Life of Mrs. Godolphin...New edition Edited by Edward William Harcourt of Nuneham Park Oxon. Esq. London: Sampson Low, Marston, Searle, & Rivington. 1888.

18·5 cm, pp. xxiv, 287, [9]. Frontispiece as before. Issued in smooth red cloth.

114 The Life of Margaret Godolphin by John Evelyn Alexander Moring Ltd The de la More Press 32 George St. Hanover Square London W 1904 [The King's Classics]

15 cml ppi xxxix, [i], 169, [3]. Frontispiece as before. Issued in paper boards with paper label on the spine.

114*a* The Life of Mrs. Godolphin By John Evelyn Edited by Harriet Sampson Oxford University Press London New York Toronto MCMXXXIX

18·5 cm, pp. xxxiii, [i], 282, [2]. With Commentary, four Appendixes, Biographical Supplement, and four illustrations. Issued in dark blue cloth.

115 The Saintly Life of Mrs. Margaret Godolphin abridged by permission from 'The Life of Mrs. Godolphin by John Evelyn of Wootton Esq. Edited by Samuel Lord Bishop of Oxford' [*Pickering's device*] London William Pickering 1853

11 cm, pp. 32. Issued in printed paper wrappers.

116 The Saintly Life of Mrs. Margaret Godolphin, by John J. Daniell,...compiled from 'The Life of Mrs. Godolphin, by John Evelyn, edited by Samuel, Lord Bishop of Oxford', And from other Sources. Second Edition. Oxford and London: John Henry and James Parker. 1864.

15 cm, pp. [iv], 57, [1], 2.

Note: Evelyn's friendship with Mrs Margaret Godolphin occupied an important place in his life from 16 October 1672, when their relationship was cemented by a pretty ceremony, until her death on 9 September 1678. She was the daughter of Colonel Thomas Blagge, Groom of the Bedchamber to Charles I, and was born in August 1652. She became Maid of Honour to Queen Catherine, and married Sidney Godolphin on 16 May 1675. Her son, Francis, was born on 3 September 1678, and she died of puerperal fever 6 days later. Evelyn first mentions Margaret Blagge in his Diary under the date 30 June 1669.[1]

Their friendship ripened during the next three years and by 31 July 1672 Evelyn refers to her as 'one I did infinitely esteem for her many and extraordinary virtues'.[2] There are many references to her thereafter in the Diary, from which it is clear that her piety, wit, modesty and beauty made a very deep impression on Evelyn's mind. A small volume of *Privat Devotions and Offices*, which Evelyn had composed for his own use and had caused to be written out by Richard Hoare in 1650, he afterwards gave to Mrs Godolphin, who added some notes of her own.[3] Probably one or two other manuscripts extant in the Evelyn Collection, such as one entitled *Oeconomis to a married friend*, were also composed for the use of Mrs Godolphin.[4] Evelyn was heartbroken at her premature death,[5] and later accepted as a pious duty the suggestion made by his friend Lady Sylvius that he should write an account of her life. The actual date at which he wrote his *Life* is uncertain, though it was probably written about 1678 and revised ten years later. A manuscript remained in Evelyn's

[1] de Beer, III, 530. [2] *Ibid.* 622.

[3] See a description in Wheatley, I, cxxii–cxxiv. The volume was sold at Puttick and Simpson's, 7 March 1873, for £36. 10*s*.

[4] In the Houghton Library, Harvard University, are several sheets from this MS, which had been loaned to Samuel Pepys and is headed: 'April 13th 1675. A copie of Mrs Evelyn's Instructions to Mrs. Blague for setting up and keeping house.' They are written in Richard Hoare's hand.

[5] de Beer, IV, 148.

To the Rt Hon:ble the Lord Godolphin, Lord High=Treasurer of England.

My Lord,

I neede no Kalendar to Mind me of the Approch of this Anniversary; The Remembrance of our this-Days mutual Losse (tho' after so many yeares Revolution) must never cease to leave the ~~the~~ most Indelible Impressions in Me I am sure; and I am perswaded, in your Lo.p also; which neither the Sublimity of your Station, nor the nature of your High Office (the Highest this World can Advance a Subject to) will be altogether able to put out of your Thoughts: And you have taken Care it should not, by preventing, & taking off the Excuses I us'd to make for Troubling you with my Letters upon this Occasion, by one of yours; wherein you tell me, "That as oft as I make them, you will as often "Repeate it, That Nothing in the World, gives you "so much Satisfaction, as the Hearing from me an "hundred things of the Vertue & perfections of that "Blessed-Creature who is gon before us; The Contem-"plation of whose goodnesse & felicity, is the greatest "Comfort you are Capable of.

'Tis the Continuance of that my Ld. and that you may never Forget her (and the Blessings you Injoy by Her) which induces me to offer you this little Present, in this Manner, and no sonner. Besids an Obligation I bound my-selfe in; That I would write the Life of that Saint: And the prohibition your Lp. layd on me; That I would not do it Hastily. Both which I have observ'd, it being now about sixteene yeares, since I sent this Copy to my Lady Sylvius, who Assures me she never Communicated it to any Creature living, save to your Lp's Sisters.

What it was I wrot to y Lp concerning this Matter, indeed I know not; But, what you were pleas'd to write back to me about it, I must never forget as it remaines a Record in the CHARTER (that MAGNA

The Life of Mr[is] Godolphin.

Madame,

I am not unmindfull of what y[r] Lady[p] suggested to me concerning that Blessed Saint now in Heaven: Do you believe I need be Invited to preserve y[e] Memory of One whose Image is so lively imprinted in my Heart? But you would have a more permanent Record of her perfections, and so would I; not onely for the Veneration we beare her precious Ashes but for the Good of those who emulous of Virtue, would persue the worthyst Instance of it in this, or perhaps, in many Ages before it. 'Tis Certaine the Materials I have by me, would furnish one who were Master of a Style becoming so admirable a Subject, and wish'd I have a thousand times, y[e] person in the World, who knew her best (and best she Loved) would give us the Picture of a Lady, his Pencil could best delineate. If such an Artist as He is, decline the Undertaking, for feare that even with all his Skill, he should not reach ye Original; how far short am I like to fall, who cannot pretend to the meanest of his Talents! But, as Indignation (they say) sometimes Creates a Poëme, where is no natural Disposition in the Composer; so a mighty Obligation, a holy Friendship, & y[r] L[p] Comands, irresistibly prevaile with me, rather to hazard the Censure of my Imperfections, than to disobey you, or suffer those precious Memoires to be lost, which deserve Consecration to Eternity. 'Tis then the least, & last Service I can Expresse to a dying Friend, for whom I should not have refused even my-Selfe to die.

But Madam, you will not Expect I should be so Exactly particular in the minuter Circumstances of her Birth, & what pass'd in her Infancy, and more tender Yeares. Because, tho' I have sometimes told her pleasantly, I would Write her Life (when God knows) little thought of Surviving her, whom often I have Wish'd, might be at the Closing of mine owne Eyes) I had not the honour of being Acquainted with her, 'til about the last seaven Yeares of her Life. I say, the little Expectation I had of Erecting to her a Monument of this Nature, made me not so Industrious to Informe my Selfe, of what pass'd in her minority as I should have ben: For I am perswaded, that (from the very Beginning) something of Extraordinary Remarkable was all-along Conspicuous in her, Nor was it possible, that my Admiration of her Virtues (when I came to know her) should not have prompted me to Inquire concerning the particulars of her Life before I knew her: Something I learned Casualy Conversing with her; divers things from the Keepers of ...

cated

possession and he referred to it in his list of 'things I would write out fair and reform if I had the leisure'—an intention which was carried out, for there are two MS versions in existence. One was kept in the family archives and so came into the possession of Evelyn's great-great-grandson, Edward Harcourt, Archbishop of York, by whom it was entrusted to Samuel Wilberforce, Bishop of Oxford, for publication. It was accurately transcribed and edited by the Bishop, and was printed for William Pickering at the Chiswick Press in 1847. It was at that time believed to be in Evelyn's hand. After passing through three editions the text was re-edited by the Archbishop's grandson, Edward William Harcourt, who seems never to have seen the original MS, since it was not returned by the Bishop of Oxford. It was then printed for Sampson Low in 1888 and again for the King's Classics in 1904. The MS came to light again as the property of Dr Octavia Wilberforce, the Bishop's granddaughter, who sent it to Sotheby's for sale on 8 May 1956. It then proved be in the hand of a copyist, bound in contemporary black morocco gilt, gilt edges, 19·8 × 15 cm, with book labels of Martha and Ann Venables Vernon (lot 422 in Sotheby's catalogue). The volume has 90 leaves, of which 32 are blank.

It was a different MS, and certainly in Evelyn's hand, which was in the Morrison collection of autographs and was acquired by the late Howard C. Levis in 1919. In 1924 this was bought by Dr A. S. W. Rosenbach of Philadelphia. Both manuscripts are now in the Richmond Collection in the Houghton Library, Harvard University. Comparison of the second text with the first shows that they differ throughout in minor details, and that the Morrison MS contains much additional matter. At the beginning is a letter from Evelyn addressed to Lord Godolphin, Lord High Treasurer of England (see pp. 248–9). Godolphin did not attain this office until 1702, so that the gift-letter must have been written after this date, near the end of Evelyn's life. He states in it that it is 'now about sixteene yeares, since I sent this *Copy* to my *Lady Sylvius*', having been enjoined by Godolphin not to 'do it *Hastily*'. The revision, represented by this MS, may therefore be dated about 1688, and the handwriting is so clear that it cannot have been written much later (see facsimile). Evelyn has inserted after his letter a copy of one from Godolphin to him dated 22 September 1678, containing the injunction not to proceed too hastily, and this may indicate the approximate date of the first draft. The Morrison MS is written in a volume of 65 leaves of which 17 are blank. It is in an elaborately tooled red morocco binding, 19 × 13·5 cm, with Evelyn's cipher in the centre of the design (see reproduction, Plate 14). This text, which is obviously to be preferred to the one previously printed, was the source of a new edition edited by Miss Harriet Sampson of New York in 1939. The frontispiece used in all the previous editions of the *Life* was made from a portrait of Mrs Godolphin formerly at Wotton House, stated to be the work of Gaspar Netscher.

PLATE 14

Binding for Evelyn's *Life of Mrs. Godolphin*

117 The History of Religion. A Rational Account of The True Religion. By John Evelyn,...now first published, by permission of W. J. Evelyn, Esq. M.P., from the original MS. in the Library at Wotton. [*quotations*] Edited, with notes, by the Reverend R. M. Evanson, B. A., Rector of Lansoy, Monmouthshire. In two Volumes. Vol. I. [II.] London: Henry Colburn, Publisher, Great Marlborough Street. 1850.

20 cm, Vol. I, pp. xxix, [i], 443, [1], Vol. II, pp. v, [i], 386. Issued in brown embossed cloth with yellow end-papers.

118 The History of Religion...By John Evelyn,...Edited, with notes, By the Revd R. M. Evanson, B.A. In Two Volumes. Vol. I. [II.] London: Henry G. Bohn, York Street, Covent Garden. 1859.

As in no. 117, with new title-pages and a frontispiece (Christ blessing the bread) added to Vol. I. Issued in brown cloth, with yellow end-papers.

Note: The MS of this book was preserved at Wotton, and was included by Evelyn in the list of his projected works in *Memoires for my Grandson* (p. 64). He called it 'a larger Booke intitled the History of Religion, being a Congestion, hastily put into Chapters many years since, full of Errors'. According to the title-page of the MS it was begun in 1657, and a note shows that it was revised at some later date, probably about 1683. It consists of a rough draft, a second copy, and marginal notes added during revision. The publication of a new edition of the Diary by Colburn in 1850-2 suggested the simultaneous issue, in modernized spelling, of this rather heavy treatise. At the date of its publication Evelyn's 'congestion' may have had some interest, as it is stated[1] to anticipate 'all the arguments of Butler, Warburton, Waterland, Paley, and Magee'. At the present time its chief attraction lies in the author's brief preface, in which he explains how his observation of the decay of religion, first under the Commonwealth, and later following the Restoration, led him to examine for himself the grounds upon which his religious beliefs were founded.

119 Memoires for My Grand-son by John Evelyn ¶ Transcribed and furnished with a Preface and Notes by Geoffrey Keynes 1926 Printed at Oxford for the Nonesuch Press, 16 Great James Street Bloomsbury

15 cm, pp. xii, [ii], 104, [4], the last leaf blank. Issued in limp parchment in marbled-paper slip-case.

Note: Evelyn wrote these brief *Memoires for my Grandson* in 1740 at the age of 84. His son John had died in 1699, and his grandson was soon to inherit the family estate at Wotton. The *Memoires* give an intimate account of how a country gentleman should conduct his

[1] In a notice among the advertisements inserted at the end of vol. II.

Memoires

for my Grand-son

BY

JOHN EVELYN

¶ *Transcribed and furnished with a Preface and Notes by* GEOFFREY KEYNES

1926

Printed at *Oxford* for the *Nonesuch* Press, 16 Great *James* Street *Bloomsbury*

Title-page of no. 119

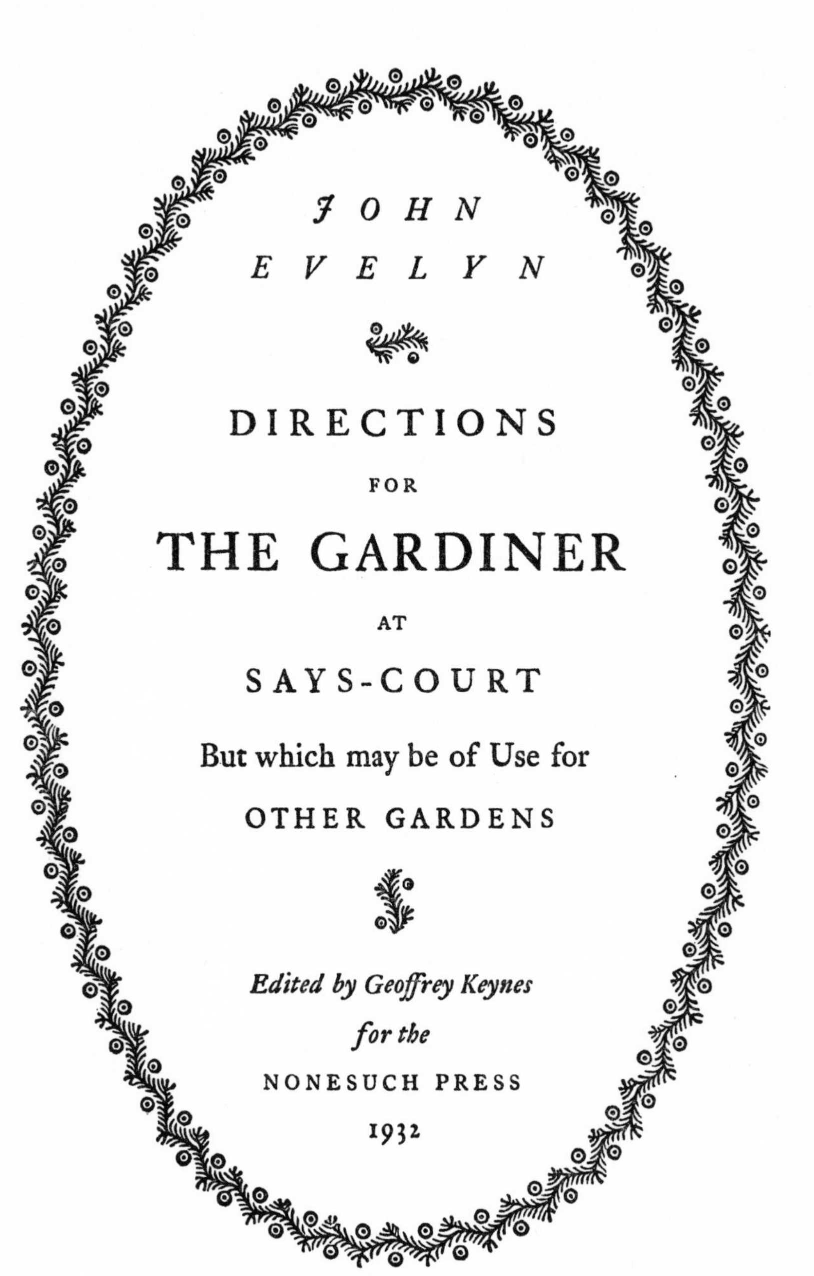
JOHN
EVELYN

DIRECTIONS
FOR
THE GARDINER
AT
SAYS-COURT
But which may be of Use for
OTHER GARDENS

Edited by Geoffrey Keynes
for the
NONESUCH PRESS
1932

Title-page of no. 120

life and affairs, and form the most personal record of Evelyn, other than the Diary, that we possess. A limited edition of 1250 numbered copies printed in Fell types on French handmade paper was issued by the Nonesuch Press.

120 John Evelyn Directions for the Gardiner at Says-Court But which may be of Use for other Gardens Edited by Geoffrey Keynes for the Nonesuch Press 1932

21 cm, pp. 109, [3]. Issued in marbled-paper boards and orange wrapper.

Note: The MS of this work, which was evidently not seriously intended for publication, was preserved in the library at Wotton House. It forms a pleasantly personal record of Evelyn's gardening activities. 800 numbered copies were printed at the Fanfare Press for sale in England and America. It was set in Janson types and free use was made of typographical ornaments. The paper of a grey tint was made by Van Gelder.

121 A Devotionarie Book of John Evelyn of Wotton, 1620–1706 Now first published with an introduction by Walter Frere, C.R., D.D. Lately Bishop of Truro London John Murray, Albemarle Street, W. [1936]

21·5 cm, pp. [ii], viii, 65, [5], the first leaf and the last two leaves blank. Frontispiece, collotype reproductions of two pp. of the MS. Issued in quarter cloth.

Note: This small book of devotions consists of three parts, (1) an introduction 'Of Frequent Communion', (2) 'Mental Communion', (3) 'Entertainements', that is, meditations with prayers. Evelyn explains at the end of the introduction the circumstances during the Commonwealth in which he composed the greater part of the book. Taking the Communion in public was forbidden, and Evelyn describes in his Diary how on Christmas Day 1657 he and others were arrested in Exeter Chapel while communicating.[1] He therefore composed these Devotions for his own use as a means of Mental Communion. He afterwards wrote them out in their present form, addressing all three parts to an unnamed friend. It may be surmised that this friend was Margaret Blagge, wife of Sidney Godolphin, who was on terms of close friendship with Evelyn from 1672 until her death in 1678 (see p. 247). The book was probably then returned to Evelyn, who gave it to his wife, her name, Mary Evelyn, being written in pencil on a fly-leaf. In 1780 the MS was in the possession of the Hon. Mrs F. Boscawen, granddaughter of John Evelyn's sister, Jane Glanville. Mrs Boscawen had married the grandson of Sidney Godolphin's sister, so that she had a double claim to possession of the MS. From Mrs Boscawen the book descended to the eighth Viscount Falmouth.

The MS is written in Evelyn's neatest hand on 66 leaves, duodecimo, bound in tooled red morocco with a clasp. The editor of this transcript provides a genealogical table showing the relationships of the successive owners of the book. It was published in December 1936 in an edition limited to 250 numbered copies.

[1] de Beer, III, 204.

121*a* John Evelyn London Revived Consideration for its rebuilding in 1666 Edited by E. S. de Beer *Omnia explorate, meliora retinete* Oxford At the Clarendon Press 1938

19·5 cm, pp. [viii], 61, [3]. With two plates from Evelyn's plans engraved by Vertue inserted and a reproduction of Hollar's Plan of London on the back endpaper. Issued in white parchment.

Note: A reprint of Evelyn's paper from the *Journal of the Royal Institute of British Architects*, 1919–20 (see p. 167 n. 3).

OCCASIONAL CONTRIBUTIONS

122 TUKE'S ADVENTURES OF FIVE HOURS [W. T 3230] 4° 1664

The Adventures of Five Hours. A Tragi-Comedy. The Second Edition... London, Printed for Henry Herringman,... 1664. A⁴ a⁴ B–O⁴ P².

A3*b*–A4*a*: 'Upon my Worthy Kinsman Colonel Tuke, His Incomparable Play', 28 lines of verse signed *J. Evelyn.*

Note: Col., later Sir, Samuel Tuke, a prominent royalist officer during the Civil War, was a friend of Evelyn and a relative of his wife, and is frequently mentioned in the Diary. His tragi-comedy, first published in 1663, enjoyed much contemporary favour and was greatly praised by Pepys. Evelyn's verses, with those by Abraham Cowley and several others, did not appear in the first edition, and were omitted from later editions. (First edition, fo. 1663; third edition, 4° 1671; fourth edition, 4° 1704.) The lines on a2*b*–a3*a*, 'To the Author, upon his finish'd Poem', signed *MElpomene*, are possibly by Evelyn's wife, Mary.[1]

123 BOYLE'S HISTORY OF COLD [W. B 3996] 8° 1665

New Experiments and Observations touching Cold, or, An Experimental History of Cold, begun...By the Honorable Robert Boyle,...London. Printed for John Crook,... MDCLXV. [Fulton, *Bibliography of Boyle*, no. 70]

Dd4–5, pp. 407–9. An account by Evelyn of 'snow pits in Italy', with an engraving showing their structure facing p. 407.

Note: Evelyn was closely associated with Boyle in the early days of the Royal Society and mentions him so frequently in the Diary that it is unnecessary to enlarge here upon their long friendship. A second edition of the *History of Cold* was published in 1683, 4°, Evelyn's contribution being on pp. 160–1.

123*a* HOOKE'S MICROGRAPHIA [W. H 2620] f° 1665

Micrographia: or some Physiological Descriptions of Minute Bodies made by Magnifying Glasses...By R. Hooke,...London, Printed by Jo. Martyn, and Ja. Allestry,... MDCLXV.

Dd4*b*–Ee1*a* (pp. 200–2). 'Obs. xlviii. Of the hunting Spider...Some other properties of this Spider, observ'd by the most accomplish'd Mr. Evelyn, in his travels in Italy, are most emphatically set forth in the History hereunto annexd, which he has pleased upon my desire to send me in writing.' A note by Evelyn follows.

[1] See *The Adventures of Five Hours*, edited by A. E. H. Swaen, Litt.D. (Amsterdam, 1927), p. 255.

124 PHILOSOPHICAL TRANSACTIONS 4° 1665–1684

Philosophical Transactions:

(1) Vol. I, no. 6, 6 Nov. 1665, pp. 99–100. 'An Advertisement of a way of making more lively Counterfeits of Nature in Wax, then are extant in Painting: And of a new kind of Maps in a low Relievo. Both Practised in France.'

(2) Vol. I, no. 22, 11 Feb. 1666, p. 398. 'Advertisement', requesting 'that if any Person have any Material Additions or Reformations' for a second edition of *Sylva*, he will communicate with Mr H. Oldenburgh, one of the Secretaries of the Royal Society.

(3) Vol. V, no. 60, 20 June 1670, pp. 1055–7. ' A Letter of John Evelyn Esq;...Concerning the Spanish Sembrador or New Engin for Ploughing, and Equal Sowing all sorts of Grain, and Harrowing, at once...together with a Description of the Contrivance, and Uses of this Engin, English't out of Spanish,...'

Reprinted in *Miscellaneous Writings*, 1825, pp. 621–2.

(4) Vol. XII, no. 158, 20 April 1684, pp. 559–63. 'An abstract of a Letter from the worshipful John Evelyn Esq; sent to one of the Secretaries of the R. Society concerning the dammage done to his Gardens by the preceding Winter,' dated Says Court, Deptford, 14 April 1684.

Reprinted in *Miscellaneous Writings*, 1825, pp. 692–6.

(5) Vol. XXIII, no. 280, July and August 1702, pp. 1177–1201. 'An Account of divers Schemes of Arteries and Veins, Dissected from Adult Human Bodies, and given to the Repository of the Royal Society by John Evelyn, Esq; F.R.S. To which are subjoyn'd a Description of the Extremities of those Vessels ...With some Chirurgical Observations, and Figures after the Life, by William Cowper, F.R.S.'

Cowper's description is preceded on pp. 1177–9 by a letter to him from Evelyn recounting the circumstances in which the anatomical tables were made at Padua by Veslingius and Leoncenas, and purchased for Evelyn by George Rogers for 150 scudi. At the end are two folding plates, signed *M. vdr Gucht Sculp.*, which include three figures drawn from Evelyn's tables. (For a full description of these and an account of the tables see no. 180.)

Note: Evelyn made other contributions to the Royal Society's proceedings that were not printed in the *Transactions*. Thus the Register Book of the Royal Society, vol. I, contains:

i. 'An Exact Account of the making of Marbled Paper By Mr Evelin' (no. 32).
ii. 'The Construction of the Rowling Press and manner how to work off the Plates. By Mr Evelins' (no. 39).

Copies of these are in the BM: Sloane MS 243, fols. 96–98 and 127b–141b.

125 SMITH'S ENGLAND'S IMPROVEMENT 4° 1670

England's Improvement Reviv'd: Digested into Six Books. By Captain John Smith. In the Savoy. Printed by Tho. Newcomb for the Author, An. Dom. 1670. A^4 a^4 A–Z^4 Aa–Ll^4.

A2*b*: 'The Report of Iohn Evelyn Esquire, by Order of the Royal Society, concerning the Following Discourse.' A brief letter dated *Sayes-Court, Feb.* 10. 68, and signed *J. Evelyn.*

Note: John Smith had studied trade and industry since 1633, and in 1661 published a work on the fishing and other industries of the Orkneys and Shetlands.[1] The present work on forestry and the use of waste land was completed in 1668, but not published until 1670 for lack of means. Evelyn in his commendatory letter refers to the second edition of his *Sylva*, then preparing, but observes that the two books may be published 'without the least prejudice to each other'. Smith's book was re-issued with a cancel title in 1673.

Copies: BM (1670, G.19287; 1673, 441.c.10), K (1670).

126 LANGFORD'S FRUIT-TREES [W. L 388] 8° 1681

Plain and Full Instructions To raise all sorts of Fruit-trees That prosper in England;...By T. Langford, Gent. London, Printed by J. M. for Rich. Chiswell...1681. A^8 a^2 B–K^8 L^6.

A5*a*: Commendatory letter addressed to *Mr Chiswel* and signed *J. Evelyn.*

Note: Langford is not mentioned in the *D.N.B.* or in Evelyn's Diary. Another edition of his book was published in 1696, and this was re-issued with a new title-page in 1699.

Copies: BM (966.a.9), CCE,[2] K (1681 and 1696).

127 HOUGHTON'S LETTERS 4° 1681

A Collection of Letters For the Improvement of Husbandry & Trade, By John Houghton, Fellow of the Royal Society. London, Printed for John Lawrence, ...1681. (Vol. 1.) A–Z^4 Aa^4.

[1] *The Trade & Fishing of Great-Britain Displayed: With a Description of the Islands of Orkney and Shetland. London, W. Godbid* [for] *N. Webb*, 1661.

[2] Presentation copy in red morocco gilt, rubricated.

Numb. 12, Tuesday, January 16, 1682/3, pp. 127–36: 'An Account of Bread, from the Learned John Evelyn, Esquire; Entituled, Panificium, or the several manners of making Bread in France. Where, by universal consent, the best Bread in the World is eaten', signed *J. Evelyn.*

Note: John Houghton (d. 1705) is not mentioned in the Diary, but was no doubt acquainted with Evelyn, having been elected F.R.S. in 1680. His *Letters* appeared weekly and were collected in two volumes, 1681–3. He was the first to notice the potato plant as an agricultural vegetable, and in many ways actively promoted the progress of agricultural science. Evelyn's short treatise on bread is in his most solemn manner.

Copies: BM (1029.c.2), K, ULC (Syn.7.68.51).

128 ROGERS' HARVEIAN ORATION [W. R 1803]. 4° 1682

Oratio Anniversaria, habita In Theatro Collegii Medicorum Londinensium, Decimo octavo die Octob. Et divi Lucæ Festo. 1681. In Commemorationem Beneficiorum à Doctore Harveio,... à Georgio Rogers, ejusdem Collegii Socio. Necnon & Oratio In Gymnasio Patavino Habita Prod. Cal. Maii An. CIↃIↃCXLVI....Londini, Sumptibus Benj. Tooke, ad Insigne Navis in Cœmeterio Divi Pauli. MDCLXXXII. A–G⁴ (F3 cancelled).

G2*a* (p. 39) four Latin couplets to Rogers, signed *Joan. Euelinus Anglus.*

Note: Under the date 15 August 1682 Evelyn wrote in his Diary: 'Came to visite me Dr Rogers, an acquaintance of mine long since at Padoa. He was there Consul of the English Nation students in that Universitie, where he proceeded Dr in Physic; presenting me now with the Latine oration he lately made upon the famous Dr Harvey's Anniversarie in the Coll. of Physicians in London.'[1] George Rogers (1618–97) was President of the College of Physicians in 1688. Evelyn's lines were probably written in 1646, when Rogers delivered his first oration in Padua.

Copies: BM (1184.b.23), etc.

129 CREECH'S LUCRETIUS [W. L 3448] 8° 1683

T. Lucretius Carus. The Epicurean Philosopher, His Six Books De Natura Rerum Done into English Verse, With Notes. The Second Edition, Corrected and Enlarged...Oxford, Printed by L. Lichfield, Printer to the University, For Anthony Stephens...1683. A^4 b–e^4 f^2 B–Z^4 Aa–Ee^4 a–g^4 h^2, engraved frontispiece.

C2*a–b*: 'To Mr Creech. On His accurate Version of Lucretius', 22 lines dated *White-Hall Decem.* 15. 82, and signed *J. Evelyn.*

[1] de Beer, IV, 291.

Note: Evelyn refers in these lines to his own translation of Lucretius, part of which had been published in 1656 (see no. 4). Thomas Creech (1659–1700) was a fellow of All Souls, Oxford, in 1683, and afterwards became headmaster of Sherborne. His translation of Lucretius was first published in 1682, and he afterwards translated a number of other authors. Evelyn's lines were printed again in the third edition, London, 1683, and many more editions appeared up to 1776. His verses contain fine imagery and it has even been suggested that they may have influenced Keats in some of the phrases in his sonnet 'On first looking into Chapman's Homer'.[1]

Copies: BM (3rd edn, 11375.b.22), K (2nd and 3rd edns), ULC (3rd edn, L.12.21).

130 CASE OF GEORGE EVELYN [W. E 3477] [1698]

The Case Of George Evelyn of Wotton, in the County of Surrey, Esq; With some Remarks thereon, by Iohn Evelyn of Deptford, Esq; only Brother of the said George. [*broadside*]

Note: This broadside, measuring about 34 × 32 cm., has the above title printed on one side, and on the other *The Case of George Evelyn* and *Remarks on the Case* printed in two columns. The appeal is addressed to the House of Commons, and apparently the sheet was intended to be laid folded on the seats of the members of the House. It was occasioned by a family quarrel which is not mentioned in the Diary, but is referred to as 'an unexpected controversy' in *Memoires for my Grandson* (p. 2 and note, pp. 93–4), first printed in 1926 (see no. 119). In the left-hand column of the broadside the circumstances are recounted in which George Evelyn in 1692 left his estate by deed to John Evelyn and his male issue, and a complaint is made that these heirs were taking steps to prevent the reversion of the estate to the descendants of George Evelyn if their own male line failed. George Evelyn therefore asks leave of the House to bring in a bill enabling him so to resettle the estate that this reversion may take place. In the right-hand column John Evelyn replies to this that there was perfect understanding between him and his brother when the settlement was made, and that no alteration has taken place since. Further, that George Evelyn was at the time pressed to reserve to himself power of revocation but positively refused, foreseeing 'what clamours he might be subject to from his Grand Daughters (all of which had been very largely provided for; yet one of them lately Marrying one Dr Fulham, a Clergyman, he has raised this Clamour after so many Years Satisfaction under the Settlement)'. He pleads that no misunderstanding exists except in the imagination of Dr Fulham and that therefore no such bill may be passed. Evelyn mentions in his Diary 'Dr Fulham who lately married my niece' under the date January 2, 1697–8.[2] The bill was brought up at the House of Lords on 14 March 1698/9 and John Evelyn's petition on 16 March. The hearing was put off until 22 March, and no

[1] See a letter by John H. Wagenblass in *The Times Literary Supplement*, 25 January 1936.

[2] de Beer, v, 282.

further proceedings were taken.[1] George Evelyn died on 4 October 1699, and his estate passed to John Evelyn and his male heirs as originally intended.[2]

Only three copies of the broadside are known to have survived. One of these is in the Bodleian Library, which also possesses a broadside giving George Evelyn's complaints only.[3]

Copies: BLO (Gough, Surrey. 30 (26)), BM (Cup. 645. e 1(1)), K.

THE

CASE

Of GEORGE EVELYN of Wotton, in the County of Surrey, *Esq; With some Remarks thereon, by* Iohn Evelyn *of* Deptford, *Esq; only Brother of the said* George.

Title-page of no. 130

131 HOOKE'S PHILOSOPHICAL EXPERIMENTS 8° 1726

Philosophical Experiments and Observations Of the late Eminent Dr. Robert Hooke, S.R.S. And Geom. Prof. Gresh. And Other Eminent Virtuoso's in his Time. . . . Publish'd by W. Derham, F.R.S. London: Printed by W. and J. Innys, . . . MDCCXXVI. A^4 B–Z^8 Aa–Cc^8.

(1) Pp. 186–8. 'The Genuine Recept for making Orvietano', and 'The Virtues', with a note on the history of the receipt, signed J. Evelyn.

(2) Pp. 188–90. 'Ink for the Rolling Press', signed J. Evelyn.

Note: These notes were found by Derham among Hooke's papers, and so came to be included here. Evelyn had made a communication to the Royal Society on printing copper-plates (see no. 124, note).

Copies: BM (234. g. 33), K.

[1] See House of Lords MSS, vol. III, n.s., 1905, pp. 380–1.

[2] See Hiscock, pp. 203–5.

[3] *The Case of George Evelyn of Wotton, in the County of Surrey, Esq;* [W.E 3478] BLO (B.S. 4°. 239).

DIARY, LETTERS AND MISCELLANEOUS WRITINGS

PREFACE

THE manuscript of Evelyn's Diary was preserved at Wotton House, the main text being contained in a bound volume and some loose sheets, the whole of which is in Evelyn's hand. A second volume contains an amplified version of the Diary from the beginning to October 1644, this being all that was accomplished of Evelyn's intended revision. It is again in his own hand except for the last few lines. The earlier part of the second version was copied out by Sir John Evelyn in 1737, though this rescript clearly has no authority. Evelyn's *Kalendarium*, as he himself headed it, is not in the strict sense of the word a diary, that is to say, it does not consist of day-by-day entries always made immediately after the events as they happened. Although some of his experiences may have been recorded at once, Evelyn tended rather to write up his diary at intervals, probably using sometimes full memoranda made at the time, though also inserting passages from memory. The result is that events are not infrequently recorded under the wrong dates, or are telescoped into shorter periods than they actually occupied. Additions were also made at varying intervals and sometimes in the wrong places, so that the Diary, regarded as an historical record, presents many discrepancies. It is nevertheless a document of such importance that a full and accurate transcript was greatly to be desired; yet its textual history has been singularly unsatisfactory until recent years.

The first printing of the Diary was due to the initiative of William Upcott, Assistant Librarian at the London Institution, to whom the MS was shown by Lady Evelyn about the year 1814. He was engaged upon an exhaustive investigation of the papers at Wotton, the value of which was not appreciated by their somewhat irresponsible owner, and there can be no doubt that the labour of editing the Diary devolved largely upon him, though Lady Evelyn preferred that the nominal office of editor should be assumed by William Bray, whose name carried weight by virtue of his reputation as an antiquary. He had been born, however, in 1736, and so was aged 82 when the Diary was first published in 1818. The work was at least done under his supervision, and Upcott's name did not appear on the title-page, though he was thanked by the editor at the end of the preface 'for the great and material assistance received from him in this Publication, besides his attention to the superintendance of the Press'.

The editor did not claim that the Diary, or *Memoirs* as he preferred to call it, as printed in 1818 was complete, and he refers to it in his preface as a 'selection'. He does not mention that the editor's task included alteration as well as selection, though perhaps that was assumed in 1818 to be part of any editor's duty. The Bray–Upcott selection occupied the whole of one large quarto volume and part of a second, which was amplified by the inclusion of some miscellaneous papers and correspondence. A second edition of the two quarto volumes was printed in 1819 with improvements, and this text has been several times reprinted (Murray, 1870; Chandos Classics, 1879; Newnes, 1903, etc.).

In 1827 Bray's text was printed for the third time, in five volumes octavo, without any indication of revision, though it is stated by a later editor, John Forster, to have been 'superintended for the press' by Upcott, except for the earlier sheets of the first volume. This, the third text, was reprinted by Wheatley in his editions of 1879 and 1906.

The fourth text was edited in four volumes in 1850–2 by John Forster, who claimed that he had incorporated in it Upcott's final additions and corrections, relating particularly to the early portion printed in 1827 before he had begun his task of revision. Forster also modernized the spelling and added more than a hundred letters, transcribed by Upcott, to the correspondence. This text was included in Bohn's Historical Library in 1859 with some further revisions by Forster, and the Diary by itself was taken from this source for Austin Dobson's edition, 1906, Dent's Everyman edition, 1907, and Macmillan's Globe edition, 1908.

With these texts the public has hitherto had to be content, though none of the later ones was really much of an improvement upon Bray's second text of 1819, produced according to a standard of scholarship long obsolete. During the last quarter of the nineteenth century the unsatisfactory state of the text was realized, and attempts were made, notably by H. B. Wheatley, to obtain access to the original MS for the purpose of preparing a new version. All approaches, however, were barred by W. J. Evelyn, the owner of the Wotton estate at that period, and Wheatley had to be content with the cold assurance that 'Colburn's third edition of the Diary was very correctly printed from the MS and may be relied on as giving an accurate text'. W. J. Evelyn made some amends for his persistent refusal to satisfy the just demands of scholarship by printing a full text of the Diary from 4 October 1699 to the end, a large part of this having been omitted from the previously printed text. He chose, however, to bury his contribution in the pages of an obscure periodical, *The Abinger Monthly Record*, in brief instalments from 1889 to 1893.

Matters rested in this unsatisfactory position until 1921, when the late A. T. Bartholomew and myself, through the good offices of Captain Evelyn Broadwood and the late Miss Joan Broadwood, obtained an introduction to Wotton House. We then found the late John Evelyn and his wife anxious to listen to reason and to do what was right and public-spirited, and as a result of our conversations the MS of the Diary was deposited for ten years at the Bodleian Library in order that a full and accurate transcript could be made and verified. This new text has been edited for the Clarendon Press by Dr Esmond de Beer, and Evelyn's Diary has at last been made accessible in a complete and accurate text.

Evelyn's letters have never been collected in their entirety, though many have been printed among the miscellaneous correspondence given with the first and some later editions of the Diary. The chief printed sources of letters, apart from the Diary, are listed below, but the list is certainly not exhaustive. The most important sources are those containing letters between Evelyn and Pepys.

So full an account of Evelyn's life is to be found in the printed portions of the Diary and his editors' prefaces that very little independent biographical study has been made of him. Before the appearance of the *Memoirs* in 1818 articles concerning him had been printed in such works as Wood's *Athenæ Oxonienses*, Walpole's *Biographical History of England*, the *Biographia Britannica*,[1] and Chalmers' *Biographical Dictionary*. Subsequently Hone included Evelyn in his *Lives of Eminent Christians*, 1833, and a short life by 'J. F. R.' was published together with those of Alfred the Great and Sir Thomas More in 1845. An article was written for the *Dictionary of National Biography*, 1889, by Leslie Stephen, but no other life was published until 1933, when Heinemann issued *John Evelyn* by Lord Ponsonby of Shulbrede, who made no fresh research, basing his study on 'the ample existing material'. In 1951 the late W. G. Hiscock, librarian at Christ Church, Oxford, and so in charge of the Evelyn books and papers removed from Wotton, published a book, *John Evelyn and Mrs Godolphin*. In this he sought to question the purity of Evelyn's motives in his relations with Margaret Blagge, later Mrs Godolphin, but this did not carry conviction with other students of Evelyn's life. This section of the Bibliography does not, therefore, extend beyond the Diary and selections from it. It concludes with the two issues of Upcott's collection of *Miscellaneous Writings*, because the volume was originally designed to range with the quarto editions of the *Memoirs* and has never been reprinted.

[1] The author of the article on Evelyn in *Biographia Britannica* was Dr John Campbell, 1708–75. See *Gentleman's Magazine*, vol. L, p. 33.

It is certain that the list of editions of the Diary, with abridgments and selections, is incomplete, for many of these books are not to be found even in the great public libraries. It contains, however, all that are of importance, and we are perhaps the less concerned with them now that we have Dr de Beer's new text.

THE DIARY

132 Memoirs, illustrative of The Life and Writings of John Evelyn, Esq. F.R.S. Author of the 'Sylva', &c. &c. comprising his Diary, from the year 1641 to 1705–6, and a selection of his familiar letters. To which is subjoined, The Private Correspondence between King Charles I and his Secretary of State, Sir Edward Nicholas, whilst His Majesty was in Scotland, 1641, and at other times during the Civil War; also between Sir Edward Hyde, afterwards Earl of Clarendon, and Sir Richard Browne, Ambassador to the Court of France, in the time of King Charles I. and the Usurpation. The Whole now first published, from the original MSS. In Two Volumes. Edited by William Bray, Esq. Fellow and Treasurer of the Society of Antiquaries of London. Vol I. [II.] [*Evelyn's monogram*] London: Printed for Henry Colburn, Conduit Street. And sold by John and Arthur Arch, Cornhill. 1818.

31 cm, vol. I: pp. xxxii (should be xxxiv), 620; vol. II: pp. viii, [iv], 366, [2], 335, [1]. Folding table of pedigrees inserted in vol. I between pp. viii and ix. The additional correspondence in vol. II is separately paginated. Issued in brown paper boards, untrimmed, with paper labels on spines (not seen) and half-titles in both volumes.

Illustrations:

i. Vol. I, frontispiece. Portrait of Evelyn engraved by T. Bragge after Kneller.
ii. Vol. I, p. 2. Wotton House (in 1818).
iii. Vol. I, p. 241. Portrait of Evelyn, engraved by Nanteuil.
iv. Vol. I, p. 315. Plan of Deptford, 1623, from a sketch by Evelyn.
v. Vol. II, frontispiece. Portrait of Mrs Evelyn engraved by Meyer after Nanteuil.
vi. Vol. II, p. 121. Wotton House, etched by Evelyn in 1653.
vii. Vol. II, part ii, p. 1. Portrait of Sir Edward Nicholas.
viii. Vol. II, part ii, p. 177. Portrait of Sir Richard Browne.

Additional plates in separate wrapper dated 1819:

ix. Vol. I, p. xiv. Exterior view of Wotton Church.
x. Vol. I, p. xiv. Interior view of the same.
xi. Vol. I, p. xxvii. Burial place of the Evelyn family in Wotton Church.

Note: There were only eight plates in the volumes as first issued. The second edition of the following year has eleven plates, and the three additional plates were also issued separately in a printed paper wrapper: *Additional plates, &c. to the First Edition of Memoirs of John Evelyn, F.R.S.... London: Printed for Henry Colburn, Conduit Street; and sold by John and Arthur Arch, Cornhill.* 1819. An example of this wrapper is bound up in one of the BM copies. The second BM copy has india-paper proofs of seven of the plates before letters; a note states that no proofs were taken of the remainder (nos. ii and ix–xi). Plate no. iii is the engraving by Nanteuil, first used in the fourth edition of *Silva*, 1706. It has been retouched and constitutes the fifth state of the engraving (see p. 138).

133 Memoirs, illustrative of The Life and Writings of John Evelyn, Esq. F.R.S.... [etc. as in no. 132]. Second Edition.—Vol. I. [II.] [*Evelyn's monogram*] London: Printed for Henry Colburn, Conduit Street; and sold by John and Arthur Arch, Cornhill. 1819.

31 cm, vol. I: pp. xxviii, 671, [1]; vol. II, pp. v, [iii], 342, [2], 336. Issued in brown paper boards, untrimmed, without half-titles, with paper labels on the spines: MEMOIRS | AND | CORRESPONDENCE | OF | JOHN EVELYN, | AUTHOR OF | 'SYLVA,' &C. | WITH | LETTERS | OF | K. CHARLES I. &C. &C. | [*short rule*] VOL. I | DIARY, &C. [VOL. II. | DIARY AND CORRESPONDENCE, | LETTERS OF CHARLES I. &C.]

Illustrations as in the first edition, vol. I facing title-page and pp. xii (2), xxiv, 2, 245, 328; vol. II facing title-page and p. 94, pt. II, pp. 1, 177. Folding leaf of pedigree in vol. I facing p. ix. List of plates on p. viii.

134 Memoirs of John Evelyn, Esq. F.R.S. Author of the '*Sylva*', &c. &c. comprising his Diary, from 1641 to 1705–6, and a selection of his familiar letters. To which is subjoined, The Private Correspondence...Edited from the original MSS. By William Bray, Esq. F.A.S. A New Edition, in Five Volumes. Vol. I. [etc.] London: Henry Colburn, New Burlington Street. 1827.

22 cm, vol. I: pp. [ii], xl, 394, [2]; vol. II, pp. [iv], 464; vol. III, pp. [ii], 441, [3]; vol. IV, pp. [ii], 552, [4]; vol. V, pp. [iv], 399, [1]. Issued in brown paper boards, half-titles in vols. I, II, and V, and paper labels on the spines: MEMOIRS | OF | JOHN EVELYN. | [*rule*] | NEW EDITION, | IN FIVE VOLUMES. | [*rule*] | VOL. I. [etc.]. Folding table of pedigree inserted in vol. I facing p. ix.

Illustrations:

i. Vol. I, frontispiece. Portrait of Evelyn engraved by T. Bragge after Kneller.
ii. Vol. I, p. xv. Exterior view of Wotton Church.
iii. Vol. I, p. xxxiii. Interior view of same.
iv. Vol. II, frontispiece. Portrait of Mary Evelyn, after Nanteuil.
v. Vol. II, p. 51. Wotton House, etched by Evelyn, 1653.

vi. Vol. II, p. 221. Cornbury, seat of second Earl of Clarendon.
vii. Vol. III, frontispiece. Wotton House in 1827.
viii. Vol. IV, frontispiece. Portrait of Sir Richard Browne, after Nanteuil.
ix. Vol. V, frontispiece. Burial-place of the Evelyns in Wotton Church.

Nos. ii, iii, iv, v, and viii are printed, with some alterations, from the same plates as were used in the previous editions. The remainder have been newly engraved.

Note: There is no statement in this edition concerning the text. It is recorded, however, in the *Advertisement* to the edition of 1850 that, with the exception of the earliest sheets of the first volume, the text was revised by Upcott, who compared it with the MS and supplied many omissions and corrections. The text therefore differs considerably from that of the quartos, except at the beginning, the first sheets having been printed off before Upcott began his revision. This text was reprinted by Wheatley, 1879 and 1906.

135 Diary and Correspondence of John Evelyn, F.R.S., Author of the 'Sylva'. To which is subjoined The Private Correspondence... Edited from the original MSS. at Wotton. By William Bray, Esq., F.A.S. A New Edition, in Four Volumes. Corrected, revised, and enlarged. Vol. I. [etc.] London: Henry Colburn, Publisher, Great Marlborough Street. 1850. [Vols. III and IV, 1852.]

20 cm, vol. I, pp. xl, 429, [3]; vol. II, pp. [iv], 396; vol. III, pp. xii, 399, [1]; vol. IV, pp. iv, 448. Folding table of pedigree inserted in vol. II, facing p. 376. Issued in embossed brown cloth, with the Evelyn arms in gold on the sides, and gold lettering on the spines. Half-titles in vols. I and III. Advertisements inserted at end of vol. II.

Illustrations:
i. Vol. I, frontispiece. Portrait of Evelyn after Kneller.
ii. Vol. I, p. 1. Wotton House (in 1827).
iii. Vol. II, frontispiece. Portrait of Mary Evelyn, after Nanteuil.

Nos. i and iii are printed from the same plates as were used in 1827, the dates at the bottom being altered to 1847. No. ii has been re-engraved with alterations.

Note: The editor of this edition, whose name does not appear, was John Forster. According to his *Advertisement* further revision was carried out by Upcott, who was engaged on the task at the time of his death. This edition contains additional notes and over a hundred letters, transcribed by Upcott, which had not been printed before. The spelling has been modernized. Re-issued in 1854. This text was reprinted by Austin Dobson, 1906, and in Everyman's Library.

136 Diary and Correspondence of John Evelyn, F.R.S. to which is subjoined The Private Correspondence... Edited... by William Bray, Esq, F.A.S. A new edition, in four volumes. Corrected, revised, and enlarged. Vol I. [etc.] London: Henry G. Bohn... 1859.

18 cm, vol. I: pp. xxxviii, 434; vol. II: pp. [iv], 398; vol. III: pp. xii, 399, [1]; vol. IV: pp. viii, 469, [3]. Folding table of pedigree in vol. II, and 45 plates.

Note: 'Bohn's Historical Library', frequently re-issued by Bell and Daldy. The editor, John Forster, states in his preface dated June 1857 that the text has been further revised since it was printed in 1850–2.

137 Memoirs illustrative of the Life and Writings of John Evelyn, Esq., F.R.S.... Edited by William Bray, Esq.... Reprint of second edition.—London, 1819. London: Alex. Murray & Son, 30, Queen Square, W.C. 1870.

18·5 cm, pp. xvi, 17–783, [1]. Issued in purple embossed cloth.

Note: Re-issued in 1871.

138 Diary of John Evelyn, Esq., F.R.S. to which are added a selection from his familiar letters and the private correspondence between King Charles I. and Edward Nicholas and between Sir Edward Hyde (afterwards Earl of Clarendon) and Sir Richard Browne, Edited from the original MSS. by William Bray, F.S.A. A new edition in four volumes with a Life of the Author by Henry B. Wheatley, F.S.A. with numerous portraits. Vol. I. [etc.] London: Bickers and Son, 1, Leicester Square. 1879.

29 cm (large paper), or 22 cm. Vol. I: pp. [ii], cxxv, [i], 299, [1]; vol. II: pp. [vi], 491, [1]; vol. III: pp. [vi], 487, [1]; vol. IV: pp. [vi], 497, [1]. Folding table of pedigree inserted in vol. I.

Illustrations: Vol. I, 7 plates; vol. II, 6 plates; vol. III, 5 plates; vol. IV, 6 plates.

Note: Wheatley did not add to the notes already in the edition of 1827, but contributed to the preliminary matter and greatly lengthened the index.

139 Chandos Library, Memoirs of John Evelyn, Esq F.R.S.... Edited by William Bray, Esq.... London: Frederick Warne and Co.... New York: Scribner, Welford and Co. [1879]

17·5 cm, pp. xvi, 17–783, [1]. Frontispiece.

Note: A reprint from stereotypes of Murray's edition, 1870; frequently re-issued. The BM copy (and presumably others) ends at p. 619, omitting the correspondence.

140 The Diary of John Evelyn, Esq., F.R.S. . . . with memoir Edited by William Bray, Esq. . . . London W. W. Gibbings, 18, Bury Street, W.C. Exeter: J. G. Commin 1890

22 cm, pp. xvi, 17–619, [1], 4. Issued in red cloth, gilt.

Note: Reprinted from the stereotypes of Murray's edition, omitting the Correspondence.

141 The Diary of John Evelyn, edited . . . by William Bray, with a biographical introduction by the Editor, and a special introduction by Richard Garnett New York 1901

2 vols. 8°, with coloured frontispieces and 3 plates (not seen).

142 The Diary of John Evelyn Esquire F.R.S. Edited by William Bray London George Newnes Limited [1903]

16·5 cm, pp. [iv], xx, 809, [3].

143 Diary of John Evelyn Esq., F.R.S. to which are added a selection from his familiar letters and the private correspondence. . . . Edited . . . by William Bray, F.S.A. A new edition in four volumes with a Life of the Author and a new preface by Henry B. Wheatley, F.S.A. . . . with numerous illustrations. Vol. I. [etc]. London Bickers and Son 1906

22 cm, Vol. I: pp. cxxxiii, [i], 299, [1]; vol. II: pp. [viii], 491, [1]; vol. III: pp. [viii], 487, [1]; vol. IV: pp. [viii], 497, [3]. Folding table of pedigree inserted in vol. I. Issued in green cloth with the Evelyn arms on the front cover.

Illustrations: Vol. I, 9 plates; vol. II, 9 plates; vol. II, 6 plates; vol. IV, 6 plates.

Note: A reprint of the edition of 1879 (no. 138), with a new preface by H. B. Wheatley commemorating the two hundredth anniversary of Evelyn's death. All references to Wheatley in the present work are to this edition.

144 The Diary of John Evelyn with an introduction and notes by Austin Dobson Hon. LL.D. Edin. In three volumes Vol. I [etc.] London Macmillan and Co., Limited New York: The Macmillan Company 1906

22 cm., Vol. I: pp. [ii], lxxiv, 355, [1]; vol. II: pp. [ii], vi, 420; vol. III: pp. [ii], vi, 479, [1]. Folding table of pedigree inserted in vol. I. Issued in red cloth.

Illustrations: Vol. I, 19 plates; vol. II, 25 plates; vol. III, 15 plates.

Note: A reprint of Forster's text, newly edited and annotated.

145 Diary and Correspondence of John Evelyn, F.R.S....Edited...by William Bray...London George Routledge & Sons...[1906]

22 cm, pp. xxxii, 952.

146 The Diary of John Evelyn F.R.S. Edited by William Bray Vol. I [2] London J. M. Dent & Sons Ltd New York E. P. Dutton & Co. [1907] [Everyman's Library, with a prefatory note by G. W. E. Russell]

17 cm, Vol. I: pp. xxxviii, 406, [2]; vol. II: pp. [viii], 400.

Note: A reprint of Forster's text, 1850–2. Reprinted in 1911–12 and subsequently.

147 The Globe Edition The Diary of John Evelyn with an introduction and notes by Austin Dobson Macmillan and Co., Limited...1908

19 cm, pp. xl, 540, [4].

147*a* The Diary of John Evelyn Now first printed in full from the manuscripts belonging to Mr. John Evelyn and edited by E. S. de Beer In six volumes Volume I [&c.] Oxford At the Clarendon Press 1955

21·5 cm, Vol. I, Introduction and *De vita propria*, with Appendixes, including pedigrees of the Evelyn family. Three illustrations: pp. xiv, 171, [1].
Vol. II, *Kalendarium* 1620–1649: pp. vi, [ii], 579, [1]. Three illustrations.
Vol. III, *Kalendarium* 1650–1672: pp. ix, [i], 639, [1]. Six illustrations.
Vol. IV, *Kalendarium* 1673–1689: pp. ix, [i], 654, [2]. One illustration.
Vol. V, *Kalendarium* 1690–1706: pp. viii, 622, [2]. Three illustrations.
Vol. VI, Additions and Corrections, Index: pp. [viii], 630, [2].

Note: These six volumes, edited by Dr de Beer with devoted scholarship, are never likely to be superseded. Every available source of information has been used and the Index volume alone occupied the editor for the best part of three years. The edition was issued in green cloth. A few copies specially bound for presentation were in hard-grain green morocco, gilt.

147*b* The Diary of John Evelyn Edited by E. S. de Beer London Oxford University Press New York Toronto 1959

18 cm, pp. xii, 1307, [1].

Note: This contains the whole of the *Kalendarium* from no. 147*a* except for the reports of sermons, 1660–1705. There is a very extensive index. Issued in dark blue cloth.

SELECTIONS FROM THE DIARY

148 An Abridgment of the History of the Great Plague in London, in the Year 1665 By a Citizen who lived the whole time in London. Together with An Account of the Fire in 1666, from the Memoirs of Evelyn. A New Edition. London . . . C. & J. Rivington . . . 1824.

17·5 cm, pp. [ii], 192. Reprinted in 1840.

149 Murray's People's Reprints. The Diary 1641 to 1706 of John Evelyn, Esq., F.R.S. . . . London: Murray & Co. [n.d., *c.* 1880]

18 cm, pp. 192. Issued in purple cloth.

Note: An abridgment by Alexander Murray from the edition published by him in 1870.

150 Voyage de Lister à Paris en MDCXCVIII Traduit pour la première fois publié et annoté par la Société des Bibliophiles François on y a joint des Extraits des ouvrages d'Evelyn relatifs à ses voyages en France de 1648 à 1661 A Paris Pour la Société des Bibliophiles. 1873

24 cm, pp. [iv], iv, xxviii, 344.

Note: 'Extraits d'Evelyn', pp. 219–314, from the *Diary* and *The State of France*, edited by E. de Sermizelles and others.

151 The Abinger Monthly Record. Vols. I–III. London: Mitchell and Hughes. July 1889–July 1893.

The Diary from 4 October 1699 to the end, 3 February 1706, is printed in monthly instalments and in several supplements edited by W. J. Evelyn.

Note: This claims to be a fresh transcript, giving for the first time the whole of the text between the dates mentioned above. There is a facsimile of the last page of the Diary facing vol. III, p. 449.

152 The Diary of John Evelyn (Reign of Charles II) With an Introduction by Austin Dobson. Cassell and Company Limited . . . MCMIV

15·5 cm, pp. 224.

153 A Passive Resister of the Seventeenth Century being a Selection from the Diary of John Evelyn with a short introduction by George Cuttle London: Elliot Stock . . . 1905

18 cm, pp. 28.

154 John Evelyn in Naples 1645 Edited by H. Maynard Smith Oxford B. H. Blackwell . . . MCMXIV

19 cm, pp. xii, 68.

155 Extracts from the Diaries and Correspondence of John Evelyn and Samuel Pepys relating to engraving with notes by Howard C. Levis Ellis 29 New Bond Street, London 1915

21·5 cm, pp. 166, [2], with 35 illustrations. Issued in quarter white cloth and grey paper.

156 Oxford Historical and Literary Studies. . . . Volume XI The Early Life and Education of John Evelyn With a Commentary By H. Maynard Smith Oxford At the Clarendon Press 1920

22·5 cm, pp. xx, 182, [2]. Issued in red cloth.

Note: The editor gives the texts of both the third and the fourth editions of the Diary where the latter gives any additional matter.

157 Selections from Evelyn's Diary Chosen and Edited by H. A. Treble, M.A. Methuen & Co. Ltd. . . . [1928]

17 cm, pp. xix, [i], 200, 8.

158 The Laurel and Gold Series Two Men See Life 17th Century life and events as seen by Samuel Pepys and John Evelyn Arranged by C. E. Wright, M.A. Collins Clear-type Press [1932]

158*a* John Evelyn's Diary A Selection from the Diary edited by Philip Francis The Folio Society London 1963

22 cm, pp. xiv, 253, [1]. With 15 illustrations.

LETTERS

159 The Natural History and Antiquities of the County of Surrey...By John Aubrey, Esq; F.R.S....In Five Volumes London, Printed for E. Curll in Fleet-street. M.DCC.XIX.

Letter: Vol. I, A3*a*–A7*a*. 'Mr Evelyn's Letter to Mr Aubrey', dated Feb. 8, 1675/6.

Note: Reprinted in *Miscellaneous Writings*, 1825, pp. 687–91.

160 The Works of the Honourable Robert Boyle [Edited by Thomas Birch]. London. 1744.

Letters: Vol. V, pp. 397–403. Seven letters from Evelyn to Boyle, including his proposals for a philosophical college dated 3 September 1659.

161 History of the Royal Society of London. By Thomas Birch D.D. London. 1756.

Letter: Vol. I, pp. 13–15. Letter from Evelyn to Dr Wilkins concerning the anatomy of trees, dated 29 January 1660/1.

162 Collectanea Curiosa;...[By John Gutch] In two volumes...Oxford, At the Clarendon Press,... M DCC LXXX I.

Letter: Vol. I, pp. 414–16. N° LXVI. 'Mr Evelin of Deptford's letter concerning the Praiers for Time of Invasion, &c, suggested by the E. of S.', dated Oct. 10, '88.

163 Gentleman's Magazine. Vol. LXVII. Part I. London. 1797.

Letter: Pp. 218–19. Letter to a Fellow of the Royal Society concerning the culture and improvement of the English tongue, dated Sayes Court, Jan. 28.

Note: A committee had been appointed by the Royal Society to consider this question. The chairman of this committee was Sir Peter Wyche, to whom Evelyn wrote an interesting letter dated June 20, 1665 (Wheatley, III, 309–12).

164 Anecdotes of Literature and Scarce Books. By the Rev. William Beloe. Six volumes. London. 1807–1812.

Letter: Vol. II, pp. 430–1, to Sir Hans Sloane concerning the errors in *Numismata* (printed at p. 232 of the present work).

165 London Magazine. Vol. x. London. 1824

Letter: pp. 589–92. Letter to Sir Thomas Browne concerning his *Elysium Britannicum*, dated Co. Garden, 28 Jan. [1657/8]. Reprinted in *Sir T. Browne's Works*, ed. Wilkin, 1836, vol. I, p. 374, and in *Works*, ed. Keynes, 1931, vol. VI, p. 299, and 1964, vol. IV, p. 271.

166 Correspondence of Richard Bentley, D.D. Master of Trinity College, Cambridge: London: John Murray. 1842.

22 cm. 2 volumes.

Letters: vol. I. Correspondence between Evelyn and Bentley from 27 March 1693 to 6 June 1700.

167 Catalogue of Historical Documents and Autograph Letters including A large and unpublished Correspondence addressed to Samuel Pepys...containing upwards of 30 Autograph Letters, etc., from John Evelyn...on sale by Samuel J. Davey, 47, Great Russell Street, London, W.C....[no. 31, 1889]

Note: This catalogue lists 28 autograph letters from Evelyn to Pepys with many extracts. The frontispiece is a facsimile of a letter dated March 15, '86/7.

168 Critical Essays of the Seventeenth Century Vol. II 1650–1685 Edited by J. E. Spingarn...Oxford at the Clarendon Press 1908

19 cm, pp. 310–29, from *Memoirs*, 1827.

Letters:

(1) To Sir Peter Wyche, Says-Court, 20 June 1665.
(2) To Samuel Pepys, Says-Court, 12 Aug. 1689.

169 Seven Letters of John Evelyn written between the years 1665 & 1703 now printed from the original copies together with a facsimile Oxford Printed for private circulation by Horace Hart at the University Press 1914

31 cm, pp. 24, with facsimile, 4 pp., inserted.

Note: Only 50 copies printed. The preface is by a descendant of the Evelyns, Frances Evelyn Rowley Heygate, who found the letters in an old box.

170 Private Correspondence and Miscellaneous Papers of Samuel Pepys. Edited by J. R. Tanner, Litt.D. London G. Bell and Sons, Ltd. 1926.

22 cm, 2 volumes.

Letters: This collection of papers in the possession of J. Pepys Cockerell includes eighteen letters from Evelyn to Pepys, some of which had not been printed before. There are also seven from Pepys to Evelyn.

171 The Times, London, 18 February 1927.

Letter: To Samuel Pepys, dated Berkley-Streete, January 14, 1698/9. Printed in an article by O. F. Morshead, 'New Light on Pepys'.

172 Letters and The Second Diary of Samuel Pepys. Edited by R. G. Howarth. London. J. M. Dent. 1932. 20 cm.

Letters: This collection includes 47 letters between Evelyn and Pepys, with one from Mary Evelyn, and two from Jackson to Evelyn. Many of these had appeared in earlier editions of Pepys's *Diary and Correspondence*.

173 Mr. Pepys and Mr. Evelyn by Clara Marburg Philadelphia: University of Pennsylvania Press London Humphrey Milford Oxford University Press MCMXXXV

23 cm, pp. [xii], 156.

Letters: In an appendix to this study are printed 37 letters between Pepys and Evelyn which had not been printed before. There is also a 'finding-list' for all those letters already printed.

MISCELLANEOUS WRITINGS

174 The Miscellaneous Writings of John Evelyn, Esq. F.R.S. Author of Sylva, or, A Discourse of Forest Trees; Memoirs, &c. Now first collected, with occasional Notes, By William Upcott, of the London Institution [*quotation*] [*Evelyn's monogram*] London: Henry Colburn, New Burlington-Street. 1825.

31 cm, pp. xxvi, 849, [3]. Issued in brown paper boards, untrimmed, with a half-title, and a paper label on spine: EVELYN'S | MISCELLANEOUS | WRITINGS. Illustrated with four engraved plates, facing title-page and pp. 243, 333, 425. The first of these is a facsimile of a letter from Evelyn to the Archbishop of Canterbury, dated November 4, 1680.

Leaf 2 L 1 (pp. 257–8) was cancelled and reprinted. Either state of the leaf may be found, or, occasionally, both.

175 The Literary Remains of John Evelyn, Esq, F.R.S. Author of Sylva, or a Discourse of Forest Trees, &c. forming a supplement to His Diary and Correspondence. Edited with notes, By William Upcott, Esq. [*quotation*] [*Evelyn's monogram*] Second Edition. London: Published for Henry Colburn by R. Bentley. Sold by all booksellers. 1834.

The sheets of no. 174 with a new title-page.

MISCELLANEA

THE MIRROUR OF TRUE *Nobility & Gentility.* BEING THE LIFE OF The Renowned *Nicolaus Claudius Fabricius* Lord of *Peiresk*, Senator of the *Parliament* at *AIX.*

Written by the Learned

Petrus Gassendus,

Professor of the *Mathematicks* to the King of FRANCE.

Englished by W. Rand, *Doctor of Physick.*

Vivit post Funera Virtus.

London, Printed by *J. Streater* for *Humphrey Moseley*, and are to be sold at his Shop at the *Princes Arms* in St. *Pauls* Church-yard. 1657.

Title-page of no. 176

176 LIFE OF PEIRESK [W. G 295] 8° 1657

The Mirrour of true Nobility & Gentility. Being the Life of The Renowned Nicolaus Claudius Fabricius Lord of Peiresk, Senator of the Parliament at Aix. Written by the Learned Petrus Gassendus, Professor of the Mathematicks to the King of France. Englished by W. Rand, Doctor of Physick...London, Printed by J. Streater for Humphrey Moseley,...1657. A^8 a^4 B–O^8 Aa–Tt^8.

A3*a*–A6*b* 'To the ingenious and learned Gentleman, the worshipful John Evelyn Esquire'. Dated: *From my House, near Cripplegate in London, January the* 30th, 1656, and signed: *The real Honourer of your Peireskian Vertues. William Rand.*

Note: Evelyn mentions in his Diary under the date 5 March 1657 that 'Dr Rand, a learned physician, dedicated to me his version of Gassendus's *Vita Peiriskii*'.[1] How this came about has already been related in the introduction to this bibliography (see p. 8). Dr Rand does not seem to be known to fame for any other achievement besides the publication of this book.

Copies: BM (614.a.18), K.

177 BROADSIDE PROCLAMATION 1662

By the Commissioners appointed by his Majesty, for the Repairing the High-Wayes and Sewers, and for Keeping Clean of the Streets, in, and about the City of London and Westminster, &c....Printed for J. G. Printer to the said Commissioners. 1662.

Note: This proclamation concerning the scavenging and maintenance of the streets was signed on 17 July 1662 by the following: Mo. Newport, Ro. Howard, Tho. Ingram, Clem. Spelman, Hugh May, A. Aeyre, A. Ashley, Jo. Denham, Will. Glasscock, Jo. Evelyn, Tho. Bales.

Copy: BM (C.21.f1 (25)).

SPRAT'S HISTORY OF THE ROYAL SOCIETY [W. S 5032] 4° 1667

178 The History of the Royal-Society of London, For the Improving of Natural Knowledge. By Tho. Sprat. London, Printed by T. R. for J. Martyn...and J. Allestry...MDCLXVII. AB^4 A–Z^4 Aa–Zz^4 Aaa–Iii^4.

Illustrations:

(i) A1*b*. Facing the title-page, an engraving of the arms of the Royal Society.
(ii) Frontispiece, a folding plate inserted between A1 and A2, or after A4 (see below).
(iii) Facing p. 173. Folding plate of scientific instruments.
(iv) Facing p. 233. Ditto.

[1] de Beer, III, 189.

Frontispiece: An allegorical subject, designed by John Evelyn and engraved by Hollar. In the centre on a pedestal is a bust of Charles II about to be crowned with a laurel wreath by an angel. To the right of the pedestal is seated Lord Brouncker, named SOCIETATIS PRÆSES; to the left is Francis Bacon, named ARTIUM INSTAURATOR. Above their heads are the arms of the Royal Society. To Lord Brouncker's right is a table carrying a diploma, with other documents, the mace given by Charles II, and a book-shelf.[1] The scene was perhaps suggested by the tiled piazzas on the north and south sides of the Green Court at Gresham College (see pl. II in *The Record of the Royal Society*, ed. 3, 1912). It is set in a tiled space with a wide arcaded verandah in which are placed various scientific instruments. Through the arcades is seen a landscape with a suggestion of Windsor Castle in the distance. In the foreground a man is kneeling at a large telescope suspended on a pole. To the right is a large building, perhaps intended to represent 'Salomon's House' in Bacon's *Atlantis*.
The print is lettered below: *Evelyn inv D.D.C. Wenceslaus Hollar f. 1667.* The plate-mark measures 21 × 16·5 cm.

Note: Evelyn's intimate connexions with the foundation and early fortunes of the Royal Society, and his friendship with Thomas Sprat, suggest that he may have had some hand in the compilation of this book. It contains, however, no visible sign except the engraved frontispiece made after his design. The print is found only in the first edition of Sprat's *History*, and by no means always in this. Perhaps it was inserted only in part of the edition, for copies occur in original condition and shewing no sign of having ever contained it. A statement by Wheatley that it was inserted only in large-paper copies I have not been able to verify. It is present in all three copies at the British Museum, of which two are on large paper (23·2 and 23·4 cm).

Copies: BM (740.c.17, G.19477 and 90.d.18, the last two on large paper, one with the Royal cipher on the binding); ULC (Rel.c.66.8, on large paper 23·4 cm, in contemp. red mor. gt.; the frontispiece has been removed, leaving parts of stub); K (2, one in contemp. red mor., from the library of H. B. Wheatley).

178*a* STILLINGFLEET'S LETTER (MS 1668) 8° 1735

Miscellaneous Discourses On Several Occasions [by Edward Stillingfleet] Ed. James Stillingfleet, D. D. Dean of Worcester. London: Printed by S. Buckley. Sold by J. J. and P. Knapton, &c., 1735. a^8 A–Z^8 Aa–Ff^8.

Note: On pp. 291–300 is Discourse XVIII, *Letter to John Evelyn, Esq*;, dated 13 August 1668, from Edward Stillingfleet D.D., later Bishop of Worcester. Evelyn had made an enquiry about a citation concerning the Invocation of Saints made by another person who seemed, Stillingfleet said, 'to have only the learning of a Fryar and the Faith of Surius'. Stillingfleet had consulted Binnius in the third part of the Ephesine Council. It appears that Evelyn had

[1] A few of the titles on the backs of the books can be deciphered and are *Harvey*, *Silva*, *Copernicus*, *Pinax* [by Christopher Merrett], *Novum Organum*, *Gilbert*, *Origin of Pole*.

PLATE 15

Frontispiece to Sprat's
History of the Royal Society

already discovered for himself 'the Impertinency of the Citation'. A letter on the same subject was addressed to Evelyn by Dr Thomas Barlow in the following year. See next entry. Stillingfleet and his sermons are mentioned many times in the Diary.

Copy: BM (1019.1.20).

179 BARLOW'S LETTER [W. B 834] (MS 1669) 4° 1679

A Letter concerning Invocation of Saints, and Adoration of the Cross, Writ Ten Years since, to John Evelyn of Depthford Esq;. By D[r] Barlow then Provost of Q. Colledge, and now Lord Bishop of Lincoln . . . London, Printed by John Macock for John Martyn . . . MDCLXXIX. A–E4.

Note: Dr Thomas Barlow (1607–91) is mentioned many times in the Diary and was evidently an old and valued friend. Evelyn first refers to him in connexion with a visit to Oxford in July 1654 when Barlow, as librarian, showed him the treasures of the Bodleian. Barlow's covering letter is dated 28 Sept. 1669. See also no. 178*a*.

Copy: BM (3936.g.4).

180 LEXICON TECHNICUM f° 1710

Lexicon Technicum: Or, An Universal English Dictionary of Arts and Sciences: . . . Vol. II. By John Harris, D.D. Secretary to the Royal Society, and Chaplain to the Lord High-Chancellor of Great-Britain. London: Printed for Dan. Brown, . . . MDCCX.

†C1*a*–†D2*b*: Arteries and Veins. 'A Description of the Veins and Arteries of a Humane Body in the two Plates annexed, as presented to the Royal Society in London, by that Generous Promoter of all Useful Learning; John Evelyn, late of Say's-Court in Deptford, Esq; and Explained and Illustrated by that Accurate Anatomist and Surgeon, Mr. William Cowper.'

Engraved plates: Two folding plates inserted before or after the two leaves of description:

(1) Figs. 1–5, inscribed at the bottom: *Place this at the Treatise of Arteries and Veins at the end of the Book.*

Fig. 1. 'Represents the Trunk and large Branches of the Arteries, Dissected from an Adult Human Body, when displayed and dryed; as they are now to be seen in the Repository of the Royal Society.'

(2) Figs. 6–8, inscribed at the bottom: *Place this*, etc.

Fig. 6. 'The Trunks of the Vena Cava, with their Branches Dissected from an Adult Humane Body, done from the Original Scheme in the Repository of the Royal Society.'

Fig. 8. 'The Trunks of the Vena Portæ dissected and displayed; done from the Original Scheme in the Repository of the Royal Society.'

This plate is also inscribed alongside fig. 6: *Venas has et Humani Corporis Arterias Geminis Tabulis adplicitas Patavio a se pridem deductas Regali demum Societati dedit Johannes Evelynus ejusdem Socius MDCLXVII.*

The remaining figures were drawn from subjects supplied by William Cowper, who also wrote the description. The plates are copied from those by van der Gucht in vol. XXIII of the *Philosophical Transactions* (see no. 124).

Note: The history of Evelyn's anatomical tables, in which he took great pride, is to be found recorded in the Diary. During his travels as a young man in Italy he was for a brief period a student of medicine at Padua. In February 1645/6 he was in Venice and from there 'went to Padoa to be present at the famous Anatomie Lecture, which is here celebrated with extraordinary apparatus, & lasting almost the whole Moneth, during which I saw three, a Woman, a Child, & a Man dissected, with all the manual operations of the Chirurgion upon the humane body: The one performed by Cavaliere Vestlingius, & Dr. Jo. Athelsteinus Leoncenas, of whom I purchased those rare Tables of Veines & Nerves, & causd him to prepare a third of the Lungs, liver, & Nervi sexti par: with the Gastric vaines, which I transported into England, the first of that kind had ben ever seene in our Country, & for ought I know, in the World, though afterwards there were others.'[1] He returned to England in October 1647 and wrote on 2 April 1649, 'My Italian collection being now ariv'd, came Moulins [Molines] the greate chirurgion, to see & admire the Table of Veines & Arteries which I purchasd & caused to be drawne out of several humane bodys at Padua.'[2] The dissections aroused much interest and were in request for demonstrations in London: '10 Nov. 1652. Dr Scarbrough was instant with me to give the Tables of Veines & Arteries to the Colledge of Physitians, pretending he would not onely reade upon them, but celebrate my curiositie as having ben the first who caus'd them to be compleated in that manner, & with that cost; but I was not so willing yet to part with them, as to lend them to the Colledge during their Anatomical Lecture, which I did accordingly.'[3] Fifteen years later, in 1667, Evelyn handed the Tables over to the Royal Society: 'Oct. 31. I was this day 47 years of age: Blessed [be] God for his mercys: I went to Lond: dined with my Bro: made the Royal Society a present of the Tables of Veines, Arteries, & Nerves, which with greate Curiositie I had caused to be made in Italy, out of the natural humane bodies, by a learned Physit: & the help of Vestlingius professor at Padoa, from where I brought them 1646, for which I received the publique thanks of the Society, & are hanging up in their Repositary; with an Inscription.'[4] The Tables are mentioned in Nehemiah Grew's *Catalogue of the Rarities Belonging to the Royal Society, and preserved at Gresham College. London*, 1681, f°, p. 4. It was not until many years later that William Cowper, surgeon and anatomist, wrote his description of the veins and arteries: 'Jan. 21, 1701/2. At the Royal Society there was read & approved the delineation & description of the Tables & Veins [and Arteries],

[1] de Beer, II, 475.
[2] *Ibid.* II, 553.
[3] *Ibid.* III, 77.
[4] *Ibid.* III, 501.

by Mr Cooper the chirurgeon, in order to their being Ingraven.'[1] This reading was recorded in the *Philosophical Transactions*, vol. XXIII, 1702, under Cowper's name, though Evelyn is said to have drawn up a description of the Tables in his own hand. This MS, signed by Evelyn and intended for Cowper's use, was still extant in 1906.[2] The plates were duly engraved from Cowper's drawings for the *Philosophical Transactions* (see no. 124), and were copied for the second volume of Harris's *Lexicon Technicum*, 1710, the first of which had appeared in 1704 (second edition, 1708).

The four dissections of vessels and nerves, dried and mounted on large pinewood panels, may be seen at the present time in the Hunterian Museum at the Royal College of of Surgeons in Lincoln's Inn Fields. They were transferred by the Royal Society to the British Museum in 1782, and from there to the College of Surgeons in 1809. They have recently been cleaned, varnished, and glazed, and appear to be quite undamaged in spite of their vicissitudes since 1646.

Copies: BM (12216.h.2), etc.

[1] *Ibid.* v, 487.

[2] Wheatley, I, xxviii.

APPENDIX I

WORKS BY JOHN EVELYN JUNIOR AND HIS SON

PREFACE

THE younger John Evelyn was born at Sayes Court on 14 January 1654. He was sent to Oxford in 1666 to be under Dr Bathurst's tutelage at Trinity, and was entered as a Gentleman Commoner in 1667. He does not seem to have taken a degree, though he was a somewhat precocious classical scholar and composed a set of Greek lines for the second edition of his father's *Sylva* at the age of fifteen. His translation of Rapinus was published in 1672, when he was eighteen, and his father reprinted Book II of this in the third edition of *Sylva*, 1679 (see no. 42). He was admitted of the Middle Temple in the same year, and held the office of Commissioner of Revenue in Ireland from 1692 to 1696. He married a daughter of Richard Spencer, Esq., and had two sons and three daughters. He died some years before his father on 24 March 1699, so that his son John, created baronet in 1713, inherited the family estate at Wotton.

The younger Evelyn shared his father's interests and, as was natural, acquired a considerable degree of culture, so that his English poems published in Tate's *Miscellany* of 1685 have excited some little admiration. Many of the books now in the Evelyn Collection at Christ Church were added by him, including much of the poetry. He does not seem, however, to have possessed very distinguished qualities, and his writings would not merit description except in order to prevent their being confused with his father's. His signature, as seen in books formerly in his possession, closely resembles his father's. It is usually associated, however, with the motto *Durate, etc.* taken from the family arms, which was never used by his father.

In my collection is a manuscript[1] entitled : *Rules and Observations In the / Propagation and Planting / Of / TREES*. It is written on eighteen leaves (20 × 13·5 cm) of seventeenth-century paper in a clear hand resembling Evelyn's; closer examination suggests that the hand is much influenced by Evelyn's, though less mature. It can scarcely be doubted that it was written by John Evelyn junior. The instructions, divided into seven chapters, are composed concisely and with authority, and there can be little doubt that they were written by John Evelyn senior and copied by his son. The manuscript has never been printed, though the *Rules and Observations* are likely to be still valid.

[1] Formerly Phillipps MS 1365.

181 OF GARDENS [W. R 268] 8° 1672

Title: Of Gardens. [*rule*] Four Books [*rule*] First written in Latine Verse by Renatus Rapinus, And now made English By J. E. [*engraved panel with arms between rules*]
London, Printed by T. R. & N. T. for Thomas Collins and John Ford at the Middle-Temple Gate, and Benjamin Tooks at the Ship in St. Pauls Church-yard, 1672.

Collation: *4 A–Q8 [R]8; 140 leaves.

Contents: *1 title; *2 (sign. A2)*a*–*4*b* *The Epistle Dedicatory* to Lord Arlington (engraved panel, as on title, at top of *2*a*); A1*a*–A8*a* *The Preface*; A8*b* blank; B1*a*–Q7*a* (pp. 1–237) *Of Gardens*; Q7*b*–Q8*b* blank; [R]1*a*–[R]8*b* *The Table.*

Note: Under the date January 3, 1672/3, Evelyn wrote, 'My Sonn now published his version of *Rapinus Hortorum*.'[1] The book is entirely by John Evelyn junior as appears from the dedication, although this is reprinted by Upcott, in the *Miscellaneous Writings*, 1825, pp. 623–4, as Evelyn's own work. The engravings on the title-page and at the head of the dedication bear the arms of Lord Arlington, to whom the book is dedicated. *The Table*, which I have seen only in the ULC copy, is preceded by corrections of seven mistakes in the pagination, pp. 92, 84, 76, 77, 89, 78, 79 having been misprinted 29, 48, 66, 67, 68, 79, 78.

Copies: ULC (Ff.20.27), K.

182 OF GARDENS [W. R 269 A] 8° 1673

Title: Of Gardens. . . [etc. as in no. 181] 1673.

Collation: *4 A–Q8; 132 leaves with 1 leaf inserted.

Contents: *1*a*–Q8*b* as in no. 181. Leaf with *errata* on recto inserted between Q7 and Q8.

Note: The book is more usually found with this date on the title-page than with 1672, the alteration having been made while the book was in the press. The quire with *The Table* is not found in the copies I have seen although the errors in pagination have not been corrected. The leaf of *errata* is not found in all copies.

Copies: BM (11405.aa.37), CCE,[2] K, ULC (Y.11.2); CH, CLC, HCL (2).

[1] de Beer, IV, 1.
[2] Bound for Sir Richard Browne with his ciphers.

183 HISTORY OF THE GRAND VISIERS [W. C 3728] 8° 1677

Title within double lines: The History of the Grand Visiers, Mahomet, and Achmet Coprogli, Of the three last Grand Signiors, their Sultana's and Chief Favourites; With the most secret Intrigues of the Seraglio. Besides several other particulars of the Wars of Dalmatia, Transylvania, Hungary, Candia, and Poland. [*rule*] Englished by John Evelyn, junior. [*rule*]
London: Printed for H. Brome, at the Gun at the West-end of St. Pauls. 1677.

Collation: A4 B–S8 T4; 144 leaves.

Contents: A1*a* blank; A1*b* *Imprimatur*, dated Nov. 24, 1676; A2 title; A3*a*–A4*b* *The Epistle Dedicatory* from De Chassepol, the author, to the Prince Godefroy Maurice De la Tour d'Auvergne; B1*a*–T3*a* (pp. 1–277) text; T3*b*–T4*b* blank.

Frontispiece: Engraving of two swordsmen engaged in mortal combat, with tents, etc. in the background. Inscribed at the top: *Battels*, and signed below: *W. Dolle scl.* Plate-mark 15 ×o cm.

Copies: BLO (Art. 8° O.21), BM (1053.a.16), K, ULC (U.4.72); CLC, HCL.

184 PLUTARCH'S LIVES [W. P 2639] 8° 1685

Title: The Fourth Volume of Plutarch's Lives. [*rule*] Translated From the Greek, by Several Hands. [*rule*]
London: Printed for Jacob Tonson, . . . 1685.

Translation: pp. 257–391. 'The Life of Alexander the Great. English'd from the Greek', by John Evelyn [junior].

Note: This was published by Tonson in five volumes, 1683–6, the life of Plutarch being by Dryden. There is an engraved frontispiece to each volume, and an engraving to each Life.

Copy: BM (609.b.4).

185 TATE'S POEMS [W. T 210] 8° 1685

Title: Poems by Several Hands, and on Several Occasions [*rule*] Collected by N. Tate. [*rule*, *ornament*, *double rule*]
London: Printed for J. Hindmarsh, at the Golden Ball, over against the Royal Exchange in Cornhil, 1685.

Collation: A–Z8 Aa–Ff8; 232 leaves.

Poems: G5*b*–H7*b* (pp. 90–110):

1. The Immortality of Poesie. By Mr Evelyn. To Envy. Ovid. Amor. Lib. 1. Eleg. 15.
2. Out of Martial Lib. 8. Epigr. 56. *Temporibus nostris Ætas.* By the same.
3. To Mr. &c. By the same.
4. Out of Horace, Ode 8. L. 1. *Lidia dic per omnes,* &c. By the same.
5. The Punishment. By the same.
6. Part of Ajax's Speech. Ovid Metam. l. 13. By the same.
7. Out of Sannazar. By the same.
8. Remedy of Love. By the same.
9. Written on her Mask. By the same.
10. To Mr. S. G. By the same.

Note: All except one of these were reprinted, with a biographical note, in John Nichols's *Select Collection of Poems,* vol. II, London, 1780, pp. 127–40, and again in Helen Evelyn's *History of the Evelyn Family,* London, 1915, pp. 145–52.

Copies: BM (11626.d.60), K.

185*a* POEM TO THE KING [Not in W.] f° 1685

Title: To the King: A congratulatory Poem. [*rule*] Virg. Æn.1.6.

——Tu maximus Ille es
Unus qui nobis cunctando Restituis Rem.

[*ornament between rules*]
London, Printed for R. Bentley in Russel-Street in Covent-Garden. MDCLXXXV.

Collation: A1 B1 C–D2; 6 leaves.

Contents: A1 title; B1*a*–D2*a* (pp. 3–9) text; D2*b* blank.

Note: The second leaf, though with signature B, was probably imposed with the title-page. The reference for the quotation on the title-page should be *Æn.* VI, 845–6

Copy: CCE (marked in Evelyn's hand: *By Jo Evelyn Jun:*).

185*b* GROTIUS HIS ARGUMENTS [W. G 2085] 8° 1686

Title within double lines: Grotius His Arguments For the Truth of Christian Religion; Rendred into plain English Verse...London: Printed for Jonathan Robinson,... MDCLXXXVI.

Collation: A–L8 M4; 92 leaves.

Contents: A1 title; A2*a*–*b* address to *Robert Boyle*; A3*a*–A4*a To the Reader*; A4*b*–A8*b* poems to the translator, with *errata,* 10 lines, on A8*b*; B1*a*–M4*b* (pp. 1–168) text.

Contribution: On A5*b*–A6*a*, lines 'To my Learned, and Ingenious Friend—on his Translation of *Grotius de veritate Religionis Christianæ*, into English Verse', signed *J. E.*

Note: The translator was William Attwood (d. 1705?), a barrister of Gray's Inn and later Chief Justice and Judge of Court of Admiralty, New York. Evelyn's poem in praise of Attwood's work was no doubt inspired by their friendship contracted as young lawyers at the Inns of Court.

Copies: BLO, BM, K,[1] ULC; CH.

186 EXEQUIÆ OXON. [W. O 885] f° 1700

Title: Exequiæ Desideratissimo Principi Gulielmo Glocestriæ Duci Ab Oxoniensi Academia Solutæ. [*engraving of Oxford University arms*]
Oxonii, E Theatro Sheldoniano, An. Dom. MDCC.

Collation: π^2 A–Z^2 Aa–Oo^2; 76 leaves.

Latin poem: Ll 2*a*. *Gulielmi Glocestriæ Ducis Exequiæ*, signed, *Joh. Evelyn* e Coll. Ball. Sup. Ord. Com.

Note: By Evelyn's grandson, who had entered Balliol College as a Fellow Commoner in February, 1699, in his seventeenth year.

Copies: BLO (AA.64.Art., and Pamph. 235), BM (112.f.7), K.

[1] In contemporary red morocco gilt, inscribed by the translator to his wife.

APPENDIX II

A SECTION OF EVELYN'S LIBRARY CATALOGUE

1687

PREFACE

REFERENCE has already been made to Evelyn's catalogue of his library made in 1687, and an analysis of the contents of the library extracted from it (see pp. 14–17). If the whole catalogue were to be printed, it would form a volume of considerable interest and value. This, however, is not to be expected, and I have therefore appended to this Bibliography a single section from it as a specimen of Evelyn's manner of collecting books and listing them. This particular section has been chosen partly because it is the shortest and partly because it includes the books in his special subjects of horticulture and forestry. It occupies only five pages of the catalogue out of a total of 216, and it forms a somewhat heterogeneous collection of books. Evelyn himself seems to have been uneasy as to whether he had been quite successful in his cataloguing, for he made a note at the top of the section, '?if some of these be well plac'd.' It is true that the list shows certain incongruities, though the difficulty of fitting everything into Evelyn's simplified scheme must also be admitted.

Historiæ Materiarum & Œconom: Rei Rustici Mechanologici, &c.

1. Bayfius de Re vestiaria, Vascularia, et Navali. 8°. Lutetiæ. 1553.
2. Metallica teaching how neale, melt, & work all kind of mettle ores &c. by Tim. Sturtevania. 4°. Lond. 1612.[1]
3. Delices de la Campagne ou est enseignée a preparer pour l'usage de La vie tout ce qui croist sur la Terre et dans les eaux &c. 8°. Paris. 1654.
4. Compleat vyneyeerd according to the German & French manner by W. Hughes. 12°. Lond. 1683.
5. Art of Memory. 12°. Lond. 1654.
6. Florist's Vademecum by Sam. Gilbert. 12°. Lond. 1682.
7. Della Agricultura di Giov. Tatti libri cinque. 4°. in Venetia. 1560.
8. Le moyen de devenir Riche par Bern. Palissy. 8°. Paris. 1636.
9. L'Arte Vettraria del Ant. Neri. 4°. in Firenze. 1612.
10. Discovery of all sorts of mines & mineralls by Gabr. Plattes. 4°. Lond. desit annus.
11. Art of mettals in two books translated from the Spanish of Alb. Al. Barba by the Earl of Sandwich. 8°. Lond. 1674.
12. The lapidary, or the History of pretious stones by Tho. Nicolls. 4°. Cambridge. 1652.
13. Jo. de Caet de Gemmis, et Lapidibus libri duo cum Theophrasti libro de lapidibus. Gr. Cat. 8°. L. Bat. 1647.
14. Boetii de Boot Gemmarum, et lapidum Historia ex recensione Adr. Toll. 8°. L. Bat. 1636.[2]
15. Bellonii de aquatilibus. L. due cum Iconibus. 8°. Paris. 1553.
16. Agricultura de Herrera. fol. en Madrid. 1645.
17. Marcelli Malpighii dissertatio epistolica de Bombyce. 4°. Lond. 1669.
18. Blithes Improvement of English Husbandry. 4°. Lond. 1652.
19. Petri Laurembergii Horticultura. 4°. Francofurti ad Mornum. 1654.
20. L'Agriculture, et maison Rustique de Charles Estienne, et Jean Liebault. 4°. a Lyon. 1659.

[1] Entry repeated by no. 120.

[2] In Evelyn's special cipher binding; now in my collection. Evelyn met the author, de Boot, in Paris on 22 December 1650 (de Beer, III, 24).

21. Theatre d'Agriculture, et Mesuage des Champs d'Olivier de terres. 4°. a Rouen. 1646.
22. Uccellina overo discorso della Natura di diversi uccelli che cansono, con il modo di prendergli &c. di Gio. Pietro Olino. 4°. in Roma. 1622.
23. Flora, Ceres, & Pomona by John Rea. fol. Lond. 1665.
24. Tho. Moufeti Insectorum sive minimorum Animalium Theatrum. fol. Lond. 1634.
25. Adam out of Eden, or an Abstract of experiments to advance Husbandry. 8°. Lond. 1659.
26. Garden of Eden, or an accurate description of all flowers and fruits now growing in England by Sr Hugh Plat. 8°. Lond. 1653.
27. Musæum Tradescantium a collection of Rarities. 8°. Lond. 1656.
28. The vermin killer by W. W. 12°. Lond. 1680.
29. Instructions pour les Arbres fruictiers. 12°. a la Haye. 1655.
30. The history of propagation and improvement of vegetables by the concurrence of Art, and Nature, by Robt. Sharrack. 8°. Oxford. 1660.
31. Nature's Cabinet unlockd, discovering the naturall causes of metals, stones, precious earths &c. by Tho. Brown. 12°. Lond. 1657.
32. Humane Industry or a History of most manuall Arts &c. 8°. Lond. 1661.
33. The Anatomy of vegetables, with a generall account of vegetation founded thereon by Nehemiah Grew. 8°. Lond. 1672.
34. The comparative Anatomy of Trunks, with an account of their vegetation by Neh. Grew. 8°. Lond. 1675.
35. The ladies Cabinet of secrets in preserving, physick, Cookery, &c. 12°. Lond. 1654.
36. The compleat Angler. 8°. Lond. 1668.
37. The compleat Angler being instructions how to angle for a Trout or Grayling in a clear stream, the 2[d] part. 8°. Lond. 1676.
38. Tractatus de Arboribus coniferis, et Pice conficienda per Jo. Conr. Axtium. 12°. Jena. 1679.
39. Vinetum Britannicum, or a Treatise of Cider and such other drinks as are drawn from all manner of fruits in this Kingdom, with a description of the Mill &c. 8°. Lond. 1676.
40. Prædium Rusticum in quo cujusvis soli vel culti vel inculti, plantarum vocabula, ac descriptiones &c. 8°. Lutetiæ. 1554.
41. Salt and Fishery by John Collins. 4°. Lond. 1682.

42. Englands improvement by sea and land, by Andrew Yarranton. 4°. Lond. 1677.
43. Markhams English Husbandman the second book with a Treatise of fishing and the fighting Cocke. 4°. Lond. 1615.
44. Butlers History of Bees. 4°. Oxford. 1634.
45. Cooks Improvement of Forest Trees. 4°. Lond. 1676.
46. Columellæ de Re rusticâ l. 12 et de Arboribus liber separatus cum annotat. Phil. Beroaldi. Enarationes vocum-priscarum. Aldus de dierum generibus, de umbris et horis quæ apud Palladium. Petri Victorii explicationes in Varronem Catonem &c. Palladius de re rustica. Cato et Varro de re rustica. 8°. Parisiis. 1543.
47. Jo. Baptist. Portæ Magice naturalis l. viginti. 8°. Francofurti. 1607.
48. Instructions to raise all sorts of fruit Trees that prosper in England by T. Langford. 8°. Lond. 1681.
49. Le Floriste François traittant de l'origine de Tulipes &c. par le Sr de la Chesnea Moustereal. 8°. a Rouen. 1658.
50. Villa di Gios. Falcone opera d'Agricoltura. 8°. in Venetia. 1603.
51. Remarques necessaires pour la culture des fleurs par P. Morin. 8°. Paris. 1658.
52. The Planters manuall, or instructions for raising all sorts of fruit Trees by Charles Cotton. 8°. Lond. 1675.
53. The Art of Glasse from the Italian of Ant. Neri by Dr. C. Merrett. 8°. Lond. 1662.
54. Hartlibs legacy of Husbandry. 4°. Lond. 1655.
55. The perfect use of Silkworms, and their benefit from the french of Olivier de Serres by Nich. Geffe. 4°. Lond. 1607.
56. The Jewell house of Art and Nature by S[r] Hugh Platt. 4°. Lond. 1653.
57. Heresbackius his Husbandry english'd by B. Googe. 4°. Lond. 1596.
58. La Fauconnerie de Charles d'Arcussia &c. 4°. a Rouen. 1643.
59. Godartius of Insects. 4°. York. 1682.
60. Blakes compleat Gardiners practice. 4°. Lond. 1664.
61. Gardeners Labyrinth, or a new Art of Gardening by D. M. 4°. Lond. 1652.
62. Artificiall Embellishments, or directions to preserve or procure beauty. 8°. Oxford. 1665.
63. Le Jardinier François, avec la maniere de conserver les fruicts. 8°. Paris. 1656.

64. L'Economia del Cittadino in Villa del Vinc. Tanara. 4°. in Venetia. 1661.
65. Ferrarius de Florum cultura. 4°. Romæ. 1633.
66. Manière de cultiver les Arbes Fruictiers par le S[r] le Gendre. 8°. Paris. 1653.
67. Le Jardinier Royal. 8°. 1661.
68. Goedartius de Insectis in methodum redactus cum Notularum additione opera. M. Lister. item ejusdem Appendix ad Historiam animalium Anglia cum fig. 8°. Lond. 1685.
69. History of the first Inventers of Arts mysterys &c. 12°. Lond. 1686.
[70. Deleted.]
71. The History of Magick by G. Naudæus, englishd by J. Davies. 8°. Lond. 1657.
72. Secrets et merveilles de Nature recueillis de divers Auteurs par J. Jaques Wicker. 8°. a Rouen. 1600.
73. Essay des merveilles de Natures, et des plus noble Artifices par René François. 8°. Paris. 1609.
74. Musæum Regalis societatis or a Catalogue of the Naturall and Artificiall raritys belonging to the Royall society by Neh. Grew, with the comparative Anatomy of Stomachs and Guts. fol. Lond. 1681.
75. Parkinsons Flower garden, Kitchin garden, and Orchard. fol. Lond. 1629.
76. Malpighii Anatome Plantarum cum Appendice de Ovo incubato. fol. Lond. 1675.
77. Malpighii Anatomes Plantarum pars altera. fol. Lond. 1679.
78. The Anatomy of Plants with an Idea of a Philosophicall History of Plants &c. by Neh. Grew. fol. Lond. 1682.
79. Franc. Willoughbeii Historia Piscium ex recognitione Jo. Raij. fol. Oxon. 1686.
80. Traite du Jardinage selon les raisons de la Nature, et de l'Art par Jacques Boyceau. fol. Paris. 1638.
81. Britannia Baconica or the Naturall Raritys of Engl[d] Scotl[d] & Wales by J. Childrey. 8°. Lond. 1661.
82. Markhams Art of fowling. 8°. Lond. 1621.
83. Rusdens History of Bees. 8°. Lond. 1679.
84. Art of Gardening by J. W. 8°. Lond. 1677.
85. Englands Improvement revived by John Smith. 4°. Lond. 1670.

86. Agricoltura di Agost. Gallo. 4°. in Venetia. 1629.
87. Lawsons way to get wealth by Husbandry, Cattle, Housewifery, Planting &c. 4°. London. 1623.
88. Onomasticon Zoicon Animalium defferentias, et nomina propria pluribus linguis exponens cui accedunt Mantissa Anatomica, et de variis fossilium generibus, per W. Charleton. 4°. Lond. 1668.
89. La Physionomie Naturelle, et la Chiromance de Barth. Cocles &c. avec fig. 8°. a Rouen. 1679.
90. Sylva or a discourse of Forest Trees, and the propagation of Timber with a Philosophical Essay of Earth, to which is annexed Pomona concerning Fruit Trees in relation to Cider and the Gardiners Almanac by John Evelyn Esqr. fol. Lond. 1679.
91. Instructions concerning erecting a Library by Gabr. Naudæus english'd by J. E. 8°. Lond. 1661.
92. Gentlemans Jockey and approved Farrier. 8°. Lond. 1683.
93. History of Chalcography, and engraving in Copper, by J. E. 8°. Lond. 1662[1].
94. History of Imbanking, and draining of Fenns, and Marshes both in forein parts, and in this Kingdom, by W. Dugdale. fol. Lond. 1662.
95. Essay des Merveilles de Nature et des plus nobles Artifices, par René François. 4°. A Rouen. 1626.
96. La piazza Universale di tute le professioni del mondo di Tom. Garzoni. 4°. Venetia. 1626.
97. The Belgick Hesperides, or Culture of Orange Trees, by S. Commelyn. 8°. Lond. 1683.
98. The painting of the Antients, beginning & progress of the Art by Fr. Junius. 4°. Lond. 1638.
99. Pechams Compleate Gentleman, & Gentlemans Exercise, in which Herauldry, painting in Oyls, Miniature, & in Glasse &c. 4°. Lond. 1638, 1634.
100. Elements of portraiture, par Mr de S. Igny. 8°. Paris.
101. Sculptura or History & Art of Chalcographie, & Mezzotinto by J. Evelyn. 8°. Lond. 1662.
102. The Art of Graving & Etching, by A. Bosse, Englishd by W. Faithorne. 8°. Lond. 1662.

[1] Entry repeated by no. 101.

103. The Art of painting ordinary Works, as Timber, dials &c. Use of Vernishes, & to preserve yron from rusting, with the Mysterie of taking off prints upon Glasse or paper, & the way of painting them, by Jo. Smith. 8°. Lond. 1681.

104. A Book of sundry draughts for Glaziers, plasterers, Gardners, &c. with the Art of Anieling on Glasse by W. Gidde. 4°. Lond. 1615.

105. Idea of the perfection of the Art of painting, by Mr Freart, Englishd by J. Evelyn. 8°. Lond. 1668.

106. The value & weight of English gold. 1632.

107. An Essay for Recovery of Trade, about Wool, Lead, Tin, Fishing, &c. by W. Smith. fol. Lond. 1661.

108. Collections of Letters for Improvement of Husbandry & Trade. vol. 2 by Jo. Houghton. Lond.

109. Mechanick Exercises by Jos. Moxon viz Smith & Ironwork: num. 1 Ironwork Hinges locks screws &c: n. 2. edgd tools jacks &c: n. 3. Joynery: n. 4. 5. 6. Carpentry: n. 7. 8. 9. Turning: n. 10. 11. 12. 13. 14. printing n. [15]. } By Jos. Moxon, Lond. 1677. 1678. 1679. 1680. 1683.

110. Nurseries Ortchards Gardens vinyards encouraged by Dr Beale. 4°. Lond. 1677.

111. Stubbes Animadversions on the History of the Royal Society &c. 4°. Lond. 1670.

112. Plus Ultra, or Animadversions on Mr Glanvil, against the R. Society, Against the Mechanicall Education. Also concerning the Aire, Telescope, Chymistry, Circulation of the blood & transfusion, Baths &c. by Mr Stubbe. 4°. Lond. 1670.

113. A Vindication of the R. Society from the late misrepresentations of Mr Stubbe. 4°. Lond. 1670.

114. Observationi nella pittura di Christoporo Sorte. 4°. Venetia. 1580.

115. Description of the Ship Sovrain of the Seas, with a learnd discourse concerning ships & Navigation. 1637. 4°. Lond.

116. The Reformed Commonwealth of Bees, with the Virginian Silkworm containing many choice Seacrets: pub. by Mr Hartlib. 4°. Lon. 1655.

117. Samuel Hartlibs Legacy enlarg'd, concerning Husbandry. 4°. Lond. 1652.

118. A discourse for Advancement of our Trade of Wollen Manufacture &c. by Ri. Hide. 4°. Lond. 1660.
119. Ra. Austins Treatise of Fruit Trees, with their Alimental & physical uses and spiritual use of fruit trees &c. 4°. Oxon. 1653.
120. Metallica, or a Treatise of Metallica &c. by Sim. Sturtevant. 4°. Lond. 1612.
121. Reformation for Garbelling of Spices, cont'ing the Art of Garbelling & abuse cald the common complaint of Grievances. Lond. 1592.
122. A Treatise concerning planting of wood & Fruit trees, breeding poultry & fowls, destroying vermine &c. 4°. by Arth. Standish. Lond. 1611.
123. Designe of plenty by planting Fruit trees &c by Sa. Harlib. Lond.
124. The Art of planting & Grafting &c. by Leond Mascal. 4°. Lond.
125. Virginia, or a discourse of silkwormes & Mulbery Trees, of the Saw-mil, of Fruit trees, vine, olive, pomgrant & other rarities. 4°. by Ed. Williams. Lond. 1650.
126. Epulario il quali Tratta del modo di Cucinare ogni Carne Uccelli pesci far Sapori Torte pachelli al modo di tutte le provincie del mondo. 8°. Trevigi. 1643.
127. Original & growth of printing in England. 4°. by R. Atkins. Lond. 1664.

INDEX

The numbers refer to the pagination

PRINTED IN GREAT BRITAIN
AT THE UNIVERSITY PRINTING HOUSE, CAMBRIDGE
(BROOKE CRUTCHLEY, UNIVERSITY PRINTER)

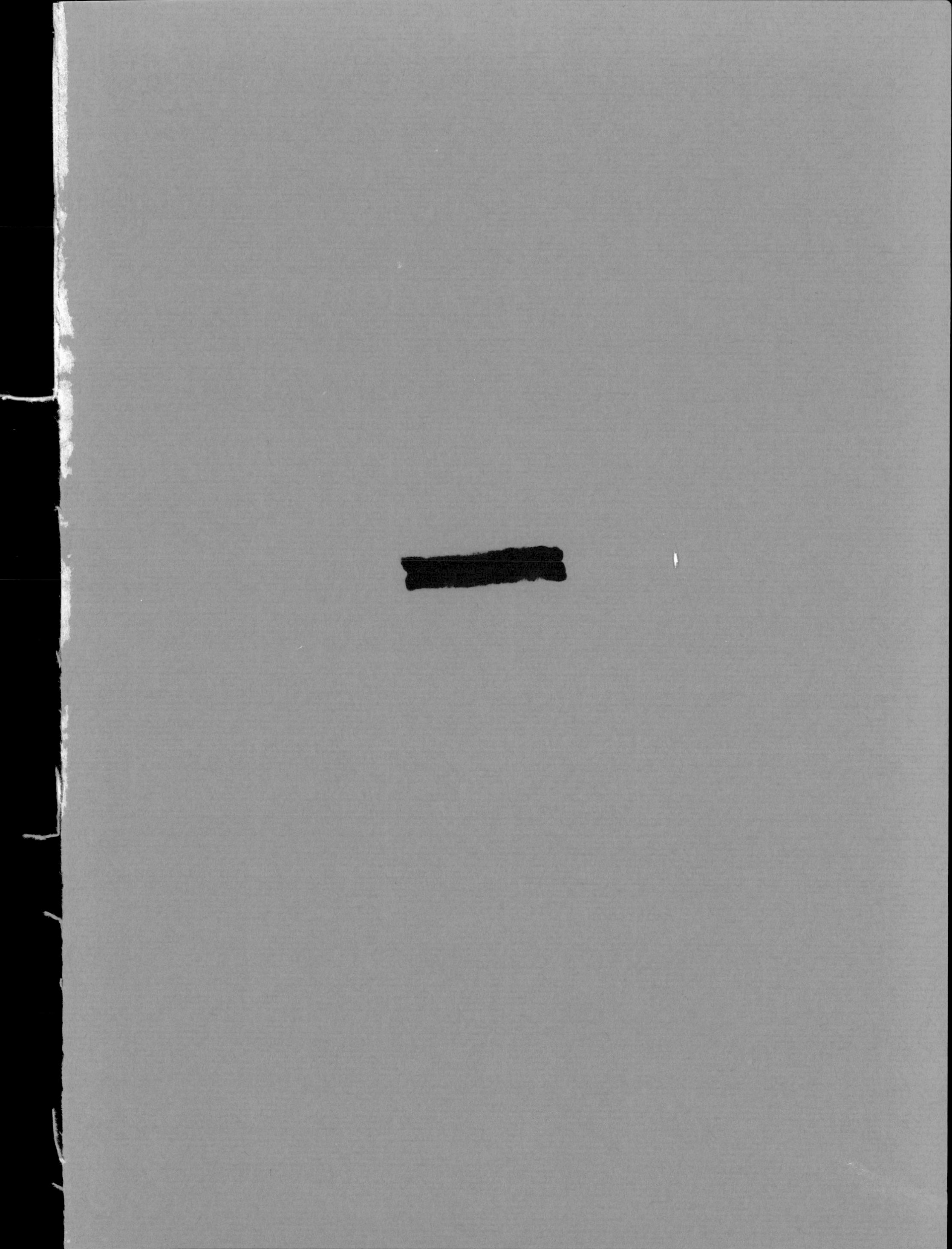